Journeys Home

Journeys Home

**The Journeys of Protestant Clergy and Laity
Coming Home to the Catholic Church
and the *Coming Home Network International,*
a Lay Ministry Committed to Helping Them**

Marcus C. Grodi, M.Div.
Author and Editor

Queenship
PUBLISHING COMPANY
P.O. Box 220, Goleta, CA 93116
(800) 647-9882 • (805) 692-0043 • Fax: (805) 967-5843

Sketch of the Vatican by Beth Hart.

© 1997 Queenship Publishing

Library of Congress #: 97-68888

Published by:
Queenship Publishing
P.O. Box 220
Goleta, CA 93116
(800) 647-9882 • (805) 692-0043 • Fax: (805) 967-5843

Printed in the United States of America

ISBN: 1-57918-001-9

Table of Contents

Foreword

by Scott and Kimberly Hahn

E ach one of us is on pilgrimage—a journey of faith which leads us closer to the God we love day by day. Some of us received the Faith on our father's knee; others converted to Christianity in the teen years or later. And many of us who began a relationship with Christ outside the Catholic Church could not imagine the riches within the Church that Christ wanted to give us.

Rather than reject the Faith given to us in our youth, we believe we have embraced the fullness that Christ died to give us within the Catholic Church. Now we recognize mystery where we previously did not know a mystery existed, such as the Eucharist and the other sacraments. More and more we appreciate the unity expressed in liturgy, doctrine and morals through the authority of the Church when previously we had only hoped for basic agreement among our fellow Christians. Daily we harness heaven through the communion of saints when earlier we pictured ourselves much more alone on our journey.

We know from first-hand experience that people in full-time Christian service who examine the claims of the Catholic Church have additional concerns and questions beyond those of other seekers. We have walked this rocky road, feeling alone in the midst of never-before-asked theological questions, unthinkable professional consequences, and emotional barriers which alternately separate us from our Protestant past, our possibly Catholic future and perhaps even each other as a married couple. Consequently, we want to accompany others along this difficult path.

As co-founders with Marcus and Marilyn Grodi and Fr. Ray and Ruth Ryland, we count it a privilege to be a part of the *Coming Home Network*. Through the *Coming Home Network* we offer practical help, prayer support and, hopefully, wisdom to those who, like us, are seriously on the "road to Rome." We are available as connectors, aiding our separated brethren however we can to understand, appreciate and cherish the fullness of the Faith in the Catholic Church. We welcome all those who are seeking regardless of where they are on their journey.

You are about to read excerpts from the spiritual journeys of people whose lives have been transformed through the grace of God in the Catholic Church. The circumstances in which each person discovered the Church—and the doctrines or moral teachings of the Church with which each person wrestled—are as individual as they are. Yet this they have in common: by the mercy of God, they have followed Christ into the Catholic Church, no matter the cost. Their accounts are invitations to join them mid-journey. Look over their shoulders, as it were, to take stock of their various backgrounds and training in Christian faith, to understand their newfound joy and wonder of discovery of the Catholic Church, and to be filled with awe at the feet of our Lord for His marvellous work on behalf of each one of us.

God bless you.

Scott and Kimberly Hahn
(authors, *Rome Sweet Home)*

Acknowledgments

Where do we begin to thank all the people God has used in our lives—whom He has used to specifically help my family and me grow in our faith, to help the *Coming Home Network International* become what it is, and to help this book come to fruition. I can only mention a few, but for all the rest who have been so caring and faithful may God bless you for your loving friendship.

First to my parents, Daniel and Dorothy Grodi who not only nurtured me with their love and discipline, but have put up with my diverse and too often unsettling spiritual journey.

Then to Reverends Elmer J. Melchert and Quentin Battiste, the two faithful Lutheran pastors who baptized, catechized, confirmed, proclaimed, and modeled the Christian faith during my childhood and youth.

To Pastor Tom Witzel who helped me return to faith during my rebellious college years. His preaching, teaching, and counseling have always been an inspiring model.

To Rev. Dr. Gary Stratman who not only ordained me, hired me as his assistant, married us, and baptized our first son Jon Marc, but also helped me understand how to minister to the great diversity of people in and outside of Christ.

To Dr. Scott and Kimberly Hahn, Fr. Ray and Ruth Ryland, Fr. Tom Cebula, Steve Wood, Scott Butler, Fr. Mitch Pacwa, Karl Keating and Dr. Mark Miravalle whose testimonies, and gifts of time and love helped the scales fall away so that Marilyn, my children and I could come home.

To Nick and Jane Healy, Fr. Michael Scanlan, Piet and Trude Dirksen, and Joseph Dublhoff whose friendship and leadership opened the doors of opportunity so that I might serve our Lord in the Church.

To Bernard Cardinal Law, Bishop Gilbert Sheldon, Bishop Paul Dudley, Bishop Donald Wuerl, Fr. William Stetson, Fr. Benedict Groeschel, Fr. Augustine DiNoia, Fr. Kenneth Roberts and Mother Angelica whose encouragement and assistance helped form the *Coming Home Network*.

To Kenneth Howell, Shannon Minch-Hughes and all our faithful *CHNetwork* members and friends in Christ, praise be to Jesus!

To my children, Jon Marc, Peter and Richard who are a great joy and a proud quiver for an unworthy father.

And now to the one who fills my life with love and meaning, an undeserved gift from God, who is certainly growing in holiness as she patiently offers up all of my foibles, my loving wife Marilyn.

Introduction

But when he came to himself he said, "How many of my father's hired servants have bread enough and to spare, but I perish here with hunger! I will arise and go to my father, and I will say to him, 'Father, I have sinned against heaven and before you; I am no longer worthy to be called your son; treat me as one of your hired servants.'" And he arose and came to his father. But while he was yet at a distance, his father saw him and had compassion, and ran and embraced him and kissed him.

Luke 15.17-20

Every single person must go through this same experience of journeying home to the Father. It is slightly or drastically different for each of us, depending upon how deeply into the pigsty we have ventured before we come to our senses. Even if we have been Christians all our lives, having been baptized, catechized, and confirmed in the Church, remaining faithful even up to the present moment, yet, as the apostle Paul reminded his Roman readers, "...all have sinned and fall short of the glory of God" (Romans 3.23).

Each one of us must recognize and confirm our own brokenness, and willfully choose to follow Jesus Christ, and aided by His grace, we can then begin advancing inch by inch along our journey of faith. And as happened to the young man in the story above, all our heavenly Father needs to see is our contrite hearts, our sincere turning homeward, and He will embrace us with His compassionate, forgiving acceptance.

The book you hold in your hand contains the stories of men and women who have all experienced this loving acceptance from God the Father. These pilgrims have all at some time surrendered their lives to Jesus Christ and, as a result, heard a call to follow Him more completely. Many of them were pastors or missionaries, or their spouses. Others were laymen who, though working in secular jobs, took their calling to serve Christ in the world very seriously.

What is unique about these stories is that each of these faithful disciples discovered, sometimes with great consternation or even horror, that continuing to follow Christ would require a journey home which they had never anticipated nor desired.

These men and women all discovered Jesus Christ in some branch of Protestantism, and remain grateful to the many faithful Protestant teachers, friends and family who helped them know Christ and grow in the Christian faith. Yet in each case, their desire to follow Christ faithfully, and to remain faithful to the truth He taught and the Church He established through His apostles, led them to consider the claims of the Catholic Church.

Many of these men and women came from Protestant faiths that viewed the Catholic Church as the "whore of Babylon," and the pope as the "antichrist." From an early age they had been taught all kinds of things about Catholics and their beliefs, sometimes horrifying, repulsive things, that made them wonder whether Catholics could even be saved. Yet in each case and in uniquely different ways, the Holy Spirit opened their hearts to realize that much of what they had been taught about the Catholic Church was never true. They learned to listen to the voice of truth speaking through history, theology, tradition, Scripture, and personal testimony.

Coming myself out of this same background, I realize that any Protestant reader may, at this very moment, be feeling cautious or skeptical, leery to go on, convinced that these men and women have instead been deceived by the prince of lies himself! However, resisting the temptation to jump into long pages of apologetic arguments, let me at least assure you that this is not the case. These stories are told by humble souls who love Jesus Christ, who desire to obey Him fully, and who have denounced completely the devil and his hoard. They have sought to follow the teachings of Scripture, as well as the teachings of the early Church Fathers and the ecumenical councils.

In doing so they were startled to discover the truth of the Catholic Church and its teachings. In the process, they also discovered that throughout its history, the Church has included not only thousands of Saints but also thousands of sinners, lay and clergy. Too often these real but less than perfect followers of Jesus dirtied the fair name of the Catholic Church, and gave fodder for the many misunderstandings and exaggerations that have led to so many schisms.

The book you hold is also unique in another way. It is not strictly a collection of conversion stories, nor does every story contain lengthy, detailed arguments in defense of their conversions. There are other, highly recommended books that accomplish this task, which are listed in *Appendix B*. Rather, this book focuses on the formation and ministry of the *Coming Home Network International* and the powerful conversion experiences of its members.

The *"Network"* was originally started to respond to the needs of the increasing number of Protestant clergy who have been "coming home" to the Catholic Church during these last years of the second millennium since Christ's birth. Unlike the hundreds of Anglican conversions that followed primarily as a result of the conversion of John Henry Newman in the 19th century, these modern day conversions are occurring as the result of no one notable precursor nor from any one denomination. Rather, they are coming from every conceivable American Christian tradition and for a great variety of reasons.

Particularly for clergy, this conversion process requires great sacrifice, including sometimes the loss of family, friends, and vocation. The *Coming Home Network International* provides needed information, fellowship and encouragement, as well as financial assistance, for these converts and their families as they become acclimated to the "strange, new world" of the Catholic Church.

I encourage you to read the following with a prayerful and charitable heart. This book basically consists of a compilation of the best articles from the *CHNetwork's* bimonthly newsletter. For this reason, the book may read less cohesively than if, for example, it had been conceived and written from scratch. However, we chose this format to hopefully convey the sense of serendipitous joy that sparked and continues to fire the growth of the *CHNetwork*.

In *Part One* you will find a collection of short conversion stories, all of which try to convey both the joys and the struggles of the journey home. The decision of a Protestant pastor to resign from his pastorate and enter the Catholic Church affects more than himself. It affects his family, particularly his spouse and their marriage. In many cases, the spouses have not shared the same convictions, and marriages have been greatly tested. In Part One you will also read about these conversions from the perspective of wives on the journey.

In *Part Two* you will discover, through the genre of journal entries, how the *Coming Home Network International* came into existence to help these men and women. You will read how the fellowship grew in response to how the Holy Spirit was working in the lives of the author and the *CHNetwork* members. You will, also, find a section of short candid responses from *CHNetwork* members as they answered a survey designed to compare their journeys and then discern how and why the Holy Spirit was bringing so many home to the Catholic Church.

Knowing that many non-Catholic readers may have urgent questions or concerns about the Catholic Church and its teachings, *Appendix A* presents *Pillar of Fire; Pillar of Truth,* a brief summary of the most commonly misunderstood teachings and practices of the Catholic Church. This was originally produced and published as a very attractive, helpful booklet by Catholic Answers.

Appendix B includes a comprehensive list of books and tapes, compiled to help any inquirer on their journey home.

Finally, in *Appendix C* you will find information on how to become a member of the *Coming Home Network International,* and how you can support its work.

Now as you turn to *Part One: Journeys Home,* I ask that you listen with both your mind and your heart, for here you will hear the whisper and work of the Spirit.

Part One
Journeys Home

Why would Jesus Christ want to throw a wrench into the lives of seemingly contented and effective Protestant clergy and their families? From the beginning of the *Coming Home Network International*, as the membership began sharing the reasons for openness to the Catholic Church, we discovered that our journeys were very similar, yet very diverse. We, therefore, began sharing our stories as words of encouragement as well as guideposts for others along the way.

The stories of many of the more well-known members of the *CHNetwork*, such as Scott and Kimberly Hahn, Steve and Karen Wood, Tom and Lovelace Howard, and Dave and Colleen Currie, have been distributed on tape, or printed in books, such as *Surprised By Truth, Rome Sweet Home, Lead, Kindly Light,* and *Born Fundamentalist: Born Again Catholic* (see Appendix B for these and other titles). These detailed accounts have served as the spiritual spark to start many non-Catholics on their journey home, as well as to rekindle the faith of thousands of Catholics.

In the following stories, you will find the witness, not only of those who have already been received into the Catholic Church, but of some who are still struggling with many of the issues encountered along the way.

As you read these stories, please remember that the decisions being considered by these men and women in Christ are much more compelling and life-changing then, say, having driven Fords all their lives and now they're trying to decide whether or not they should change to Chevys.

The decision to become Catholic often means, not only the leaving of a familiar and comfortable Protestant religious tradition and culture, but the loss of friends, family, career and ministry. Therefore, please read these stories with prayer and charity, as well as an open heart.

What Is Truth?

by Marcus C. Grodi

I am a former Protestant minister. Like so many others who have trodden the path that leads to Rome by way of that country known as Protestantism, I never imagined I would one day convert to Catholicism.

By temperament and training I'm more of a pastor than a scholar, so the story of my conversion to the Catholic Church may lack the technical details in which theologians traffic and in which some readers delight. But I hope I will accurately explain why I did what I did, and why I believe with all my heart that all Protestants should do likewise.

I won't dwell on the details of my early years, except to say that I was raised by two loving parents in a nominally Protestant home. I went through most of the experiences that make up the childhood and adolescence of the typical American baby-boomer. I was taught to love Jesus and go to church on Sunday. I also managed to blunder into most of the dumb mistakes that other kids in my generation made. But after a season of teenage rebellion, when I was twenty years old, I experienced a radical re-conversion to Jesus Christ. I turned away from the lures of the world and became serious about prayer and Bible study.

As a young adult, I made a recommitment to Christ, accepting him as my Lord and Savior, praying that he would help me fulfill the mission in life he had chosen for me.

The more I sought through prayer and study to follow Jesus and conform my life to his will, the more I felt an aching sense of longing to devote my life entirely to serving him. Gradually, the way dawn's first faint rays peek over a dark horizon, the conviction that the Lord was calling me to be a minister began to grow.

That conviction grew steadily stronger while I was in college and then afterwards during my job as an engineer. Eventually I couldn't ignore the call. I was convinced the Lord wanted me to become a minister, so I quit my job and enrolled in Gordon-Conwell Theological Seminary in suburban Boston. I acquired a master of divinity degree and was shortly thereafter ordained to the Protestant ministry.

My six-year-old son, Jon-Marc, recently memorized the Cub Scouts' oath, which goes in part: "I promise to do my best, to do my duty to God and my country." This earnest boyhood vow rather neatly sums up my own reasons for giving up a career in engineering in order to serve the Lord with complete abandon in full-time ministry. I took my new pastoral duties seriously, and I wanted to perform them correctly and faithfully, so that at the end of my life, when I stood face-to-face before God, I could hear him speak those all-important words: "Well done, good and faithful servant." As I settled down into the rather pleasant life of a Protestant minister, I felt happy and at peace with myself and God—I finally felt that I had arrived.

I had not arrived.

I soon found myself faced with a host of confusing theological and administrative questions. There were exegetical dilemmas over how to correctly interpret difficult biblical passages and also liturgical decisions that could easily divide a congregation. My seminary studies had not adequately prepared me to deal with this morass of options.

I just wanted to be a good pastor, but I couldn't find consistent answers to my questions from my fellow minister friends, nor from the "how to" books on my shelf, nor from the leaders of my Presbyterian denomination. It seemed that every pastor was expected to make up his own mind on these issues.

This "reinvent the wheel as often as you need to" mentality that is at the heart of Protestantism's pastoral ethos was deeply disturbing to me. "Why should I *have* to reinvent the wheel?" I asked myself in annoyance. "What about the Christian ministers down through the centuries who faced the same issues? What did they do?" Protestantism's emancipation from Rome's "manmade" laws and dogmas and customs that had "shackled" Christians for centuries (that, of course, was how we were taught in seminary to view the "triumph" of the Reformation over Romanism) began to look a lot more like anarchy than genuine freedom.

I didn't receive the answers I needed, even though I prayed constantly for guidance. I felt I had exhausted my resources and didn't know where to turn. Ironically, this frustrating sense of being out of answers was providential. It set me up to be open to answers offered by the Catholic Church. I'm sure that if I had felt that I had all the answers I wouldn't have been able or willing to investigate things at a deeper level.

A breach in my defense

In the ancient world, cities were built on hilltops and ringed with stout walls that protected the inhabitants against invaders. When an invading army laid siege to a city, as when Nebuchadnezzer's army surrounded Jerusalem in 2 Kings 25:1-7, the inhabitants were safe as long as their food and water held out and for as long as their walls could withstand the onslaught of the catapult's missile and the sapper's pick. But if the wall was breached, the city was lost.

My willingness to consider the claims of the Catholic Church began as a result of a breach in the wall of the Reformed Protestant theology that encircled my soul. For nearly forty years I labored to construct that wall, stone-by-stone, to protect my Protestant convictions.

The stones were formed from my personal experiences, seminary education, relationships, and my successes and failures in the ministry. The mortar that cemented the stones in place was my Protestant faith and philosophy. My wall was high and thick and, I thought, impregnable against anything that might intrude.

But as the mortar crumbled and the stones began to shift and slide, at first imperceptibly, but later on with an alarming rapidity, I became worried. I tried hard to discern the reason for my growing lack of confidence in the doctrines of Protestantism.

I wasn't sure what I was seeking to replace my Calvinist beliefs, but I knew my theology was not invincible. I read more books and consulted with theologians in an effort to patch the wall, but I made no headway.

I reflected often on Proverbs 3:5-6: "Trust in the Lord with all your heart, and lean not unto your own understanding; in all your ways acknowledge him and he will direct your paths." This exhortation both haunted and consoled me as I grappled with the doctrinal confusion and procedural chaos within Protestantism.

The Reformers had championed the notion of private interpretation of the Bible by the individual, a position I began to feel increasingly uncomfortable with, in light of Proverbs 3:5-6.

Bible-believing Protestants claim they *do* follow the teaching in this passage by seeking the Lord's guidance. The problem is that there are thousands of different paths of doctrine down which Protestants feel the Lord is directing them to travel. And these doctrines vary widely according to denomination.

I struggled with the questions, "How do I know what God's will is for my life and for the people in my congregation? How can I be sure that what I'm preaching is correct? How do I *know* what truth is?" In light of the doctrinal mayhem that exists within Protestantism each denomination staking out for itself doctrine based on the interpretations of the man who founded it—the standard Protestant boast, "I believe only in what the Bible says," began to ring hollow. I professed to look to the Bible alone to determine truth, but the Reformed doctrines I inherited from John Calvin, John Knox and the Puritans clashed in many respects with those held by my Lutheran, Baptist, and Anglican friends.

In the Gospel Jesus explained what it means to be a true disciple (cf. Matt. 19:16-23). It's more than reading the Bible, or having your name in a church membership roster, or regularly attending Sunday services, or even praying a simple prayer of conversion to accept Jesus as our Lord and Savior. These things, good though they are, by themselves don't make one a true disciple of Jesus. Being a disciple of Jesus Christ means making a radical commitment to love and obey the Lord in every word, action, and attitude, and to strive to radiate his love to others. The true disciple, Jesus said, is willing to give up everything, even his own life, if necessary, to follow the Lord.

I was deeply convinced of this fact, and as I tried to put it into practice in my own life (not always with much success) I also did my best to convince my congregation that this call to discipleship is not an option—it's something all Christians are called to strive for. The irony was that my Protestant theology made me impotent to call them to radical discipleship, and it made them impotent to hear and heed the call.

One might ask, "If all it takes to be saved is to 'confess with your lips that Jesus is Lord and believe in your heart that God raised him from the dead' (Rom. 10:9), then why must I *change?* Oh, sure, I *should* change my sinful ways. I should strive to please God. But if I don't, what does it really matter? My salvation is assured."

There's a story about a newspaper reporter in New York City who wanted to write an article on what people consider the most amazing invention of the twentieth century. He hit the streets, interviewing people at random, and received a variety of answers: the airplane, the telephone, the automobile, computers, nuclear energy, space travel, and antibiotic medicine. The answers went on along these lines until one fellow gave an unlikely answer:

"It's obvious. The most amazing invention was the thermos."

"The *thermos?*" queried the reporter, eyebrows raised.

"Of course. It keeps hot things hot and cold things cold."

The newspaperman blinked. "So what?"

"How does it *know?*"

This anecdote had meaning for me. Since it was my duty and desire to teach the truth of Jesus Christ to my congregation, my growing concern was, "How do I *know* what is truth and what isn't?"

Every Sunday I would stand in my pulpit and interpret Scripture for my flock, knowing that within a fifteen mile radius of my church there were dozens of other Protestant pastors—all of whom believed that the Bible alone is the sole authority for doctrine and practice—but each was teaching something different from what I was teaching. "Is my interpretation of Scripture the right one or not?" I'd wonder. "Maybe one of those other pastors is right, and I'm misleading these people who trust me."

There was also the knowledge—no, the gut-twisting certitude—that one day I would die and stand before the Lord Jesus Christ, the Eternal Judge, and I would be required to answer not just for my own actions but also for how I led the people he had given me to pastor. "Am I preaching truth or error?" I asked the Lord repeatedly. "I *think* I'm right, but how can I know for sure?"

This dilemma haunted me.

I started questioning every aspect of my ministry and Reformed theology, from insignificant issues to important ones. I look back now with a certain embarrassed humor at how I fretted during those trying days of uncertainty. At one point I even wrangled with doubts over whether or not to wear a clerical collar. Since there is no mandatory clerical dress code for Presbyterian ministers some wear collars, some wear business suits, some robes, and others a combination of all. One minister friend kept a clerical collar in the glove compartment of his car, just in case donning it might bring some advantage to him, "Like getting out of a speeding ticket!" He once confided with a conspiratorial grin. I decided not to wear a clerical collar. At Sunday services I wore a plain black choir robe over my business suit.

When it came to the form and content of Sunday liturgy every church had its own views on how things should be done, and each pastor was free to do pretty much whatever he wanted within reason.

Without mandated denominational guidelines to steer me, I did what all the other pastors were doing: I improvised. Hymns, sermons, Scripture selections, congregational participation, and the administration of baptism, marriage, and the Lord's Supper were all fair game for experimentation. I shudder at the memory of one particular Sunday when, in an effort to make the youth service more interesting and "relevant," I spoke the Lord's words of consecration, "This is my Body, this is my Blood, do this in memory of me," over a pitcher of soda pop and a bowel of potato chips.

Theological questions vexed me the most. I remember standing beside the hospital bed of a man who was near death after suffering a heart attack. His distraught wife asked me, "Is my husband going to heaven?" I hesitated for a moment before giving my pat Presbyterian response, as I considered the great diversity of alternative responses I could give, depending upon whether one were Methodist, Baptist, Lutheran, Assemblies of God, Nazarrene, Christian Scientist, Foursquare Gospel, Jehovah's Witnesses, etc., etc. All I could do was mouth some sort of pious but vague "we-must-trust-in-the-Lord" reassurance about her husband's salvation. She may have been comforted but I was tormented by her tearful plea. After all, as a Reformed pastor I believed John Calvin's doctrines of predestination and perseverance of the saints. This man had given his life to Christ, he had been regenerated, and was confident that he was one of God's elect. But *was* he?

I was deeply unsettled by the knowledge that no matter how earnestly he may have thought he was predestined for heaven (it's interesting that all who preach the doctrine of predestination firmly believe they themselves are one of the elect), and no matter how sincerely those around him believed he was, he may not have gone to heaven.

And what if he had secretly "backslidden" into serious sin and been living in a state of rebellion against God at the moment his heart attack caught him by surprise? Reformed theology told me that if that were the case, then the poor fellow had simply been deluded by a false security, *thinking* he was regenerated and predestined for heaven when in fact he had been unregenerated all along and on his way to hell. Calvin taught that the Lord's elect will—*must*—persevere in grace and election. If a person dies in a state of rebellion against God he proves he never was one of the elect. "What kind of absolute assurance was that?" I wondered.

I found it harder to give clear, confident answers to the "will my husband go to heaven?" kinds of questions my parishioners asked. Every Protestant pastor I knew had a different set of criteria that he listed as "necessary" for salvation. As a Calvinist I believed that if one publicly accepts Jesus as his Lord and Savior, he is saved by grace through faith. But even as I consoled others with these fine-sounding words, I was troubled by the worldly and sometimes grossly sinful lifestyles these now-deceased members of my congregation had lived. After just a few years of ministry I began to doubt whether I should continue.

Consider the sparrows

I rose one morning before dawn and, taking a folding chair, my journal, and a Bible, went out into a quiet field beside my church. It was the time of day I most love, when the birds are singing the world awake. I often marvel at the exuberance of birds in the early morning. What wonderfully short memories they have! They begin each day of their simple existences with a symphony of praise to the Lord who created them, utterly unconcerned with cares or plans. Sometimes, I'd "consider the sparrows" and mediate on the simplicity of their lives.

Sitting quietly in the middle of the dew-covered field waiting for the sun to come up, I read Scripture and meditated on these questions that had been troubling me, placing my worries before the Lord. The Bible warned me not to "lean unto my own understanding," so I was determined to trust in God to guide me.

I was contemplating leaving the pastorate, and I saw three options. One was to become the leader of youth ministry at a large Presbyterian Church that had offered me the position. Another was to leave ministry altogether and go back to engineering. The other possibility was to return to school and round out my scientific education in an area that would open even more doors to me professionally. I had been accepted into a graduate program in molecular biology at Ohio State University. I mulled over these options, asking God to guide my steps. "An audible voice would be great," I smiled, as I closed my eyes and waited for the Lord's answer. I had no idea what form *The Answer* would take, but it was not long in coming.

My reveries ended abruptly when a merrily chirping sparrow flew past and pooped on my head! "What are you saying to me, Lord?" I cried out with the anguish of Job. The trilling of the birds was the only response. There was no voice from heaven (not even a snicker), just the sounds of nature waking from its slumber in an Ohio cornfield. Was it a divine sign or merely Brother Bird's editorial comment on my worries? In disgust I folded up the chair, grabbed my bible, and went home.

Later that day when I told my wife Marilyn about the three options I was considering and the messy incident with the bird, she laughed and exclaimed with her typical wisdom, "The meaning is clear, Marcus. God is saying 'None of the above!'"

Although I'd have preferred a less humiliating method of communication, I knew nothing occurs by accident, and that neither sparrows nor their droppings fall to earth without God's knowledge. I took this as at least a comical hint from God to remain in the ministry.

But I still knew my situation was not right. Maybe what I needed was a bigger church with a bigger budget and a bigger staff. Surely, then I'd be happy. So, I struck off in the direction of the "bigger-is-better" church that I thought would satisfy my restless heart. Within six-months I found one I liked and whose very large congregation seemed to like me. They offered me the post of senior pastor complete with an office staff and a budget ten times larger than the one I had at my previous church. Best of all this was a strong evangelical

Church with many members who were actively interested in Scripture study and lay ministry. I enjoyed preaching before this large and largely approving congregation each Sunday. At first I thought I had solved the problem, but after only one month, I realized that bigger was not better. My frustration merely grew proportionately larger.

Polite smiles beamed up at me during each sermon, but I wasn't blind to the fact that for many in the congregation my passionate exhortations to live a virtuous life merely skittered across a veneer of religiosity like water droplets on a hot skillet. Many said, "Great sermon! It really blessed me!" But I sensed what they really thought was, "That's nice for other people, Pastor—for *sinners.* But I've already arrived. My name's already on the heavenly rolls. *I* don't need to worry about all this stuff, but I sure do agree with you, Pastor, that we've got to tell all the sinners to get right with God."

One day I found myself standing before the local presbytery as spokesman for a group of pastors and laymen who were defending the idea that when we use parental language for God in communal prayer, we should call him "Father," not "mother" or "parent." I defended this position by appealing to Scripture and Christian tradition. To my dismay I realized that the faction I represented was in the minority and that we were fighting a losing battle. This issue would be settled not by a well-reasoned appeal to Scripture or Church history, but by a vote—the majority of votes being pro-gender-neutral-language liberals. It was at this meeting that I first recognized the anarchistic principle that lies at the center of Protestantism.

These liberals (grievously wrong as they were in their scheme to reduce God to the mere functions of "creator," "redeemer," and "sanctifier," instead of the Persons of Father, Son, and Holy Spirit), were just being good Protestants. They were simply following the course of protest mapped out for them by their theological ancestors Martin Luther, John Calvin, and other Reformers. The Reformation maxim of "I will not abide by a teaching unless *I* believe it is correct and biblical" was being invoked by these liberal Protestants in favor of their protest against masculine names for God. All of a sudden it hit me that I was observing Protestantism in the full solipsistic glory of its natural habit: protest. "What kind of church am I in?" I asked myself dejectedly as the vote was taken and my side lost.

About this time my wife, Marilyn, who had been the director of a pro-life crisis pregnancy center, began challenging me to grapple with the inconsistency of our staunch pro-life convictions and the pro-choice stance of our Presbyterian denomination. "How can you be a minister in a denomination that sanctions the killing of unborn babies?" she asked.

The denominational leadership had bowed under the pressure from radical feminists, homosexual, pro-abortion, and other extremist pressure groups within the denomination and (though ostensibly members of individual congregations could hold pro-life views) imposed stringent liberal guidelines on the hiring process for new pastors.

When she woke me up to the fact that a portion of the donations my congregation forwarded to the Presbyterian General Assembly were most likely paying for abortions, and there was nothing I nor my congregation could do about it, I was stunned.

Marilyn and I knew we had to leave the denomination, but where would we go? This question led to another: Where am I going to find a job as a minister? I purchased a book that listed the details of all major Christian denominations and began evaluating several of the denominations that interested me.

I'd read the doctrinal summaries and think, "This one is nice, but I don't like their view on baptism," or "This one is okay, but their view of the end times is a bit too panic-ridden," or "This one sounds exactly like what I'm looking for, but I'm uncomfortable with their style of worship." After examining every possibility and not finding one that I liked, I shut the book in frustration. I knew I was leaving Presbyterianism but I had no idea which was the "right" denomination to go into. There seemed to be something wrong with each of them. "Too bad I can't customize my 'perfect' church," I thought to myself wistfully.

Around this time a friend from Illinois called me on the phone. He, too, was a Presbyterian pastor and had heard through the grapevine that I was planning to leave the Presbyterian denomination.

"Marc, you *can't* leave the church!" he scolded. "You must never leave the church. You're committed to the church. It shouldn't matter that some theologians and pastors are off the wall. We've got to stick with the church, and work for renewal from within! We must preserve unity at all costs!"

"If that's true," I replied testily, "why did we Protestants break away from the church in the first place?"

I don't know where those words came from. I had never in my life given even a passing thought as to whether or not the Reformers were right to break away from the Catholic Church. It was the essential nature of Protestantism to attempt to bring renewal through division and fragmentation. The motto of the Presbyterian Church is "reformed, and always reforming." (It should add: "and reforming, and reforming, and reforming, and reforming, etc.")

I could leave for another denomination, knowing that eventually I might move to another when I become dissatisfied, or I could decide to stay where I was and take my lumps. But then how could I justify staying where I was? Why shouldn't I return to the previous denominational group we Presbyterians had defiantly broken away from? None of these options seemed right, so I decided that I would leave the ministry until I resolved the issue one way or the other.

Returning to school seemed to be the easiest way to take a breather from all of this, so I enrolled in a graduate program in molecular biology at Case Western Reserve University. My goal was to combine my scientific and theological backgrounds into a career in bio-ethics. I figured that a Ph.D. in molecular biology would win me a better hearing among scientists than would a degree in theology or ethics. Besides, earning a Ph.D. in theology or ethics required learning Latin and German, and at 39 I figured my brain cells were a little too far in decline for that type of mental rigor.

The commute to the Cleveland campus took over an hour each way, and for the next eight months I had plenty of quiet time for introspection and prayer.

Soon I was deeply immersed in a genetic engineering research project, which involved the removal and reproduction of human DNA taken from homogenized male kidneys. The program was very challenging, but I loved it, although compared to the complexities of amino acids and biochemical cycles, wrestling with Latin conjugations and German declension endings suddenly seemed a lot easier.

The project fascinated and frightened me. I relished the intellectual stimulation of scientific research, but I also saw how dehumanizing the research lab can be. Genetic tissue harvested from the cadavers of deceased patients at the Cleveland Clinic were sent to our lab for DNA research. I was deeply moved by the fact that this tissue had come from *people*—moms and dads, children, and grandparents who had once lived and worked and laughed and loved, but who were now dead. In the lab these neatly numbered vials of tissue were just tubes of "stuff," experimental "material" that was utterly dissociated from the human person to whom it once belonged.

I wrote an essay on the ethical problems involved with fetal tissue transplantation and began speaking to Christian groups about the dangers and blessings of modern biological technology. Things seemed to be going according to plan, at least until I realized that the real reason for my return to school was not to get a degree. It was so that I might buy a copy of the local Cleveland newspaper.

One Friday morning, after a long drive into Cleveland, I was eating breakfast and killing time before class, trying to stay awake. Normally I'd squeeze in a little study time, but this morning I did something unusual: I bought a copy of *The Plain Dealer.* As I slipped the quarter into the newspaper machine I had no way of knowing I had come to a momentous fork in the road and was about to start down a path that would lead me out of Protestantism and into the Catholic Church (I suppose if I had known where it would lead I would have gone the other way). Skimming through, with only nominal interest, I came across a small advertisement that jumped out at me: "Catholic theologian, Scott Hahn, to speak at local Catholic parish this Sunday afternoon."

I choked on my coffee. "*Catholic* theologian, Scott Hahn?" It couldn't be the Scott Hahn I used to know. We had attended Gordon-Conwell Theological Seminary together back in the early 80's. Back then he was a staunch Calvinist anti-Catholic, the staunchest on campus! I'd been on the fringe of an intense Calvinist study group which Scott lead, but while Scott and others spent long hours scouring the Bible like detectives trying to uncover every angle of every theological implication, I played basketball.

Though I hadn't seen Scott since he graduated in 1982, I had heard the dark rumor floating around that he'd become Catholic. I hadn't thought much about it. Either the rumor was false, contrived by someone who was offended by (or jealous of) the intensity of Scott's convictions, or else Scott had flipped. I decided to make the hour and a half trip to find out. I was totally unprepared for what I discovered.

Much learning hath made you mad!

I was nervous as I pulled into the parking lot of the huge gothic structure. I had never been inside a Catholic Church, and I didn't know what to expect.

I entered the church quickly, skirting the holy water fonts, and scuttled down the aisle, unsure of the correct protocol for getting into the pew. I knew Catholics bowed, or curtsied, or did some sort of jig-like obeisance toward the alter before entering the pew, but I just slipped in and scrunched down, hoping not to have been recognized as a Protestant.

After a few minutes of no grim faced usher tapping me on the shoulder and jerking his thumb back toward the door—"Come on, pal, hit the road. We all know you're not Catholic"—I began to relax and gape at the strange but undeniably beautiful interior of the church.

A few moments later Scott strode to the podium and began his talk with a prayer. When he made the sign of the cross, I knew he had truly jumped ship. My heart sank. "Poor Scott." I groaned inwardly. "The Catholics got him with their clever arguments." I listened intently to his talk on the Last Supper entitled "The Fourth Cup," trying hard to detect the errors in his thinking. But I couldn't find any. (Scott's talk was so good I plagiarized most of it in my next communion sermon.)

As he spoke, using Scripture at each step to support Catholic teaching on the Mass and the Eucharist, I found myself mesmerized by what I heard. Catholicism was being explained in a way I had never imagined possible—from the Bible! As he explained them, the Mass and the Eucharist were not offensive or foreign to me. At the end of his talk, when Scott issued a stirring call to a radical conversion to Christ, I wondered if maybe he had only feigned conversion so he could infiltrate the Catholic Church to bring about renewal and conversion of spiritually-dead Catholics.

It didn't take long before I found out.

After the audience's applause subsided I went up front to see if he would recognize me. He was surrounded by a throng of people with questions. I stood a few feet away and studied his face as he spoke with his typical charm and conviction to the large knot of people. Yes, this was the same Scott I knew in seminary. He now sported a mustache and I a seasonal full beard (quite a change from our clean cut seminary days), but when he turned in my direction his eyes sparkled as he grinned a silent hello.

In a moment we stood together, clasped in a warm handshake, he apologizing if he had offended me in any way. "No, of course not!" I assured him as we laughed with the sheer delight of seeing each other again. After a few moments of obligatory "How's-your-wife-and-family?" chitchat, I blurted out the one thought on my mind. "I guess it's true what I heard. Why did you jump ship and become Catholic?" Scott gave me a brief explanation of his struggle to find the truth about Catholicism (the throng of people listened intently as he gave his mini-conversion story), and suggested I pick up a copy of his conversion story tape, copies of which were being snapped up briskly at the literature table in the vestibule.

We exchanged phone numbers and shook hands again, and I headed for the back of the church where I found a table covered with tapes on the Catholic faith done by Scott and his wife Kimberly, as well as tapes by Steve Wood, another convert to Catholicism who had also studied at Gordon-Conwell Seminary. I bought a copy of each tape and a copy of a book Scott had recommended, Karl Keating's *Catholicism and Fundamentalism.*

Before I left, I stood in the back of the church, taking in for a moment the strange yet attractive hallmarks of Catholicism that surrounded me: icons and statues, ornate altar, candles, and dark confessional booths. I stood there for a moment wondering why God had called me to this place, then I stepped into the cold night air, my head dizzy with thought and my heart flooded with a confusing jumble of emotions.

I went to a fast food restaurant, got a burger for the long drive home, and slipped Scott's conversion tape into the player, planning to discover where he had gone wrong. I didn't get half way home before I was so overwhelmed with emotion that I had to pull off the highway so I could clear my head.

Even though Scott's journey to the Catholic Church was very different then mine, the questions he and I grappled with were essential the same. And the answers he found which had so drastically changed his life were very compelling. His testimony convinced me that the reasons for my growing dissatisfaction with Protestantism couldn't be ignored. The answers to my questions, he claimed, were found in the Catholic Church. The idea pierced me to the core.

I was at once frightened and exhilarated by the thought that God might be calling me into the Catholic Church. I prayed for awhile, my head resting on the steering wheel, collecting my thoughts before I started the car again and drove home.

The next day, I opened *Catholicism and Fundamentalism*, and read straight through, finishing the final chapter that night. As I prepared to retire for the night, I knew I was in trouble! It was clear to me now that the two central dogmas of the Protestant Reformation, *sola scriptura* (Scripture alone) and *sola fide* (justification by faith alone), were on very shaky biblical ground, and therefore so was I.

My appetite thus whetted, I began reading Catholic books, especially the early Church Fathers, whose writings helped me understand the truth about Catholic history prior to the Reformation. I spent countless hours debating with Catholics and Protestants, doing my best to subject Catholic claims to the toughest biblical arguments I could find. Marilyn, as you might guess, was not pleased when I told her about my struggle with the claims of the Catholic Church. Although at first she told me, "This too will pass," eventually she too became intrigued with the things I was learning, and began studying for herself.

As I waded through book after book, I shared with her the clear and common sense teachings of the Catholic Church I was discovering. More often then not we would conclude together how much more sense and how much truer to Scripture the views of the Catholic Church seemed than anything we had found in the wide range of Protestant opinions. There was depth, an historical strength, a philosophical consistency to the Catholic positions we encountered. The Lord worked an amazing transformation in both our lives, coaxing us along, side by side, step by step, together all the way.

But, with all these good things we were finding in the Catholic Church, we were also confronted by some confusing and disturbing issues. I encountered priests who thought me strange for considering the Catholic Church. They felt that conversion was unnecessary. We met Catholics who knew little about their faith, and whose life-styles conflicted with the moral teachings of their Church. When we attended masses we found ourselves unwelcomed and unassisted by anyone. But in spite of these obstacles blocking our path to the Church, we kept studying and praying for the Lord's guidance.

After listening to dozens of tapes and digesting several dozen books, I knew I could no longer remain a Protestant. It had became clear that the Protestant answer to church renewal was, of all things, unscriptural. Jesus had prayed for unity among his followers, and Paul and John both challenged their followers to hold fast to the truth they had received, not letting opinions divide them. As Protestants we had become infatuated by our freedom, placing personal opinion over the teaching authority of the Church. We believed that the guidance of the Holy Spirit is enough to lead any sincere seeker to the true meaning of Scripture.

The Catholic response to this view is that it is the mission of the Church to teach with infallible certitude. Christ promised the apostles and their successors, "He who listens to you listens to me. And he who rejects you rejects me and rejects the one who sent me" (Luke 10:16). The early Church believed this too. A very compelling passage leaped out at me one day while I was studying Church history:

> *The Apostles received the gospel for us from the Lord Jesus Christ; and Jesus Christ was sent from God. Christ, therefore, is from God, and the Apostles are from Christ. Both of these orderly arrangements, then, are by God's will. Receiving their instructions and being full of confidence on the account of the Resurrection of our Lord Jesus Christ, and confirmed in faith by the Word of God, they went forth in the complete assurance of the Holy Spirit, preaching the Good News that the kingdom of God is coming. Through countryside and city they preached; and they appointed their earliest converts, testing them by the Spirit, to be the bishops and deacons of future believers. Nor was this a novelty: for bishops and deacons had been written about a long time earlier. Indeed, Scripture somewhere says: "I will set up their bishops in righteousness and their deacons in faith.*

(Clement of Rome,
Epistle to the Corinthians 42:1-5 [ca. A.D. 80])[1]

---

[1] *Some patristic scholars (e.g. W.A. Jurgens and J.A.T. Robinson) date this epistle as early as A.D. 80, though the traditional dating favors A.D. 96. A concise treatment of the arguments for the earlier dating is found in William Jurgens,* The Faith of the Early Fathers(Collegeville: Liturgical Press, 1970) vol. 1, 6-7

Another patristic quote that helped breach the wall of my Protestant presuppositions was this one from Irenaeus, bishop of Lyons:

When, therefore, we have such proofs, it is not necessary to seek among others the truth which is easily obtained from the Church. For the apostles, like a rich man in a bank, deposited with her most copiously everything that pertains to the truth; and everyone whosoever wishes draws from her the drink of life. For she is the entrance to life, while all the rest are thieves and robbers. That is why it is surely necessary to avoid them, while cherishing with the utmost diligence the things pertaining to the Church, and to lay hold of the tradition of truth. What then? If there should be a dispute over some kind of question, ought we not have recourse to the most ancient churches in which the apostles were familiar, and draw from them what is clear and certain in regard to that question? What if the apostles had not in fact left writings for us? Would it not be necessary to follow the order of tradition, which was handed down to those to whom they entrusted the Churches?

(Against Heresies 3,4,1 [ca. A.D. 180])[2]

I studied the causes for the Reformation. The Roman Catholic Church of that day was desperately in need of renewal but Martin Luther and the other Reformers chose the wrong, the *unbiblical,* method for dealing with the problems they saw in the Church. The correct route was and still is just what my Presbyterian friend had told me: Don't leave the Church; don't break the unity of faith. Work for genuine reform based on God's plan, not man's, achieving it through prayer, penance, and good example.

I could no longer remain Protestant. To do so meant I must deny Christ's promise to guide and protect his Church and to send the Holy Spirit to lead it into all truth (cf. Matt. 16:18-19, 18:18, 28:20; John 14:16, 25, 16:13). But I couldn't bear the thought of becoming a Catholic. I'd been taught for so long to despise "Romanism" that, even though intellectually I had discovered Catholicism to be true, I had a hard time shaking my emotional prejudice against the Church.

---

[2]   *Ibid, Vol. 1, pg 90.*

One key difficulty was the psychological adjustment to the complexity of Catholic theology. By contrast Protestantism is simple: admit you're a sinner, repent of your sins, accept Jesus as your personal Savior, trust in him to forgive you, and you're saved.

I continued studying Scripture and Catholic books and spent many hours debating with Protestant friends and colleagues over difficult issues like Mary, praying to the saints, indulgences, purgatory, priestly celibacy, and the Eucharist. Eventually I realized that the single most important issue was authority. All of this wrangling over how to interpret Scripture gets one nowhere if there is no way to know with infallible certitude that one's interpretation is the right one. The teaching authority of the Church in the magisterium centered around the seat of Peter. If I could accept this doctrine, I knew I could trust the Church on everything else.

I read Fr. Stanley Jaki's *The Keys to the Kingdom* and *Upon This Rock*, and the Documents of Vatican II and earlier councils, especially Trent. I carefully studied Scripture and the writings of Calvin, Luther, and the other Reformers to test the Catholic argument. Time after time I found the Protestant arguments against the primacy of Peter simply weren't biblical or historical. It became clear that the Catholic position was the biblical one.

The Holy Spirit delivered a literal *coup de grace* to my remaining anti-Catholic biases when I read John Henry Cardinal Newman's landmark book, *An Essay on the Development of the Christian Doctrine*. In fact, my objections evaporated when I read 12 pages in the middle of the book in which Newman explains the gradual development of papal authority. "It is less difficulty that the papal supremacy was not formally acknowledged in the second century, then that there was no formal acknowledgment on the part of the Church of the doctrine of the Holy Trinity till the fourth. No doctrine is defined till violated."[3]

My study of Catholic claims took about a year and a half. During this period, Marilyn and I studied together, sharing together as a couple the fears, hopes, and challenges that accompanied us along the path to Rome. We attended Mass together weekly, making the drive to a parish far enough away from our home town (my former

---

[3]   *University of Notre Dame Press, Notre Dame, Indiana, 1989, page 151.*

Presbyterian Church was less then a mile from our home) to avoid the controversy and confusion that would undoubtedly arise if my former parishioners knew that I was investigating Rome.

We gradually began to feel comfortable doing all the things Catholics did at Mass (except receiving Communion, of course). Doctrinally, emotionally, and spiritually, we felt ready to formally enter the Church, but there remained one barrier for us to surmount.

Before Marilyn and I met and fell in love, she had been divorced after a brief marriage. Since we were Protestants when we met and married, this posed no problem, as far as we and our denomination were concerned. It wasn't until we felt we were ready to enter the Catholic Church that we were informed that we couldn't do so unless Marilyn could receive an annulment of her first marriage. At first, we felt like God was playing a joke on us! Then we moved from shock to anger. It seemed so unfair and ridiculously hypocritical: we could have committed almost any other sin, no matter how heinous, and with one confession been adequately cleansed for Church admission, yet because of this one mistake our entry into the Catholic Church had been stopped dead in the water.

But then we remembered what had brought us to this point in our spiritual pilgrimage: we were to trust God with all our hearts and lean not on our own understanding. We were to acknowledge him and trust that he would direct our paths. It became evident to us that this was a final test of perseverance sent by God.

So Marilyn began the difficult annulment investigation process, and we waited. We continued attending Mass, remaining seated in the pew, our hearts aching while those around us went forward to receive the Lord in the Holy Eucharist and we could not. It was by not being able to receive the Eucharist that we learned to appreciate the awesome privilege that Jesus bestows on his beloved of receiving him Body and Blood, Soul and Divinity in the Blessed Sacrament. The Lord's promise in Scripture became real to us during those Masses: "The Lord chastises the son whom he loves" (Heb. 12:6).

After a nine-month wait, we learned that Marilyn's annulment had been granted. Without further delay our marriage was blessed, and we were received with great excitement and celebration into the Catholic Church. It felt so incredibly good to finally be home where we belonged. I wept quiet tears of joy and gratitude that first

Mass when I was able to walk forward with the rest of my Catholic brothers and sisters and receive Jesus in Holy Communion.

I asked the Lord many times in prayer, "What is truth?" He answered me in Scripture by saying, "I am the way, the truth and the life." I rejoice that now as a Catholic I can not only know the Truth but receive him in the Eucharist.

Apologia pro a final few words sua

I think that it is important that I mention one more of John Henry Cardinal Newman's insights that made a crucial difference in the process of my conversion to the Catholic Church. He wrote: "To be deep in history is to cease to be a Protestant."[4] This one line summarizes a key reason why I abandoned Protestantism, bypassed the Orthodox Church, and became a Catholic.

Newman was right. The more I read Church history and Scripture the less I could comfortably remain Protestant. I saw that it was the Catholic Church that was established by Jesus Christ, and all the other claimants to the title "true church" had to step aside. It was the Bible and Church history that made a Catholic out of me, against my will (at least at first) and to my immense surprise.

I also learned that the flip side of Newman's adage is equally true: To cease to be deep in history is to *become* a Protestant. That's why we Catholics must know *why* we believe what the Church teaches as well as the history behind these truths of our salvation. We must prepare ourselves and our children to "Always be ready to give an explanation to anyone who asks for a reason for your hope" (1 Peter 3:15). By boldly living and proclaiming our faith many will hear Christ speaking through us and will be brought to a knowledge of the truth in all its fullness in the Catholic Church. God bless you on your own journey of faith!

(This article was originally published in "Surprised By Truth," Patrick Madrid, ed., Basilica Press, San Diego, 1994.)

---

[4]   *Ibid., page 8.*

"I Never Wanted to be a Minister's Wife Anyway!"
by Marilyn C. Grodi

This was the tongue in cheek reply I shared at the first *Coming home Network* gathering in 1993. The statement was definitely true until I met my husband to-be at the Second Presbyterian Church of Newark, Ohio. I had only a few months before returned to the church, as in attending any church at all. Here Marcus had been called as the assistant minister and singles group coordinator.

I was a "baby" Christian struggling to live as one, becoming more and more aware of my sinfulness, as well as my inability to make *the* needed changes. I was also working in the field of alcoholism as an educator and counselor. As I sent people to Alcoholics Anonymous, I knew I needed a spiritual recovery as well as many of my clients.

A friend in our single's group gave me a verse that made sense but was difficult: "Delight in the Lord and he will give you the desires of your heart." So I began praying everyday while running, or when I'd wake up in the middle of the night. I received counseling from the minister who later married Marcus and me, and during a torturous two years of struggle and backsliding, I desired to turn my life completely over to God.

I was miserable and had been most of my adult life, living my life "my way." I had "looked for love in all the wrong places," so I really wasn't sure I knew how to recognize it when it was available. I became more involved in the church, thinking teaching high school Sunday school and things like that were reasonable requests from God. BUT marrying a minister?! This was just a little too much to ask.

The string of relationships behind me also made me feel completely unworthy of such a role. I finally prayed the prayer, "Lord, not my will but yours; if you want me to be single, that will be fine." Suddenly, I was completely released from a relationship at my work that I believe Satan had been using to keep me almost immobile. Soon after, God seemed to take a "two-by-four" to both Marcus and me, and we became engaged.

Three months later, after much reminding from my fiancé that "you are a new creation in the Lord," we were married. (I didn't even have to attend a school for minister's wives-to-be.)

Wow, was married Christian life a rewarding, exciting roller coaster ride. And with many challenges, too. I became the director of a crisis pregnancy center, and our first child, Jon Marc, was born the day after our first anniversary. Hallelujah, being a mother was the ultimate! Living with Marcus alone has always been interesting. He's always full of creative and sometimes scary ideas. I quickly learned that I need not get overly excited with every new idea. Usually, I prefer things to stay the same.

When we moved from our small, country church in central Ohio to a large evangelical congregation in northeast Ohio, I thought this is it! This active, vibrant church was quite appealing and with buying a house, my roots were down for at least ten years (or so I thought).

Being a minister's wife was actually quite fun: I was free to do whatever I wanted—teach Sunday School, redecorate the nursery, and develop relationships with many like-minded people. Then Marcus got a bazaar idea. Being restless about his ministry as well as issues in our Presbyterian denomination, he decided to incorporate his science background into his present career by studying bioethics. He left his pastoral position to study full-time while we also began looking at other denominations that might be a better fit. We both had become discouraged about how issues were dealt with at higher levels of our denomination: abortion, inclusive language, etc. Little did I know how much affect some of Scott Hahn's tapes had had on Marcus. Leaving our church was a great disappointment to me and to many in the church; it had only been one and a half years.

Marcus was now driving to Cleveland each day to Case Western Reserve University, while I was caring for our preschooler and newborn named Peter (of all names). Isolation was beginning to take place, since we still lived in our old neighborhood near our church and friends, who didn't understand what we were doing, and neither did I. We were church hopping for a summer while Marcus was studying not just genetics—he was reading every thing he could get his hands on about the Catholic Church.

Miraculously, we both found ourselves open to the truths of the Catholic Church, and much was making sense that never had before. We had never in our wildest dreams thought seriously about this historic Church, which, at least to me, had always been one of myths and misguided people. Marcus rather quickly came to the point where he felt he could no longer be a Protestant, but neither of us felt that we could actually become Catholics.

When we began attending mass, it was awful: the parish churches seemed so cold and unfriendly; there were no welcoming Sunday School programs or nurseries for the little ones. The worst part was when we would come to the sacrifice of the mass. I just wanted to break down and weep or run. Without having dealt with the issue of the Eucharist, I intuitively knew that here was the pivotal difference.

Even though Marcus stated that the kids and I were welcome to continue attending the Presbyterian Church, we did not want to go to separate churches on Sunday mornings. Fortunately, we discovered a parish across town that resembled many Protestant churches: they were a little friendlier with coffee and donuts afterwards; CCD was held on Sunday mornings for children (it felt like Sunday school). These rather superficial things actually helped a lot as I was making the transition into the world of Catholicism. So each Sunday we would drive, tearfully, past our old church, as we became more convinced about what we might have to do.

Then we ran into a most unexpected barrier. Marcus and I decided we would give the RCIA* class a look. But we backed down for two reasons. First, we were not quite ready for the world to know of our leanings towards the Catholic Church, and some of our classmates in RCIA were from our neighborhood. Second, we realized that even if we completed this class, we were at least temporarily ineligible to enter the Church because of a marital commitment I had made prior in my early 20's.

Well! Maybe here was an issue that would save us from the Church! We never dreamed we would face such an obstacle, and

---

* *Rite of Christian Initiation of Adults*

angrily thought of many worse sins we could have committed which would not have prevented us from becoming members of the Catholic Church.

After much pondering and prayer, we soon realized that this requirement of obtaining an annulment was yet another great reason for seeking this traditional Church and her teachings. I initially had been attracted to the Catholic Church because it seemed to be the only one which held fast to those things that serve to strengthen and preserve families. Every other denomination had become lax towards abortion, contraception, marriage, divorce, etc.

So I swallowed my pride and took my first big submissive step, bowing to the awesome power and majesty of the authority of the Church. We really did it together, because Marcus was there, so supportive, every stage of the process. The annulment process turned out to not be as daunting as I had imagined, but rather a blessing to both of us and our marriage.

Nine months later, after we had moved to Steubenville, Ohio (a pretty good place to learn to be Catholic), we were informed of the decree of nullity, and within a month, on December 20, 1992, we were not only received into the Church at St. Peter's parish, but our marriage was blessed with a re-exchanging of vows and rings. What a joyous occasion we shared with many new friends.

So ... Marcus isn't now known to many as Reverend. But I'm glad that I was a pastor's wife for a time, and am eternally thankful that our entire family is enjoying the riches of the one, holy, Catholic, and apostolic Church.

Catholic Inside and Out

by Dr. Kenneth Howell

Although summarizing my journey to the Catholic Church is a bit like attempting to put the internal revenue code on a postcard, I will venture to sketch the highlights of this journey. My knowledge of Catholicism in childhood was limited to my father's side of the family, some of whom were devout but most of whom were Catholic in name only. I can remember at times being impressed with the aesthetic appeal of a Catholic Church and having a sense of something greater but I was completely at a loss to know what that was.

In my late teens (college years) I had a deep sense of the grace of God in my life and loved to read the Sacred Scriptures. I read spiritual literature which stressed the importance of a daily communion with God in the Spirit and found at times an unusual degree of closeness to God which I can only describe as a gift.

During the late seventies, I attended Westminster Theological Seminary in Philadelphia, Pennsylvania where I learned the art of biblical interpretation and other theological disciplines. Although I had no interest in the Catholic Church at that time, I do remember being repulsed by the anti-Catholic attitudes of some of my conservative Presbyterian friends. To me Catholics were misguided but they were Christian.

In my seminary days, I remember formulating a theological issue that was to play a crucial role in my journey later on. I realized that the only way to justify the splitting of western Christianity that occurred in the Reformation was to see the Protestant Reformers as bringing the church back to its original purity from which it had fallen. This meant that the Protestants were the true catholics.

In 1978 I was ordained a Presbyterian minister (PCA) and served two churches while I also obtained a doctoral degree in biblical linguistics. Shortly after my ordination, I was preaching a homily on the unity of the Church and stated that the only justification for the Reformation was that the Catholic Church had left the Gospel. I further said that the demands of unity in the Church, for which our LORD prayed in John 17, required us to do this: if the Catholic Church ever comes back to the Gospel, we must go back to it. Little did I realize in 1978 that I would someday eat my words.

In 1988 my family moved to Jackson, Mississippi and I began teaching at Reformed Theological Seminary (RTS). I was not even considering the Catholic Church though two indicators were already present. I had always had a love for the Lord's Supper and I also believed that the Reformed Faith was in fact the faith of the early church, two beliefs that eventually led me to leave the Reformed Faith.

Around 1991, I began teaching a course on the Eucharist at RTS that treated the biblical foundations and history of the doctrine in the Church. After two years of teaching this course, I became convinced of the Real Presence of Christ in the Eucharist and realized that the Calvinist view of spiritual communion was deficient. This then spurred me on to study other aspects of Church history, especially concerning liturgy and the patristic period.

From this reading, I concluded two things: first, that Presbyterian worship and a lot of Protestant worship in general had reduced the ancient liturgies to their minimal form. In general, a lot of Protestantism in America represents a kind of reductionism of the Catholic faith. Perhaps the most salient point is that there can be no official worship of the Church without the Eucharist. Even Calvin seemed to recognize this truth though most of his followers would not know why he thought this.

The second conclusion involved the "why part." I have always wanted to know the reasons *why* I must believe something. I had always thought that the Reformed faith represented the teaching of the Scriptures and the ancient church. When I had to teach the process of biblical interpretation—as opposed to teaching what I thought the Bible taught—I realized that the only way to agree on a proper interpretation of a text is to have a living Magisterium in the Church.

The reason that there are so many Protestants who can't agree on what the Bible teaches is that they have no authoritative interpretative body. The analogy in law is of course the Supreme Court. The Constitution lying on the table is of no use to anyone and in the hands of each individual, it might be interpreted in a myriad of ways. So what is needed is clearly an authoritative body of interpreters who can render judgments on which meanings are permissible and which are not.

In sum, I realized that the Protestant faith was not the faith of the Ancient Fathers of the Church. The irony of all this is that John Calvin led me to the Catholic Church. Calvin in the 16th century wanted to bring the Church back to its original purity from which he and other Reformers believed the Roman Church had departed. So Calvin said in essence: go back to the ancient church! But when I did, I found that it wasn't Protestantism. So I knew in my conscience that I must leave my Protestant heritage

My journey during this period was much, much more than intellectual inquiry. Between 1991 and 1994, I met monthly with Fr. Francis Cosgrove, the Vicar General of the Diocese of Jackson for spiritual direction. It was he who guided me to the Ignatian tradition of spirituality, a very perceptive decision since so much of Ignatian spirituality focuses on discerning the will of God for our lives. In the summer of the 1993, I directed my wife in a mini-retreat in the Ignatian pattern using Fr. Andre Ravier's *Do-It-Yourself Spiritual Exercises*. This was the beginning of the end so to speak (see Ken's article, *God's Hopes in You: Ignatian Thoughts on Guidance* in *Part Two*, pg. 182).

Another Catholic friend in California paid for my travel and conference fees to attend a *Defending the Faith* conference at Franciscan University of Steubenville in June of 1992. Here God had another divine appointment for me.

One day at lunch I found myself across the table from a woman in her sixties who was from Canada. I was discussing with the man next to me the theological work of Fr. Bernard Lonergan who helped me so much to understand the doctrines of the Church. This holy and loving woman joined in our conversation with a theological sophistication that I had not found among Catholic lay people and I was intrigued. This was to be the first of many contacts with the Catholic sister who has been such an instrument of God in my journey to the Church. She is a cradle Catholic and my friendship with her was essential in understanding the process of conversion because I think that this process can often be distorted if we look at and listen to only recent converts from Protestantism.

What I needed to see was not a zealous convert but someone who had faithfully loved and served Christ her whole life in the Church. This is what Marie Jutras showed me. It was to be her friendship, love, gifts and prayers which would not only draw me to an authentic Catholic life but would also break down the misconceptions of Catholicism in the mind of my wife. Probably more than any single individual, Marie has been God's "sacrament" of love to show me the face of the Savior.

In the summer of 1994, I left Reformed seminary after six years of teaching. It was quiet and amicable but they and I knew that I couldn't remain there forever because my views had caused too much of a stir. Theologically, I was probably somewhere between Rome and the Reformation although definitely closer to Rome on many issues (e.g. Eucharist). During this time, I appreciated what had been said in the newsletter about using the time we have in a Protestant setting to clear away misunderstandings and misconceptions about the Catholic Church. I endeavored to do just that.

The greatest conviction came when one day I realized that I really believed it when the priest said, "This is Jesus, the Lamb of God who takes the sin of the world." Somehow I knew from that day on that there was no turning back and that becoming a Catholic was just a matter of time. What I didn't know was how much time it would take.

We moved to Bloomington, Indiana so I could use the excellent research facilities of Indiana University to write a book on the history of biblical interpretation. At the same time I became a good friend with the pastor of St. Charles Borrromeo Catholic Church near the university, Fr. Charles Cheesebrough. This man's patience, compassion and openness won my heart as I struggled to go through one of the most difficult years of my life.

I had fully hoped to enter the Church at Easter Vigil 1995 but conversations with my wife and Catholic friends suggested that it would be better for me to wait to see if my wife could join me in that decision.

Then on June 3, 1995 a dramatic event stunned me. An assailant shot me in the neck with a handgun and almost killed me. God miraculously saved my life. Because of the prayers of God's people on earth and the saints in heaven, I was surrounded with angelic hosts from above and human love from below and I learned, as I never had before, that in the moment of our deepest need, God's presence pervades our being.

The people of St. Charles's parish as well as many other churches in the city overwhelmed our family with love. This was only one of the many events in the last few years which have taught me the meaning of St. Paul's words, "we always carry around in our body the dying of Jesus so that the life of Jesus may be manifested in our mortal bodies (2 Cor. 4.10)."

I am so thankful that the Catholic spiritual teachings on suffering are now a part of my heritage as a Christian. Without this understanding of grace and virtue through suffering I would not have been able to endure the pains and hurts of my life. I now can say with the apostle, "I rejoice in my sufferings in hope of the glory of God."

For a long time, I was Catholic on the inside while still being a Protestant on the outside. For prudential reasons, I was delaying my entrance into the Church with the hope that my wife and I could resolve our differences so that we might join together. But God's plans were different. By God's grace and my wife's encouragement, I was able to enter into complete communion with the Catholic Church on my forty-fourth birthday, June 1, 1996, and received for the first time the body and blood, soul and divinity of my Lord. Praise and honor and glory be to God!

On Whose Authority?

by Fr. Raymond and Ruth Ryland

"**H**ow can you go into that darkness, once you have known the light?" In deep anguish, my mother-in-law asked my wife and me this question when we told her we were going to enter the Catholic Church.

There was a time when the thought of becoming Catholics would have caused us even greater distress than our news caused her. But now we were near the end of a sixteen-year pilgrimage. We could finally see the Tiber ahead, and we were eager to cross. For many years we had known ourselves as seekers. Now we realized we were pilgrims. The difference? Pilgrims know where they are going.

Whatever its hidden roots, the seeking-which-was-a-pilgrimage began not long after Ruth and I married. While the initiative was largely mine, all those years we traveled together: reading, praying, discussing, at times arguing—always just between ourselves. Yet we never walked in lock-step. Sometimes one of us would go ahead, and the other would insist on a spiritual rest-stop. (I did most of the darting ahead and the chastened retracing of steps.) But we were always together. For that, we are forever grateful.

During much of our pilgrimage we knew that we were wrestling with the problem of authority. How does one know Christian truth with certainty? We saw with increasing clarity that this issue underlies all the divisions among the thousands of competing Christian traditions. We began to recognize that the issue of authority is at root a Christological question: What has God done in Christ to communicate his truth to the world?

The quest for ultimate doctrinal authority may arise out of psychological need. Some of our friends put this interpretation on our pilgrimage. They seemed to think I was the culprit, dragging my poor wife along on my ill-fated journey. "Ray, we always knew you had a need for the authority and structure you've found in the Catholic Church."

What they said was true. It was true in a far deeper sense than they apparently meant it. With all our hearts we believe every human being needs the authority and structure of the Catholic Church. In our Episcopal years Ruth and I grew in our personal relationship with Jesus Christ, loving him and trying to serve him. Fairly late in our pilgrimage we realized that we had accepted Christ on our terms, because we had no other. In every instance of moral decision or of personal belief, we were the final authority as to what we should do or believe. This is the dilemma of all non-Catholics.

The Catholic Church was founded by Jesus Christ and claims to speak for him under carefully specified conditions. Once the truth of that claim became clear to us, after a long and arduous search, we had no alternative but to submit to the Church's authority. In that submission we knew we were submitting to Jesus Christ on his terms. No longer were "we" the final authority in matters of faith and morals. This submission is possible only in the Church Christ established and to which he gave his authority.

Looking back over the years we knew it was the Holy Spirit who long ago had put in our hearts this yearning for ultimate doctrinal and moral authority. It was in entering the Catholic Church that the yearning would know its fulfillment.

The discernible beginnings of our journey lie in my vocation to ordained ministry. The first faint sounds of a call to the ministry came to me in a summer church camp before my freshman year in college. The sounds were so faint that when I entered a college of my denomination I had no clear vocational focus. I majored in history only because it was my favorite subject.

A sophomore course in European history introduced me to details of Catholic teaching. The two textbooks were written by Carleton J. H. Hayes, who was to be the American ambassador to Spain during World War II. (Only recently I learned he had become a Catholic while a student at Columbia.)

I began to learn about popes and monks and bishops and sacraments and interdicts and penitent kings standing barefoot in the snow. Hayes's books gave far more detail about Catholic belief than the average history book. The Catholic Church was a fascinating subject, but I was not drawn to it by my study then: too remote, too utterly different from my Protestant world.

Even though entering the ministry kept coming into my mind, I never thought of praying for God to guide me. After all, it was my decision to make, or so I thought. (I thank God that he ignored my ignoring him!) In my senior year I decided to enter the seminary at my college.

In that same year came Pearl Harbor. Soon I realized that I could not sit in a classroom while my friends fought a war we all believed was necessary. After graduation I entered officers training for the Navy. I assumed that if I survived military service, and if the attraction to the ministry were valid, the attraction too would survive.

Almost all of my three years in the Navy I served as a communications and navigation officer on an aircraft carrier in the Pacific theater. We were at sea almost all that time, so in my off-duty hours I read widely and studied in preparation for seminary.

A chaplain on our ship put me in touch by correspondence with his former professor, Robert H. Pfeiffer, distinguished professor of Old Testament at Harvard Divinity School. Pfeiffer very graciously guided my study of his classic introduction to the Old Testament. My correspondence with Pfeiffer and friendship with the chaplain, himself a Harvard graduate, led me to choose Harvard Divinity School.

Ruth and I had been in college together, and we were married just before the war ended. When I was released from the Navy we moved to Cambridge, where I enrolled in the Divinity School. I soon learned that some of the faculty and students were Unitarian. Until then I had scarcely heard the word Unitarian. In my course work I made a fateful discovery. I, too, was Unitarian. In my college years and especially in my Navy years I had drifted imperceptibly into the Unitarian belief that Jesus was only a great moral teacher, nothing more.

My first theology course was taught by an elderly Dutch scholar with a very impressive name, Johannes Augustus Christopher Fagginger Auer. Without knowing it, I think, he did me a great favor by showing me the superficiality of what I actually believed.

One day, when in a reflective mood, he admitted to us in class, "It's not an easy thing to come to the end of your life and not know whether there's anything beyond death." At that moment I realized that at most I had only a vague hope that there is something, but no assurance. Ruth had retained the Trinitarianism of her Protestant upbringing, but was not strong in her faith then.

After two or three months of pondering my own situation, I told the dean I had no desire to preach and teach Christianity if what I was learning in class was all there is to Christianity. Either I must pursue some other vocation or go elsewhere to inquire further into the Christian religion. I was thinking of transferring to Yale Divinity School.

The dean was gracious and seemed to try to understand my difficulty. Though himself a graduate of Yale, he recommended that Ruth and I go instead to Union Theological Seminary in New York. He said that Union was a more cosmopolitan environment than Yale. After a trip to Union and a talk with several faculty, we decided to transfer there.

Ruth and I lived in the men's dormitory, three floors of which had been given over to married students. We took our meals in the refectory. For three years we ate, slept, drank, and breathed theology. Theological discussion was the consuming passion of everyone at Union. We were immersed in the theological bedlam that is Protestantism: all traditions to some extent contradicting each other and all claiming to be based on the Bible.

Union was indeed cosmopolitan. Dozens of denominations and many competing theological approaches created a lively, fascinating environment. Ardent Barthians argued fiercely with equally ardent Brunnerians; Niebuhrians battled with Tillichians. But everyone, so far as I knew, was Trinitarian. At Union I heard Jesus Christ powerfully proclaimed. I became a believing Christian, surrendering my life to Jesus Christ, while Ruth's faith in Christ was greatly strengthened.

Amid this bedlam we thought we heard a voice of theological sanity. We began to learn about the Episcopal Church through one of my professors, who was an Anglican clergyman and a persuasive apologist for his tradition. (Anglicanism is a generic term to designate the Church of England and all its transplanted branches, such as the Episcopal Church in this country.)

The Episcopal Church holds that to avoid theological chaos, Scripture must be interpreted by tradition; in particular, by the tradition of the early Church. Here, we thought, is a church rooted in

the past, in historical continuity with the early Church. Its theological approach seemed very sensible. We quickly came to love
the Elizabethan language of the Prayer Book the distinctive Episcopal architecture, the Englishness of the Episcopal ethos.

So we became Episcopalians. By this time I had completed
my theology degree and a year of doctoral study at Columbia and
Union. Ruth had earned a masters degree at Columbia while teaching nursery school.

To prepare for ordination and life within the Episcopal Church,
we moved to Alexandria, Virginia. For a year I attended the Episcopal seminary there and worked as a seminarian in a Washington
parish. The Episcopal bishop of Washington ordained me to the
diaconate and later to the priesthood in the National Cathedral. In
Washington I served two parishes, one as an associate rector (pastor), the other as rector. Three of our children were born during our
Washington years.

We were happy as Episcopalians, but we became increasingly
aware of theological discord within the denomination. Anglicans
claim they have no distinct theology; their theology is only that of
the early Church. But there is widespread disagreement regarding
what the early Church's theology was. A distinctive characteristic
of Anglicanism is what is called comprehensiveness: trying to
embrace a wide range of differing and even contradictory theological opinions within one communion.

The longer we lived within the Episcopal Church and the more
we studied its history, the more we saw its theological and moral
fragmentation. (We deeply regret that in recent years that fragmentation has greatly accelerated.) Initially, at Union, we were attracted
by the Anglican claim of comprehensiveness. Now we saw that
term as a euphemism for chaos.

For generations Anglicans have boasted that theirs is a bridge
church. That means they stand midway between Protestantism and
Catholicism, partaking of the good features of both and rejecting
the bad. I used to remind my colleagues that no one lives on a bridge.
A bridge is only a means for getting from one place to another.

A ray of hope did shine on us for a time, a movement within
the Episcopal Church (and other Anglican churches) known as
Anglo-Catholicism. It is based on what proponents call the branch

theory. This theory holds that the original Catholic Church is now divided into three branches, the Catholic, the Orthodox, and the Church of England. Anglo-Catholics claim that all three traditions are equally Catholic.

Anglo-Catholics believe that theological disarray within the Episcopal Church is caused by Protestant influences. The solution is to adopt Catholic ways in liturgy and (to an undefined degree) in theology. The touchstone of doctrine becomes the Catholic faith of the early centuries—Catholic, they insist, not Roman Catholic.

For half a dozen years or more we identified with the relatively small Anglo-Catholic movement. I taught my parishioners and anyone else who would listen that Episcopalians are Catholics, not Protestants. During these years we moved to Texas, where I served a newly-formed parish, and three years later to Oklahoma, where I was chaplain of an Episcopal elementary and secondary school. One of our sons was born in Texas and another in Oklahoma.

This Anglo-Catholic ray of hope finally gave out. We recognized that as a movement Anglo-Catholicism (like Anglicanism) is essentially, inescapably Protestant. The appeal to the faith of the original Catholic Church, like the appeal to the tradition of the early centuries, is futile. There is no one to say what that faith is, or what that tradition is, or what that tradition says about Scripture.

We had to admit that each individual decides for himself, or chooses a clergyman who will decide for him, what is Catholic and proceeds accordingly. There is no visible entity to which the Anglo-Catholic can point and say, "That is the Catholic Church to which I belong." That Catholic Church is only an abstraction.

In the last century John Henry Newman tried desperately for years to convince himself and others that they were part of the Catholic Church. Eventually he recognized that his Catholic Church was only a paper church, existing in the imaginations of himself and other like-minded persons.

Now where to turn?

Like most Anglo-Catholics, we looked on Eastern Orthodoxy with awe, an awe largely born, I later learned, of misunderstanding. The Anglo-Catholic logic regarding Orthodoxy goes like this. Rome denies that our church is Catholic. [That is, Rome—and also the Orthodox—reject the branch theory.] But Rome does admit that the Orthodox Churches are Catholic. [Today I know this is incorrect.] Therefore, the Orthodox tradition is living proof that one can be Catholic without having to be a papal Catholic. We wondered, is Orthodoxy the answer to our seeking?

At this stage of our journey, as a chaplain I had summers free. A generous friend and benefactor made possible our family's spending several summers at the University of the South in Sewanee, Tennessee. There I studied in the Episcopal graduate school of theology.

In our first summer in Sewanee, a well-known Byzantine scholar offered an introductory course in Eastern Orthodoxy. Ruth and I saw this opportunity for me as purely providential. I found the course and the work on a required research paper to be intensely interesting. I decided the paper should be the basis of a graduate thesis in theology. Both Ruth and I were drawn to Orthodoxy by our reading and study. But there was ambivalence in our thinking about the Eastern Churches. The Orthodox ethos is utterly foreign to Americans. Whatever its ethnic background, an Orthodox Church is a very different world to those raised in this culture. How could we, an Okie and a Texan and our five children, ever be truly at home in any of these other cultures?

More and more, the essentially ethnic nature of the various Orthodox traditions stood out in our thinking. No other Christian tradition is so deeply rooted in a particular culture as are the several Orthodox churches.

All the Orthodox churches have been ingrown for centuries. None has evangelized any significant part of the world in recent centuries. Their spread to this country and elsewhere has been due almost entirely to the immigration of Orthodox people from their various homelands. Not one of these ethnic churches has demonstrated universal appeal.

Orthodox theologians agree that an ecumenical council is their highest authority. Yet in over 1,200 years they have never conducted one. Now that there is no Christian emperor, who can convoke a council for them? If the patriarch of any of the ethnic churches presumed to call for an ecumenical council, he would be opposed immediately as having asserted unauthorized jurisdiction over the other churches.

But most importantly of all, Orthodox churches have no real solution to the problem of doctrinal authority. The bishop, they say, speaks for Christ, and the ecumenical council is the ultimate authority, and conciliar decrees can be called infallible only after they have been received by the whole church, but there is no way of determining whether and when that has happened.

From within the Catholic communion we now can see other fundamental problems in the Orthodox churches. First, the term Orthodoxy commonly designates the Orthodox churches as a whole. But both Orthodoxy and Anglo-Catholicism have this in common: in differing degrees, perhaps, both are abstractions.

There is no entity, no institution to which one can point and say, "There is Orthodoxy." There is no Orthodoxy; there are only separate Orthodox churches. All hold basically the same faith, but they are not organically united. Indeed, jurisdictionally they are divided. In a given city in this country one may find two or three or more different Eastern Churches, each with its own bishop. But where is Orthodoxy? As the Eastern churches gradually separated themselves from Rome, under the influence of powerful Eastern emperors, they became more and more subservient to the secular authority in their countries. This is the problem of caesaro-papism, which has characterized the life of the Eastern Churches ever since they began to break with Rome. The communist secret police's admitted control of the Russian Orthodox Church for generations is only the latest example.

Earlier I referred to the Anglo-Catholic opinion that Rome regards the Orthodox churches as Catholic. This is incorrect. Vatican II documents, for example, always refer to the eastern churches, never to the Orthodox Church, and certainly never refer to Orthodox churches as being Catholic. True, they do have Catholic sacraments and hold most of the Catholic faith, but they are in schism from the Catholic Church.

Again, it was back to the search. We loved the Lord Jesus, we wanted to be in his Church, we wanted to do his will. Where should we look next?

Almost before we dared ask the question one more time, we knew the answer: Rome.

Frequently, in television coverage of baseball games, the camera will focus several times alternately on the pitcher and the catcher, just before the pitcher throws across the plate. The catcher signals for a certain pitch. The pitcher shakes his head, waits for another signal, then another. Finally, when he gets one he likes, the pitcher winds up and delivers.

How many signals from the Holy Spirit dared we turn down? But Rome? Idol-worshiping, power-hungry, priest-ridden, thought-controlling Rome?

From our upbringing and from our seminary training we imbibed all the prejudices, all the stereotypes. But these had to be put aside. We already knew the outlines of Catholic teaching from our Anglo-Catholic days. Now we admitted to ourselves we had to listen to the details of Rome's claims. Our reading and discussion resolved most of our objections, which were almost entirely based in misunderstanding.

The last major hurdle between ourselves and submission to Rome was the papacy. We read Newman's *Apologia* avidly and devoured Meriol Trevor's two-volume biography of Newman in large bites. Our journey was much like his, though on a small scale. We saw ourselves as pygmies trying to follow a giant. We continually invoked his prayers in our behalf. We received much help from what may be the best single book about the Catholic Church, Karl Adam's *Spirit of Catholicism*.

Sixteen years after beginning our search for the full truth of Christ we admitted to one another that we had to submit to Rome. Neither of us really wanted to be a Catholic, but God's call was unmistakable. We submitted to his will and eventually to his Church.

Our decision had to be kept secret to spare embarrassment to the school of which I was chaplain. Each week for months we drove to another city to spend an evening in instruction by a Benedictine monk whose friendship has been a rich blessing to us. With his help I began seeking employment to support our family. We knew that God never leads anyone down a blind alley. We cast ourselves as completely as possible upon his mercy. Then doors began to open, and the way became clearer.

The day we were received into the Church, Ruth and I wanted to have a party in our home. The problem was that we had no one to invite. Our Episcopal friends were either greatly saddened or resentful. We did not know any Catholics. But we had our party:

Ruth and I, our children, the two priests who received us, and, Ruth reminded us, the angels and archangels.

On the third day after our family was received into the Church, I went to early Mass in our parish church. As I knelt in the pew after receiving Communion, the words suddenly came to me, half-aloud, in a burst of joy: "Now I'm ready to die!"

For seven years I was a layman in the Church. During that time we moved to Milwaukee where I completed course work for a doctorate in theology. Back in Oklahoma, I taught and worked for the diocesan educational department and completed my dissertation. Then came a move to San Diego to join the theological faculty of a Catholic university. While teaching full time, I was ordained a permanent deacon in the Church and entered law school at night.

Several years after passing the bar I was preparing to begin part-time practice, which I intended would become full-time after I stopped teaching. Then the Church announced the Pastoral Provision for this country. Under its terms, married Catholic laymen who had formerly been Episcopal clergy were allowed to apply through their bishops for a dispensation from the rule of celibacy and for ordination to the priesthood.

My application was the first to be sent to Rome, though not the first one acted on. Thirteen months later my bishop received a letter from Cardinal Ratzinger, telling him the Holy Father had approved my being ordained. Several months later, after a series of written and oral exams, I was ordained to the priesthood. That was twelve years ago.

Each time I stand at the altar, at least once the thought suddenly comes, "Can this be real? Am I a Catholic priest, offering the Holy Sacrifice?" Then comes that blessed answer: "Yes! Thanks be to God!"

(Fr. Ray and Ruth's journey was originally published in This Rock Magazine, January 1995)

I Never Dreamed I'd be Married to a Roman Catholic Priest!

by Ruth Ryland

In the July issue of the *Network* Newsletter, Marilyn Grodi said that she never had wanted to marry a minister anyway. Well, I never dreamed I'd be married to a Roman Catholic priest.

The thirteen years Ray served as an Episcopal priest were exciting, fulfilling years. We had both come from a Disciples of Christ background and we found the intellectual and liturgical ethos of the Episcopal Church very satisfying. Our five children came along during that period. We loved the people in the various parishes and the school where Ray served. The people were great, good people who struggled along with us to live the Christian life. There were, of course, the usual ups and downs, joys and sorrows of living and serving, but through it all we felt most blessed by our Lord in all the important ways.

Through these years of study, prayer and simply living with God's people, we gradually moved to a more "catholic" view of the Church ("low church" to "high church"). There began a search for the historical "roots" of the Church. We became more and more aware of conflicting views and teachings on the Episcopal Church, not only in doctrinal maters but in moral ones as well. Some teachings were quite heretical. Questions arose: who was right? Which were the teachings faithful to the gospel? Who was to say what teachings were true or false? Where was the locus of authority?

When we began to see where the search was leading, we resisted. We didn't want to go. We didn't want to turn our comfortable life upside down. We didn't want to go into the "unknown," into a "foreign land." We loved the Episcopal Church and all it meant to us: the people, the beautiful churches, the grand music and liturgy. Then there were all the questions of how to support our family, of leaving dear friends. (When we entered the Church we knew not even one Catholic, only the two priests who instructed us.) What about our families who would grieve and be shocked that we had "lost our minds," etc.? Those who have traveled this road know all about the sufferings. And yet, and yet ... we could hear the insistent beat of the "following feet" of the Hound of Heaven as He pursued, keeping their steady and unhurried pace.

When the Holy Spirit showed us, through sheer grace, beyond the shadow of a doubt, that the Catholic Church is indeed the true Church, founded by Jesus Christ himself on the Rock of Peter, could we say anything but "yes!" to Him? Praised be to Jesus Christ for his mercy and grace!

In 1963, together with our five young children, we were received into the Catholic Church. We had truly come home. In those days it was rather rare for a Protestant clergyman to take that step. Except for the angels and archangels, we had no one with whom to celebrate our joy. But joy it was and is.

Dear brothers and sisters who are on the Way, or contemplating the Way: the path may be dark for you, the problems seemingly insurmountable, the sufferings great. But if you are looking to Jesus, the Author and Finisher of your faith, you can be certain of this: He will never betray your trust. **Trust Him.**

Breathing Catholic Air
by David Palm

My wife and I were raised Evangelical Protestants, and if you would have told us a year ago that we would be Catholics today, we would have laughed. Becoming Catholic was not a prospect we were particularly happy with. When we first began to be influenced positively by things Catholic, our feeling could probably best be summarized as, "We have met the enemy, and it is us."

I am sorry to have to portray the relationship between certain Evangelical Protestants and the Catholic Church in adversarial language, but that is how we were raised. We were taught that the Catholic Church had usurped the Bible by adding layers of "human tradition" to it and that the Church deceives millions by teaching them that they are saved by their good works. We were nothing if not staunchly Protestant. But now, by God's grace, we have come to see that only in the Catholic Church does the fullness of the Christian faith reside.

My own journey to Catholicism started when, fresh out of college, I attended a prominent Evangelical Protestant seminary: Trinity Evangelical Divinity School. This school is well known in Evangelical circles for its commitment to the Bible as the sole authority for Christian faith and practice. The faculty and students staunchly and enthusiastically defend the Bible's authority, inspiration, and inerrancy. This is not done in a dogmatic, unintellectual, "Fundamentalist" fashion. We learned Greek and Hebrew, methods of exegesis and principles of hermeneutics, history and theology. We read the works of liberal scholars and learned to engage them on their own intellectual grounds. In short, we took our Bible very seriously. It was a stimulating environment in which we were encouraged to think for ourselves and formulate theological positions well grounded in the objective evidence available in Scripture.

Interestingly, we never read the early Church fathers, nor any Catholic theologians except Augustine (because he is considered a sort of proto-Calvinist) and Aquinas (because his impact on Christian thought was so profound as to be difficult to ignore). Generally we just skipped straight from the apostles to the Reformers, so my exposure to Catholic ideas was virtually nonexistent. Yet two things significantly influenced my thinking with respect to Catholicism, although I didn't know this at the time.

First, as I wrestled with the Bible and studied it in detail, I began to realize that it didn't support the theology that I had been brought up to believe. I changed from premillennial to amillennial eschatology; I ceased believing in the common Protestant belief of the eternal security of the Christian; I abandoned the doctrine of justification by faith alone, one of the pillars of the Reformation; and I began to hold a sacramental view of baptism and the Lord's Supper.

I felt like a bit of a theological "misfit" because no Protestant denomination held precisely the same views that I held, and this bothered me. Some of my professors assured me that it was fine to hold independent opinions on various issues, so long as one's views were consonant with the Bible and lay generally within the broad spectrum of "orthodox" Christian belief. But this sort of maverick approach to Christian doctrine concerned me; what is the basis of Christian unity if we formulate customized doctrines? Isn't it precisely because of these differences that Protestants have been fragmenting and dividing for centuries?

Although I didn't feel called to start my own denomination, I didn't feel theologically comfortable in the existing ones either. In fact, I chose to keep some of my personal views to myself in my local church, for fear of others' reaction. This confusion over Bible interpretation among Protestants made me question—at least on a semi-conscious level—whether commitment to the inspiration and authority of the Bible is really the unifying factor that Evangelical Protestants think it is.

The second factor that changed my thinking was exposure to unorthodox views propounded both by liberal Protestant theologians and by conservative Protestant groups. The proponents of these views appeal to the Bible for support, but many of their doctrines are innovative; they have never been held in the entire history of the Church.

Instinctively I knew that these ideas were unorthodox; many of them ran directly against the great creeds of the Church. But what was my standard of orthodoxy, the Bible or the creeds? If I appealed to creed or "the universal belief of the Church" in order to declare something unorthodox, was I not following something besides Scripture alone? This raised questions that I couldn't answer: What is orthodoxy? What is the standard of Christian orthodoxy?

I began to suspect that it couldn't be just the Bible, because none of us could agree on what the Bible says. All appeals to the Bible can be countered with a different interpretation or an outright rejection of the authority of the Bible. Increasingly I turned to the creeds and to a nebulous collection of the "universal beliefs of the Church" to assure myself that what I believed was orthodox.

I didn't know it at the time, but my wife, Lorene, also was being prepared for our journey to the Catholic Church. While in college she attended a Reformed Baptist church. This exposed her to a sacramental understanding of the Lord's Supper; in turn she influenced me on this doctrine.

One of her sisters—whose husband was raised Catholic—would occasionally point to the disarray among Protestants and ask how they could all claim to hold true Christian doctrine, yet disagree on so many things. My wife had no good answer to this question and, because of her Protestant upbringing, didn't think there really was an answer. She stuck to the idea that a person should read the Bible and ask for the Holy Spirit's guidance. That response seemed inadequate, but it was all that she knew.

About two years ago I was in a Salvation Army-like thrift store, rummaging through the used books. I saw a copy of *Catholicism and Fundamentalism* by Karl Keating and leafed through it out of curiosity. It was only one dollar, but I almost put it back since it was, after all, about Catholic theology. Still, I thought to myself, the chapter headings are interesting, and it couldn't hurt to know what Catholics say about these things.

I purchased the book and began to read it on my morning train ride into Chicago. I tried to read sympathetically, and conceded that if I stepped into Catholic shoes—especially with regard to how Catholics view Scripture—then Catholic theology seemed coherent and made sense. The book cleared up misconceptions I had about what Catholics really believe.

I shared these observations with my wife. That was a mistake. We got into an argument right there on the train. "You're not going to become a Catholic, are you?" she blustered at me. She told me later that all she could think was, "How am I going to explain this to my family? I married a Protestant seminary student and he turns Catholic!" Backpedaling quickly, I told her that I was just playing devil's advocate, and the whole topic went on a back burner for a while.

Still, my respect for Catholics grew steadily. I very much admire Pope John Paul II—his unequivocal stand against immorality, his refusal to water down his message to our President and to the people of the United States, and his calling the youth of America back to Christianity, inspired me. I read Charles Colson's book *The Body* and was impressed by the role the Catholic and Orthodox Churches played in bringing down Communism. I saw Catholics reaching out and meeting so many physical needs in the name of Christ. I had for a long time been disappointed with our Evangelical churches because we complained a lot about the problems in our society, but didn't do much about them. I saw Catholics in our town putting their faith into practice—feeding the hungry, giving shelter to the homeless, caring for unwed mothers and their children.

In May 1993, because of some pro-Catholic statements I made in a Bible study, a couple that we knew from the Baptist church we attended told us that they were exploring Catholicism. Dave had attended the same seminary that I graduated from, so we had similar theological backgrounds. We talked for an afternoon about things that we found attractive about the Catholic Church. I ended up lending Keating's book to Dave, and he lent me a tape series by Scott Hahn, a former Presbyterian minister who has become Catholic. I enjoyed the tapes, but at the time was not fully persuaded by Hahn's arguments (only later would I realize how much he had influenced me).

Nothing much happened, seemingly, until September, when Dave brought the book back. He told us that he had resigned from the deacon board at our church and that he and his family had begun to attend Mass. We were surprised, but curious. I look up to Dave as a spiritual role model. He is a solid man, and I knew that he would not do something like this lightly. Lorene and I knew that

Dave's news would not get a warm reception at our Baptist church, and we were determined to maintain the friendship and to support him and his wife in their decision.

We invited them over a few weeks later to talk. We just asked questions, not trying to talk them out of their decision to become Catholic, but trying to find out what had compelled them to make such a move. The more we talked the more excited we all got. On point after point Catholic doctrine was biblical, logical, and consistent. It seemed to encompass the entire Bible, including the problem passages, rather than focusing on a select group of verses to support a particular position. It seemed that within a Catholic framework, many of these problem passages were no longer a problem.

We found too that we have seriously misunderstood much of what the Catholic Church actually teaches, and that there were good answers to all the questions we had. Our friends stayed until midnight, and, when they left, my wife and I were like the disciples on the road to Emmaus; our ears burned with this new knowledge. That weekend neither of us could get it out of our heads; we could barely sleep.

My wife—much to my surprise—began talking about the "inevitability" of us becoming Catholic. I was shocked that she, of all people, was so moved toward Catholicism. But once she understood and believed the basic principles of papal authority, the role of the magisterium, and the place of tradition in Christian doctrine, she understood that all the rest must follow. I was not there yet; I had too many questions, although I had to admit that in my heart I wanted it to be true.

We began a serious exploration of this new faith. As a result of this study, I found that in all of the areas of theology in which I had changed my views, I had either arrived at or was on the way toward orthodox Catholic doctrine. I confirmed that much of my prior "knowledge" about Catholic doctrine was at best distorted and at worst simply wrong.

In the past, when I bothered to read about Catholicism at all, I consulted Protestant sources. These tended to cast Catholicism in an unfavorable light and often, whether wittingly or unwittingly, misrepresented what the Catholic Church teaches. Reading from orthodox Catholic sources about Catholic doctrine and the support for it was eye-opening and challenging. I was forced to rethink issues I had taken for granted.

Through this study I came to see that, although the Protestant Reformation was touted as a return to "Scripture alone" over against Catholic "traditions," in fact the major theological tenets of the Reformation cannot be supported from the Bible. The Reformers made their break with the Catholic Church based primarily on three doctrines: justification by faith alone, sola scriptura or the Bible alone as our authority, and a repudiation of the doctrine of transubstantiation.

While still in seminary I had abandoned the doctrine of justification by faith alone because it was unbiblical (see James 2:21-26; Rom. 2:6-13; Gal. 5:6; Matt. 12:36-37). The next watershed for me was when I began to believe in the Real Presence of Christ in the Eucharist. Already I viewed the Lord's Supper as a sacrament, but now I saw that Scripture teaches something greater, that the bread and wine actually become the body and blood of our Lord. Even more compelling to me was the fact that this was the orthodox view of the Church for 1,500 years, before the Protestant reformers came along and convinced our branch of Christianity that it just wasn't so, that what the Church had for all those centuries held as her deepest and most precious mystery was, in fact, no mystery at all but just a memorial service!

I went back and read the writings of the earliest Church Fathers—Ignatius, Justin Martyr, Irenaeus, Tertullian, Hippolytus, Augustine—and found that they all believed in the Real Presence. I could no longer swallow our Protestant assertion that millions upon millions of Christians, including some who knew the apostles personally, had been misled by the Holy Spirit until Calvin and Zwingli came along and set everybody straight. Although these Reformers couldn't agree among themselves what the Lord's Supper meant, they all insisted that the Catholics must be wrong.

The last straw for my status as a Protestant was when sola scriptura—the doctrine that the Bible alone is our authority in matters of faith—fell apart. I had read in Keating's book and had heard in Hahn's tape that the doctrine is not taught in Scripture, that Scripture nowhere claims to be the sole rule for our faith. Many passages indicated that the traditions of the apostles, whether written or oral, are authoritative and that Christians should believe and follow them (see especially 1 Cor. 11:2; 1 Thess. 2:13; 2 Thess. 2:15; 2 Tim. 2:2; 2 Pet. 3:1-3).

The Catholic Church teaches that the Church is the guardian of this deposit of God's revelation to the apostles. So does Paul, when he calls the Church (not the Bible) "the pillar and foundation of the truth" (1 Tim. 3:15). Always I shrugged off this argument, although I could not counter it. (2 Timothy 3:16 came to mind immediately, but this verse only says that the Bible is profitable for correction, training, and so on, which is not the same as saying that it is the only source for these things.)

One afternoon the consequences of these facts hit home. The foundation of my Protestantism was kicked out from under me. We Protestants insisted that all of our doctrine must be found in the Bible, but the doctrine of sola scriptura is itself not found in the Bible. Then I realized that the Protestant position was based fatally on a logical incoherence.

Once I became convinced that the Reformers were wrong in these three areas, there was very little support left for the Reformation at all. While virtually everybody, whether Catholic or Protestant, will admit that the Catholic Church needed reform during Luther's day (even the popes said so), it was difficult for me to see how reforming the Church consisted of smashing it into thousands of splinter groups, all claiming to hold true doctrine but interpreting the Bible differently and rarely if ever cooperating with each other. The continuous division and rupture, schism upon schism, that characterizes Protestantism is impossible to justify and is profoundly unbiblical (John 10:16; 17:20-23 and 1 Cor. 1-3).

Having worked through these and many other issues, my wife and I felt that there were only two paths left: a descent into rationalistic agnosticism or an ascent into the fullness of the Christian faith found in the Catholic Church. This was no choice at all, since we loved Jesus too much to become agnostics. We were confirmed and received into the Catholic Church on February 8, 1994. We are thrilled to be Catholic, even though the transition—particularly telling family and friends about our decision—was difficult.

Because culturally the Catholic Church is different from Evangelical Protestantism, we are still in a process of acclimation, but I feel much like Cardinal Newman, who said after his conversion to Catholicism that he felt as if he had finally come into port from rough sea. No longer do we have to be "blown about by every wind of doctrine" (Eph. 4:14). We don't have to wonder any longer if what we believe is orthodox.

A wonderful group of Catholic priests and lay people have rallied around us and have ministered Christ's love through their prayers and support during our pilgrimage into the Church. Our journey has opened up for us new vistas of Christian worship in the liturgy, the incredible richness of the sacraments, and the vast treasury of Catholic spirituality. All these confirm to us that we have truly come home.

(Dave and Lorene's journey was originally published in This Rock Magazine, April 1994.)

A Journey Home
by Rosalind Moss

May He guide thy way, who Himself is thine everlasting end:
That every step, be swift or slow, still to Himself may tend.

A s I set out to do the unthinkable—to study the claims of the Roman Catholic Church—I clung to the prayer above, fearful that the enemy of our souls would deceive and render me useless for the kingdom of the Christ I had come to know and love.

I was raised in a Jewish home, one which celebrated many of the traditions, at least in our younger years. I remember having a special sense that the one God was our God and that we were His people. Yet as we grew and went out on our own, much was left behind. Eventually my brother, David, became an atheist, and I, perhaps, an agnostic.

In the summer of 1975 (we were now in our thirties) I visited David. For years David had been searching for truth, for the meaning of life, and to know if there really was a God. Many times I had thought to myself,

> *What makes you think there is such a thing as truth?! ... that there is one thing that is truth? And what makes you think you could find it? Wouldn't it be like looking for a needle in a haystack? And how would you recognize it?*
>
> *But even if there was such a thing as truth, and you could find it, and you knew when you had it ... and even if the truth meant that there is a God—then what? How would knowing that make a difference in your life? I figured, "I am because of what is. If what is means there's a God, therefore I am; if what is means there's no God, then therefore I am. My knowledge or lack of it doesn't determine what is, so why know?"*

In our conversation this same visit, David told me he had come across an article that said there are Jews—Jewish people—alive, on the face of the earth, who believe that Jesus Christ is the Jewish Messiah—the Messiah(!) the rest of us were still waiting for. I'll never forget the shock that went through my system at that moment. I thought back to all the years we sat at the Passover table in expectation of the Messiah's coming, knowing He was the only hope we had. And now David was telling me that there are people—Jewish people—who believe that He came?!

I said to David, "You mean they believe He was here—on earth—already!? And n-o-b-o-d-y knows??? The world isn't changed? And He left???!"

Now what? There would be no hope, nothing left. It's insane. And besides, you can't be Jewish and believe in Christ.

Within three months of that conversation, I had moved to California and met some of these Jews who believed in Christ. They didn't just believe that Jesus Christ was the Jewish Messiah, but that He was God come to earth! How can anyone even compute that? How could a man be God? How could you look on God and live?!

One life-changing night I was together with a group of these Jewish believers, all Christians—all Evangelical-Protestant Christians. They told me that God required the shedding of blood for the forgiveness of sin and they explained how, under the Old Testament sacrificial system, individuals would come daily to offer animal sacrifices for their sins—bulls, goats, lambs. If it was a lamb, it had to be a male, one-year-old, and absolutely perfect, without blemish or spot. The individual would put his hand on the head of the lamb, symbolic of the sins passing from that individual on to the animal. And that lamb—who was innocent but who symbolically had taken upon itself the sin of that person—was slain, and its blood was shed on the altar as an offering to God in payment of that person's sin.

I couldn't understand why God would put an innocent animal to death for my sin? But it began to get through to me that sin was no light matter to God. They explained further that those animal sacrifices were temporary, that they needed to be repeated, and that they could not perfect the offerer. Those sacrifices pointed to the One who would one day come and take upon Himself—not the sin of one person for a time—but the sins of the entire world, for all time.

And with that they pointed me to one verse only in the New Testament, John 1:29, when Jesus came and John the Baptist, looked at Him and said, "Behold, the Lamb of God who takes away the sin of the world!" The Lamb of God—the final, once-for-all sacrifice to which all Old Testament sacrifices pointed. It shattered me. I couldn't believe what I had just begun to understand. My biggest hang-up was the thought that a man can't be God! But I realized that night that—if God exists—He can become a man! God can be anything or anyone He wants to be; I'm not about to tell Him how to be God!

It was not long after that that I gave my life to Christ. And God transformed my life—overnight. I knew little, if anything, about Evangelicalism, or Protestantism for that matter. I had become a Christian. I had a relationship with the God of the universe and a reason to live for the first time in my life. I wanted to take a megaphone to the moon and shout to the world that God is and that they could know Him.

My first Bible study as a new Christian was taught by an ex-Catholic, who himself was taught by an ex-priest. So I learned from the start that the Catholic Church was a cult, a false religious system leading millions astray. For years I taught against the Catholic Church, trying to help people, even whole families, by bringing them out of such man-made religion into a true relationship with Christ through the only Christianity I knew and believed with all my heart.

It was about a year after my commitment to Christ that David called to tell me that he had come to believe that Christ was God and that, for him, it also meant giving his life to Christ. But he was not ready to commit himself to any church at the time (though he had been attending a Baptist congregation). The increasing number of Protestant denominations and splinter groups stood to David as a poor testimony to Christ's words that He would build His church. Where was the unity? How, he would ask, could sincere, born-again, Bible-believing Christians, indwelt and led by the same Holy Spirit, come out with such varying interpretations of Scripture?

These among other concerns led David to the study of the Roman Catholic Church. I was horrified, and frightened for him. How could he be a true Christian and buy into that!

It was Christmas 1978 when I visited David again. He took me first to meet the monk with whom he was studying and who I was sure was an agent of the devil on a mission to lead my brother astray. And then we went to a midnight Christmas-Eve Mass. It was the first time I had ever entered a Catholic Church. I sat in shock through the entire Mass, and also through the car trip home. When I could finally speak, I said to David: "It's like a synagogue, but with Christ!!" He said, "That's right!" To which I answered, "That's wrong!!!!" Christ fulfilled the Law; all that ritual and stuff was done away with! I was sick inside. How could David fall for that? Did he have some hang-up? Was he drawn to the liturgy, to the aesthetics, from our Jewish background? Could he not see Christ as the end to which it all pointed?

David entered the Catholic Church in 1979. Our phone bills between California and New York were hefty over the years that followed. The more he plunged into what I believed was error, the more I devoured what I knew was truth. Having completed the Bible institute at my church, I entered graduate studies at Talbot Theological Seminary in La Mirada, CA, while serving as full-time Chaplain of a women's jail facility in Lancaster, CA. My deepest desire upon graduation was to be on staff at a local church teaching women, helping them to raise godly families and to reach others with the gospel.

The God who gives us the desires of our hearts is the same God who brings them to fruition. Upon graduation from Talbot in May 1990, I was called to the staff of an evangelical Friends (Quaker) Church in Orange County, CA, as Director of Women's Ministries. Doctrinally, the Friends denomination did not align fully with my beliefs, since they had done away with baptism and communion. This particular church, however, under the leadership of a new pastor, of Baptist (and ex-Catholic) background, had reinstituted both for this single congregation within the denomination.

In the fateful month of transition from the jail ministry to that local church, I had time to visit David in New York. It was June of 1990. In one of our marathon conversations David asked, "How is it that Evangelicals don't seem to want to work toward unity? Didn't Jesus pray that we'd all be one ...?" I saw red. "Yes, Jesus prayed we'd be one, as He and the Father are one ... but not at the expense of truth!"

With that David asked me if I had ever seen the publication sitting on his table entitled, *This Rock*, which he described as a "Catholic apologetics" magazine. I couldn't even fathom those two words modifying each other. I never knew Catholics had a defense of their faith—no Catholic ever told me the gospel. But more, I never knew Catholics cared that anyone else know it.

I took the magazine back with me to California out of curiosity, and also out of some measure of respect for people who would want others to know what they, at least, believe is the answer to life—even if they are wrong. Inside was a full-page advertisement that read: Presbyterian Minister Becomes Catholic. There's no way, I thought to myself. I don't care what he called himself, or what he functioned as ... there's no way this "Presbyterian Minister" could have been a true Christian if he entered the Catholic Church. How could he have known Christ and been so deceived?

I ordered the four-part tape series of this ex-Presbyterian minister (whose name was Scott Hahn) which included a two-part debate with a professor from Westminster Theological Seminary on the issues of justification (faith alone vs. faith plus works) and authority (Scripture alone vs. Scripture plus Tradition). Hahn's concluding statement summed up 2,000 years of church history and climaxed with the thought that to those who will look into the claims of the Catholic Church and judge the evidence will come a "holy shock and a glorious amazement ..." to find out that that which he had been fighting and trying to save people from is, in fact, the very Church Christ established on earth.

Holy shock are the only words to describe what went through me at that moment. "Oh no," I thought, "don't tell me there could be truth to this." The thought paralyzed me. I couldn't believe what I was thinking. And it came at a most inconvenient time. In two weeks I would begin at the new church.

I reread the doctrinal statement of the Friends denomination I was about to enter. It included the story of its founder, George Fox, whose dramatic conversion in the 1600's filled him with a deep love for God and zeal to counter the abuses of his day. In his desire that God be worshipped in spirit and in truth, Fox did away with the only two sacraments, or "ordinances," that Luther had left—baptism and communion—lest faith be placed in the elements of wine, bread and water rather than in the God to whom they pointed.

I loved the heart of George Fox, but I believed he was wrong. Baptism and communion were clearly commanded in Scripture, though I believed they were symbolic. The thought seized me: What if Luther did what Fox did? What if Luther, out of love and zeal for God's honor, also discarded what God intended? My stomach sank as my fear rose. Were my thoughts from God? Were they from Satan? I knew only that, before God, I had to find out what the Catholic Church taught.

During the next two years on staff with the Friends church I ordered books, tapes, even a subscription to *This Rock* magazine, even though I dreaded the thought of anything Catholic coming to my mailbox. When I told David of my search, he challenged me concerning the doctrine of sola scriptura. "Ros, where does the Bible teach sola scriptura?" The very question annoyed me. I had heard it before and chose to ignore it. "If," I thought, "you truly knew Christ, if you believed Scripture to be the very Word of God, if the Holy Spirit were operative in your life, illuminating and confirming His Word to you, you wouldn't even ask such a question. Why would you have as your focus challenging the authority of Scripture rather than clinging to them as your food?"

He tried to assure me that he did believe the Scriptures to be the Word of God, infallible, inerrant and authoritative. "But," he asked, "where does the Bible say it is the only authority? And where does Scripture say the Word of God is confined to what was written?"

I ran through several verses of Scripture (2 Timothy 3:16,17; 2 Peter 1:20,21, and others), but none answered his questions. In fact they posed a further question: "How do we know the New Testament is Scripture? Those verses can refer only to the Old Testament since the New was not written as yet, at least not in its entirety. As I delved into the matter I came face to face with the fact that the Scriptures nowhere teach "sola scriptura."

Without revealing the nature of my search, I asked several pastors and Bible study leaders the same question. No one had an answer from Scripture. Each one came up with the same verses I had looked at and when I countered that they really don't teach that the Bible is the only authority, they each reluctantly agreed, and "the verse that eludes me at the moment" never came to anyone's memory. "How amazing," I thought. "We are teaching the doctrine of 'Scripture alone' which Scripture alone does not teach! Still, neither does that prove there is another authority!"

But the thought hovered: Evangelicals were teaching a doctrine outside of Scripture while denying that anything outside of Scripture was authoritative. Something was wrong. And if we were wrong about this, could we be wrong or blind about other issues? How is it, I thought, that Protestants accept the Canon of Scripture—believing that God, who inspired Scripture, also led, by His Spirit, chosen men of the 4th and 5th century councils to recognize that which He inspired—and yet discard or disregard what those same men believed about other major doctrines: the Eucharist, baptism, apostolic succession, etc.? Further, in the first 400 years—prior not only to the completion of the Canon, but also prior, by over 1,000 years, to the invention of the printing press—the faith was preserved, being passed on orally from one generation to the next. Again, how is it that in these last 400 years of Christianity since the Reformation, with the Canon in hand and with printing presses galore, the faith has been splintered into thousands of denominations, each with its distinctive and competing doctrines, each "holding forth the Word of life?"

I began reading all that I could, whenever I could, until I knew after two years that I needed to leave my church in California and devote myself to finding out if the Catholic Church was what it claimed to be. I moved to New York and began what turned out to be a two-and-a-half-year intensive and heart-wrenching search. For months I read every Protestant Evangelical work I could find against the Catholic Church. I wanted to be rescued from such a fate as ever becoming Catholic. To my deep disappointment, I discovered that these authors, for the most part, were fighting something other than Roman Catholicism. They were arguing against what they thought the Catholic Church teaches, and it seemed their various understandings or misunderstandings reflected the Protestant perspective from which they came. Archbishop Fulton Sheen's insight became evident:

> *There are not over a hundred people in the United States who*
> *hate the Catholic Church. There are millions, however, who hate*
> *what they wrongly believe to be the Catholic Church—which is,*
> *of course, quite a different thing.*
> *Radio Replies* (1938; Rockford, Ill., Tan Books, 1979), I:ix.

Each "discovery" of Catholic teaching led me to reexamine a multitude of Evangelical doctrines. And with every thought that drew me closer to the Church, a sense of death, of mourning, ripped through me as I considered being severed not only from my church in California, but from the only Christianity I had known and loved for eighteen years.

Prior to leaving California, one very beloved pastor with whom I shared my quest asked: "If there were no Roman Catholic Church, would your understanding of the New Testament lead you to invent Catholicism?" My answer at the time was, "That's what I'm setting out to find out." One year later, I would say, "No, I wouldn't come up with Roman Catholicism, but nor would I any longer come up with Evangelical Protestantism." I had become a Christian without a home. I could not fathom being Catholic, but nor could I return to the Evangelicalism from which I came.

Three books were extremely helpful to me along the way: John Cardinal Newman's *Essay On The Development of Christian Doctrine*, Dietrich Von Hildebrand's *Liturgy and Personality*, and Karl Adam's *The Spirit of Catholicism*. The more I read, the more I began to sense a beauty, a depth, a fullness of God's design for His Church beyond all I had known. On every issue, including those three most famous cries of the Reformation—sola gratia, sola fide, sola scriptura—I came to believe that the Catholic Church was in harmony with Scripture. All that I read of Catholic teaching and life drew me to the Church; most of what I observed made me want to run from it. Where was the Church I read about? Where was the Church called "home"?

One Sunday, as I sat in the back pew of a Catholic parish I had visited for the first time, I heard the priest say what I had never heard any Catholic say before. At the conclusion of the gospel message, he said to the congregation, "We need to tell the whole world!" My heart stood still. It was the first time I had sensed a passion for souls from the pulpit of a Catholic Church.

I burst into tears. Since the day I met Christ, I've lived to tell others of Him. I thought, if the Catholic Church is true, why aren't Catholics evangelical?! Evangelical is not a synonym for Protestant. To be an evangel is to be a messenger; it's to reach out to a lost and hurting world to tell them the good news of Christ—that there is a Savior who came for sinners and who gives life to all who will come to Him.

I met with that priest, Father James T. O'Connor, Pastor of St. Joseph's in Millbrook, NY, at the beginning of March 1995. In two meetings he helped me immeasurably with some key areas of difficulty, particularly concerning the Mass and the sacramental nature of the Church. I realized, soon after, that the question of three years prior was answered at last: My understanding of the New Testament would not lead me to invent Catholicism, but my understanding now would lead me to embrace it as true to the Scriptures much more than it would lead me to embrace Evangelical Protestantism. And I knew that, before God, I needed to enter the Catholic Church ... which I did that Easter of 1995. I had found the Church called "home."

I'm still a bit awkward. I feel like I've embarked on an enormous ocean and don't quite know how to navigate yet. But I know it's true. It is not doctrinal differences only that separate Evangelical Protestants from Catholics; it's a whole different way of seeing. My entire world has opened up. All of creation has taken on new meaning for me.

I have embraced all of the Church's teachings because I have embraced that Church which Christ Himself established 2,000 years ago. It is that Church, founded on the apostles and prophets, the mustard seed grown into a tree, that has preserved and passed on the faith once delivered to the saints; that Church that has stood the test of time through every age, every heresy, confusion, division and sin. And it is that Church that will stand to the end of time, because it is truly His Body, and, in its essence, therefore, holy, immutable and eternal.

And gift upon gift it is that Church that has restored to me the reverence, the majesty, the awe I knew as a child in the synagogue. I said to David at one point, "I feel like I have God back." How strange a statement from one who came to know Him so wonderfully and truly through Evangelical Protestantism. Yet in the freedom and familiarity of the Evangelical expression and worship, a sense of the transcendence of God is often lost. It is good to bow before Him.

And yet I have come to see that God, who IS transcendent, has given us in His Son, and in His Body, the Church, more of Himself than I could ever have imagined—not more than Christ, not other than Christ, but the whole of Christ.

Oh, the depth of the riches both of the wisdom and knowledge of God!
How unsearchable are His judgments and unfathomable His ways!
Rom. 11:33

As long as God gives me breath, I want to tell the world of such a Savior and of His one, holy, Catholic and apostolic Church.

Love Compelled Me to Wait

by Dr. Paul Thigpen

"**W**hy do we have to go to the Catholic church, Dad? Why?" Tears were spilling off my daughter's face onto her dinner plate. "I don't know anybody there," she went on. "The way they do things is so weird that I can't understand what's going on. They don't dance and shout like the charismatic churches we've belonged to. And week after week, nobody says a word to us when we go. Why do we have to become Catholic?"

My wife, Leisa, sat across the table in an angry silence that echoed my daughter's protest. How could I do this to them? Our family's spiritual home had always been a major concern for us; most of our life together had revolved around the church. I'd even been a pastor! But now I'd brought chaos into our home by insisting I had to become a Catholic.

Leisa and I had always agreed that a husband and wife should belong to the same church; if a couple couldn't meet on theological fundamentals, how could they possibly agree on anything else of importance? Having a religiously "mixed marriage" was simply out of the question for us. But for Leisa, becoming Catholic was out of the question as well.

Working on a Ph.D. in historical theology, I'd had the high privilege of reading Augustine, Aquinas, Newman, Chesterton, Merton, and a host of others whose arguments and personal example had pressed me, over a period of years, closer and closer to the Catholic Church—until finally I felt I had nowhere else to go. But Leisa had spent those same years caring for our kids and for me and serving in the congregations where we'd made our spiritual home, with precious little extra time to read the heavy old tomes on my shelves. Without our realizing it, we'd drifted apart theologically. But the distance hadn't been apparent for a long time because we'd remained close spiritually: that is, we'd continued to pray together, worship together, have fellowship with the same Christian friends, rear our children in a friendship with God, and minister to others together in practical ways.

But now the hidden shifts in the tectonic plates of my theology had built up so much pressure underground that an earthquake was inevitable. The surface of my everyday religious practice was at last feeling the tremors, causing panic in my family and forging an unfamiliar landscape for us all. I had begun attending Mass, saying the Hail Mary, praying to the saints, and making the sign of the cross. In my office at home I had placed a little statue of St. Joseph on my desk and a crucifix on the wall. My wife and children thought all this new behavior was strange, and they chided me about it—first gently, then with increasing anxiety.

In my times alone with God, I wept, I struggled, I interceded, I asked the help of St. Joseph (the patron saint of families), St. Anne (the patron saint of homemakers), and the local parish. In the occasional quiet moments when Leisa and I could try to lay aside our emotions and talk rationally about the issue, I laid out my reasons for taking this new direction. But nothing seemed to be working. We were at an impasse.

I felt as if God had put me in an impossible dilemma: I believed it was His will for me (and my family) to become Catholic. But I also believed that He wanted me to care for my family, to hold it together, to protect it from the devastation that would result if I parted ways with them theologically. Could the Lord possibly want me to "divorce" my wife and children spiritually—to head for Rome and abandon them?

The struggle stretched on for weeks, and the weeks became months. Leisa said one day that if I became Catholic, she would leave me. I didn't think she would actually carry out the threat; even in the worst of times before, we had always considered our marriage vows inviolable. But her words were a cry of pain that told me just how deeply the battle was hurting her and the kids.

At last I came to a difficult decision: I would wait.

I told Leisa and the children that for the time being, we would take no more steps in the direction of the Catholic Church. They were visibly relieved. Though I didn't promise them that I would never become Catholic, I said I wouldn't fight them or try to drag them down that road any longer, and I wouldn't tear the family apart.

For the months following, I stopped attending Mass and retreated to my prayer closet to ask for wisdom and grace. Throughout this difficult period, I wrestled with all the theological issues again. Was it really necessary for me to associate with the institution? Couldn't I simply pray to the saints in private, attend Mass occasionally, wear a crucifix under my shirt and be a closet Catholic? I even tried to forge some kind of compromise with my wife in which we would plant a new congregation that would draw liberally from Catholic sources for its belief and practice—similar to the high Anglican tradition—without actually being Catholic.

During these months, we rarely attended church of any kind; wherever we might visit on Sunday morning, no place seemed right. We gathered as a family every Sabbath to read Scripture, sing and pray. But it felt as if we were simply playing at church, and I could see our spiritual life withering. I kept praying and trying to be patient. But I knew we couldn't survive spiritually if we remained long as we were.

In the meantime, no matter how I twisted and turned, I couldn't escape the conviction, once again strengthening its grip on me, that the Catholic Church was the Church Jesus had established through His apostles. No compromise, no middle way was possible. And I began to hunger for the Eucharist as never before.

Then, one day I received word that an old family friend had a terminal illness. I asked myself, "If you too discovered that you only had a short time to live, what would you do immediately and without fail?"

The answer leapt to mind: I would join the Catholic Church. At that moment I knew that even if I were in the best of health, I couldn't wait any longer.

January and a new year had just rolled around, and Leisa knew as well as I did that our family's spiritual life had to change. I don't remember who first brought up the subject, but I do remember the look of resignation in her eyes when she asked me: "You'll never be happy outside of the Catholic Church, will you?"

I shook my head. "It's becoming a matter of conscience. I feel as if I'll be disobeying God if I don't."

The calmness of her reply shocked me. "Then I guess you'd better go along with your conscience. But I just can't take that step myself."

We talked awhile longer, and we each made concessions that we believed were reasonable and loving. RCIA classes would begin at the local parish soon (they had a rather short course of instruction), so I would start attending them and Mass with the firm intention of entering the Church at Easter. Leisa agreed to attend with me and to keep an open mind, but she was making no commitments. If I would not pressure her to come along on this road, she would stand aside and let me proceed.

The local priest who directed the RCIA classes was a Christlike, Christ-centered man—just the person my family needed in this new close encounter with the Catholic faith. He led us gently through the basics and gave Leisa the freedom to attend without making any commitment until close to the class's conclusion. By the time my preschool aged son began greeting the priest with a warm hug, my hope had grown that by some miracle, Easter would see us all in the Catholic Church.

I was not disappointed.

In less than three months, Leisa had passed from resignation to interest to conviction, if not enthusiasm. She read, prayed, asked countless questions. She left some things on the shelf for the time being. ("Even if I'm Catholic, I may never pray to Mary," she once said. I just smiled.)

So much that was Catholic still seemed alien to her, yet she was finding a home in the Church nevertheless. And the children, with that marvelous flexibility God graciously gives to youth, were coming around as well.

On Palm Sunday eve—the day we entered the Church—Leisa still couldn't bring herself to "pray to Mary." But she took her leap of faith with grace and even a sense of peace that passed her understanding. The children took their part excitedly, happy to be settled at last in a spiritual niche that felt surprisingly comfortable.

In the year and a half since we took the plunge together, God has done more for us than I could have dared to ask. When we had to move to another state so I could do my dissertation research, I asked St. Joseph to pray that we would find a parish where we could grow as a Catholic family. We had much of our theology in place, but we needed Catholic friends who could show us how to pray the Rosary as a family, teach us Catholic table blessings, tell us how to celebrate our children's confirmations. We needed up-close models of godly Catholic manhood and womanhood, people for whom practicing the Catholic faith was so natural that we could learn from them just by watching.

That's exactly the kind of parish we've found in our new home. The community is warm, the liturgy is magnificent, the theology is orthodox, the pastor is wise. Several families have befriended us and helped us learn the everyday practices of Catholic family life. We've become Eucharistic ministers; Leisa and my daughter are helping out with sacristy responsibilities; and the two of them have just helped to found a new sodality in our congregation for young girls and their mothers.

During Lent, God gave Leisa a deep hunger for spiritual reading. I was amazed to see how much she grew in a few short weeks as she devoured biographies of the saints. Ever since then, her conviction has been fired with enthusiasm as well; sometimes she's the one pulling me farther down the road, exploring new paths of Catholic tradition and introducing them to me.

Meanwhile, my daughter's perspective has been transformed as well. I could tell she was enjoying herself in church, but my heart almost broke with joy on the day when she came to me quietly and said almost in a whisper: "Dad, I'm so glad we're in the Catholic Church now. I have such a sense of peace in the Church that I never had anywhere we've been before. When I go to Mass, I can feel the presence of God and a spirit of worship in the people."

I weep even now to realize how far we've come so quickly. In fact, at times I find myself wishing that I hadn't delayed entering the Church, that I hadn't wrestled through those long months till my family was ready to consider joining me. Think of how much farther along we might be by now if I hadn't hesitated! And think of how terrible it would have been if one of us had died while I was waiting!

And yet ... it seems to me at the same time that the timing was all in God's providence. I suppose I could look back and conclude that my hesitation reflected weakness or cowardice on my part.

But even if those were truly factors in the situation, I know for sure that at the heart of my decision was an overriding pastoral concern, a desire to lead my family without bludgeoning them, to allow God to woo them to the Church as He had wooed me. If I had walked over my wife and children to get to Rome, they might never have followed me; bitterness might well have sent them running the other way instead.

Above all, I know now that it was love that finally enabled us to conquer our dilemma. The very fact that the issue was so explosive for our family indicates how much we cherished one another: we simply couldn't bear the thought of being separated, spiritually or otherwise. It was my love for my wife and children that gave birth to my patience; and it was their love for me that pressed them at last to risk letting go of me so that I could find peace.

Perhaps much of this story sounds all too familiar to you. Perhaps you too are caught in a demoralizing battle with your family over your conviction that Rome is home. If so, I want to encourage you that the most important thing you can do just now is simply to love your spouse and children. God may want you to wait for them, or He may not; that depends on the details of your situation. Only you and He know. But whatever God calls you to do, He wants you to do it compassionately, gently, sensitively.

I can't help thinking that our Lord is more than willing to honor such love by working out all the messy details in spite of us. In any case, of this much I'm certain: whatever my family may have lost in those months of uncertainty, when love compelled me to wait and compelled them to let go, we have more than regained in the glorious days that have followed, and our love for one another is stronger than ever.

Paul Thigpen is Associate Professor of Religious Studies at Southwest Missouri State University in Springfield, MO., where he, his wife Leisa, and their two children are now members of St. Joseph's Parish. A more detailed account of their journey can be found in the book Surprised By Truth (see Appendix B).

JOY

by Dr. Douglas Lowry

There is a scene in the Alistair Sim version of The Christmas Carol which describes my feeling about being received into the Catholic Church. The movie setting was the morning after the visit of the three spirits of Christmas. Scrooge stood grinning at himself in the mirror, amazed that he was still alive and that he had a chance to start fresh. He tousled his hair and muttered wonderingly about how ridiculously joyous he felt. It didn't seem right to feel that good, but he did, he did!

I feel the same. On February 7, 1993 my wife Margaret and I took the final step in a 30-year pilgrimage toward Rome. Through this step, we have found a joy that goes on and on, a surprising, ridiculous, but very real joy.

For more then 27 years I was a minister of The Presbyterian Church in Canada. From 1975-1992 I served as one of the three Clerks of the General Assembly. The Clerks draft laws, advise on procedure, take minutes, and come along side conflict situations. Somewhere along the line I began to grieve over the disunity that seemed woven into the fabric of our denomination's life. It became apparent that every conflict in congregations and every political maneuver in committees and Church courts had its root in failure to obey the Gospel. Why did we not give priority to the things that make for peace and unity? Couldn't we as a denomination come to terms with the command to love one another? I watched, and listened, and prayed.

These concerns lead finally to a decision to reconcile with the Catholic Church. This was the only solution to a growing hunger for unity. The outcome ... a burden lifted, a sense of celebration, and joy.

This is written to encourage people, particularly clergy, who are considering reconciliation with the Catholic Church. The stumbling blocks seem so large ... perhaps a need for repentance over harsh judgments in the past, fear of causing hurt to those we love, discomfort in our childlike unfamiliarity with Catholic ways, uncertainty on how to make our way, and for some of us, our living. In spite of these stumbling blocks, some of us are attracted.

Our reasons for considering the Catholic Church are varied. My wife was attracted most by the Eucharist. For me, the primary motive was obedience to the command of unity. Whatever reason or constellation of reasons puts us on this path, the destination is one in which we find ourselves at home among the family of God.

Joy is not a Catholic preserve, or something new to those of us who journey toward Rome. But in reaching the destination, I have found the quality of joy enriched. Joy is set in a new dimension. The new dimension flows directly from reconciliation with the church. Here are some perspectives on Christian joy as I experienced it in earlier life. Then I want to show why that joy has become more full.

There is joy in gratitude, a capacity to receive gifts. Gratitude is the foundation of a good marriage. My wife and I learned early to receive each other as gifts from God. Our thirty-four years together have been marked with a sense of wonder, a belief that God has been outrageously kind to us.

There is joy in servanthood. This understanding came to me through thousands of hours as a volunteer ambulance attendant. The 40 members of our service took pride in serving the community. We underwent constant training so we could serve even better. For me, the inspiration was Mother Theresa, coming along side those most in need, and serving each person as if he or she were Jesus. Monitoring vital signs of a person in mid-heart attack, talking gently with a fear filled child after being struck by a car, efficiently bandaging, caring, listening, watching ... at times we were rewarded by watching the fear drain away to be replaced by peace, even in the midst of pain.

Somehow in the early years I was lead to read *The Practice of the Presence of God*, the classic book filled with the insights of Brother Lawrence. In coming to grips with his spirituality, I began to learn the joy of the presence of God. God is not sequestered in church. God is wonderfully active in the marketplace ... in management and computers and dealings with all manners of people. God comes to us in creative solutions to problems, in the strength to stand for right in the face of powerful wrongs, in Christ-filled people, and in the midst of even the greatest difficulties. God is there. We need only to watch and to listen. In finding Him, there is joy.

Joy is a normal part of the Christian experience, the result of conscious choices. Joy does not depend on whether we are Presbyterian, Methodist, or Catholic. But I find that joy is deeper and enriched now that my wife and I are part of the whole family of God. Celebration of the unity of the Body of Christ adds a new dimension to joy.

Why this greater joy? Because I do not have to be the judge in judgment of the Catholic Church, of the Scriptures, or even of myself. It's not my job. Millions of people over a period of two thousand years have reflected on our holy faith, and struggled with it, some cases even given up their life for it. Shall I improve on their combined insight, as it is shared with us through the Magisterium? Shall I pit my few decades against millions and million of man years? No!

No indeed! I am too busy celebrating. And daily mass is the center of the celebration. I am surrounded by good people. I join with them: "Lord, I am not worthy to receive you. But only say the word, and I shall be healed." And later in the service, a sense of wonder, new every time: "This is my body for you." For me? Yes, for you. No more symbols. Now the reality. The vast humbling, wondrous reality of being part of his Church and of receiving His life, day by day. "Take, eat."

Was it difficult to come into the Catholic Church? Yes, I could not lightly set aside service on behalf of The Presbyterian Church in Canada and of the many people there whom I have learned to love. But the call to unity and to the Eucharist gradually outweighed the service that I could give to them.

My progress toward the Catholic Church was very public— my picture appeared with John Paul on the cover of the denominational magazine. The secular press picked up on the suggestions by zealots of a heresy trial. ("Does a Clerk of Assembly not know that the Pope is the Anti-Christ?") Some Presbyterians would still like to debate my decision; perhaps in Heaven we might find the time (if the subject seems relevant any more). But for the most part there has been an understanding, an acceptance. My farewell address to the 1992 General assembly was received with remarkable good will.

Have there been any regrets? None. I hope that you may be blessed as much as my wife and I. Life is full. In my new work, sharing the life of Christ with business students at Franciscan University, I find immeasurable joy. There is a wondrous sense of being at home and at peace.

To non-Catholics who love Christ and are thinking about entering the Catholic Church, my message is simple: "Come on in, the water's fine." Here is the place of unity with the whole body of Christ. Here is celebration. Here is joy.

The Price of Obedience
by Kristine Franklin

One of the most difficult aspects of our journey into the Catholic Church was wondering how our decision would impact not only ourselves and our two children, but the lives of extended family and good friends as well. We were choosing the Catholic Church. They were not. Yet they could not remain untouched.

We knew our becoming Catholic would bring confusion and disappointment to many, in addition to bringing real pain and a certain sense of shame to certain family members. Coming from a strongly anti-Catholic fundamentalist sect as I do, I knew the potential existed for us to be shunned and possibly disowned by those closest to us. This was not easy to face.

Though my fundamentalist siblings do not see the connection, our decision to become Catholic was no different from our decision to be evangelical missionaries. In both cases there was no option but to obey. Our allegiance to Christ was paramount and following Him, even to a war-torn, poverty-stricken nation, had preeminence over all other considerations. We followed His leading to Guatemala. And when the same Jesus who led us to Guatemala led us into the Catholic Church, we followed. In both instances, other people were affected by our decision.

Once while we were raising money to go overseas a young mother approached me and obviously wanted to talk. "I don't see how anyone could think of raising their children so far away from grandparents," she said hotly. "I would never deprive my parents of their grandchildren." I was surprised at the vehemence of her words, especially since she was a total stranger. Still, her words stuck with me.

Of course we had added up all the costs of mission life, costs to ourselves that is. We believed we were following God's will by becoming missionaries. We understood and accepted responsibility for the fact that we were choosing the missionary lifestyle for our children. But I think up until my conversation with that young woman, we had not seriously calculated the costs to others, those unwilling participants in our decision, those people who had had no part in our decision yet for whom our decision was bound to have an effect. The ramifications were clear. If God was calling us to foreign missions, our obedience, our leaving America to live in another country, was as much a part of God's plan for our families and friends as it was for us. If our obedience brought pain to others, we had to leave it in God's hands and assume it was part of His plan for them. Our job was to follow Christ. That fact has never changed.

To become Catholic is to leave the comfortable, familiar country of Evangelical Protestantism behind forever. It is a choice that creates a lot of ripples, small and large, ripples which touch many people outside our own family circles. When we made the decision to enter the Catholic Church it was one of obedience, just as when we chose to live overseas as missionaries. Comfort, convenience, what other people thought, or even how our choice might change the lives of others, did not figure into the ultimate decision to go to Guatemala. Peter and James and John laid down their nets and followed. When we were faced with the choice to enter the Catholic Church, the issue was the same. Who were we to cling to our nets, or to a secure place in evangelicalism, or to the comfort of family approval? There was no excuse, not even the discomfort of others, no reason big enough to keep us out of the Catholic Church. When we laid down our Protestant nets, that decision changed forever the paths of many, many people, all of them unwilling participants in our journey to Rome. It was not an easy decision, as all who have trod this path know. Still, as before, there was no valid reason to say no to Jesus Christ.

To say yes to God's call into the Catholic Church is to pay a price. My brother, a fundamentalist minister, only recently communicated with me for the first time in nearly a year. For me, his missionary sister, to convert to Catholicism was one of the lowest points of his life. He compared the feelings to grieving over a divorce or death. Indeed, in his mind we have repudiated the Faith and have dragged our innocent children off the straight and narrow. To minimize his deep feelings of loss would be insensitive, yet I can't help but hope and pray that God might use this pain to bring him all the way home.

To say yes is also to know unsurpassing joy. Some of our friends have been influenced in a distinctly positive way by our conversion. Several have begun a fervent study of the Catholic Faith. At the Christmas Eve Mass we had the incredible privilege of sponsoring two of these people as they were received into the Church. Several more are on the way home, and we get sincere "tell us why" inquiries every month, thanks be to God!

The decision to lay down our old nets and follow Christ changes us forever. It carries a high price. Consider the Apostles. As we pick up the new nets Christ offers us in His True Church, the lives of all whom we touch will necessarily be changed because we ourselves are changed. My prayer is that like good servants, we would obey God with eagerness and joy, and that we would trust Him for the grace to allow the result of our obedience in the lives of others to be His divine business. Our responsibility is to follow where Christ leads.

For more details about Kris and Mary Franklin's journey, turn to their survey responses on pages 229-235.

Journeys Home

A Difficult Journey of Joy!

(A letter from an anonymous pilgrim to her priest shortly before her entry into the Church. This was submitted for the newsletter to illustrate the many difficulties encountered by some along the road to Rome.)

Dear Father,

Once in a while I am racked by fear when I think of my imminent conversion. I wake up from a nap and I'm immediately sized in horror at the thought. I feel like I'm abandoning my family, my husband, and my sons, my father, my friends. But then I wonder if it isn't that I am made to feel this way by imagining them thinking the worst; or by the outburst of rage that I imagine from my husband, or have actually felt from him in the past. Car doors slammed. Screaming. Objects thrown. Storming out into the wood or over the hill. "I hate you! You've destroyed everything! None of our friends are Catholic. How could you do this to me!"

I pray. I ponder. I live with it. It lingers. It fades. It returns once more. And then, again, I wake up to it. There it is in his voice, his eyes, his bodily form sitting there. On edge. Ice. It is there even in his recumbent form beneath the blankets when I wake up to leave for Mass on Sunday mornings. An abyss. A deadness. Something unforgiving.

Perhaps I am too sensitive. There have been probably as many good days as bad. The light has danced in his eyes. I have seen his smile. We have laughed together once or twice. Our thoughts have ranged from games of Scrabble to themes of stories and Somalia. Guests have come and gone, and we have been in other homes, sipping coffee, talking about our sons and family reunions.

I am afraid. I am afraid of upsetting this precarious balance. Of tipping the scale-barely, but disastrously. By my choice. By my simple choice. I browbeat myself for my cowardice. I understand full well my convictions. Am I ashamed of them? No. But grateful.

Are they not all that I hold dearest? Of all I know, the greatest consolation? But how can I begin to explain? "Say, I've been meaning to tell you: I've become a Catholic." "Where does that leave my husband? Well I'm not sure. He won't have anything to do with it." How can I begin to explain, with the four hundred years of incomprehension behind and about us. What to say to relatives and family? Or to say nothing at all and remain ever on guard, tiptoeing gingerly around our dark, heavy secret?

Even my hairdresser has an opinion on the matter. "God is one thing," she says, "but churches are another. Allegiance to any one church is like having your favorite soap opera. You shouldn't put too much stock in it, because someday you could wake up to find that life has passed you by while you've been watching the soaps. In any case, none of it really matters much. Your family and friends—they're what really count." Some truth in that. Plenty of misunderstanding, too.

My conscience speaks. Deny yourself, take up your cross and follow me. You are not your own. You are brought with a price. God's grace is sufficient for you. I know. But to whom do I turn at the family reunion? I can visualize the bewilderment. "A holy day of obligation? What's that? It sounds so legalistic. You mean just any old church wont do? What kind of a God is it that can't hear you wherever you are?" And then there's his reaction: "See? I told you, she'll do what ever they tell her to, no matter what it does to her family! I feel like she's inviting a lover to move in with us."

I sometimes sit amazed, listening to the strange energy of his speech. I am overwhelmed with pity and love. He is suffering. I know it is such needless suffering, when all is said and done. But so inevitable and understandable, too. How is he to face his family and friends? "She's becoming a Catholic." How trivial a thought in any other context! Yet how utterly wrenching here! Something like saying: "She's a good wife and mother, but she spends every Sunday with her lover on the other side of town."

I long to see him happy. I know that I am a large measure the cause of his unhappiness. I know how absurd and inordinate this desire to become a Catholic must appear—not only to him, his parent, and Protestant supporters, but even to my Catholic friends. Yet, I also know what I believe the Lord wants of me and that it is neither prudent nor safe to hold out indefinitely against conscience. And I know that I must be willing in some sense, to commit his happiness to the Lord, whose alone it is to protect us from all anxiety and grant us peace in our day.

Please do not think that I am severely cast down. Any clouds that darken my day are very quickly scattered by the rays of sunlight and hope. I know that you and a host of others are praying for us. I know that God is gracious and will not tarry forever. Even now, in small and silent ways, I am frequently surprised by joy—in myself, my husband, in our family, and in God.

Journeys Home

A Leap of Faith

by Don Bennette

In the mental image forming in my mind, I saw myself standing at the edge of a great chasm like Indiana Jones in the movie *The Last Crusade* looking for the Holy Grail to save his father. I knew that the Holy Grail was on the other side of that chasm, but I was too afraid to take the leap.

That was the vision the Lord gave me just seconds before sharing with my wife that I had decided to lay aside my clerical collar as a Protestant minister and become Roman Catholic. All glory be to God who started us on our journey beginning with my wife Terri. It was her courage and hunger for the truth that lead our family into the Catholic Church.

Terri began her conversion to the Catholic Church in 1992 two years before I did. During Terri's conversion there were many truths that she shared with me, but none required action until question 121 of the Baltimore Catechism: *"All are bound to belong to the Church, and he who knows the Church to be the true Church and remains out of it, cannot be saved."*

Because Terri truly believed this, she asked me for permission to leave our church and become Roman Catholic. She asked my permission because in our old church, the husband made all the major spiritual decisions for the family. At first I would not allow her to convert, but when I saw her humble submission and the toll staying out of the Catholic Church was taking on her soul, I gave her my permission.

Although my spiritual fathers were sure it was not God's will for Terri to convert, I was not sure, and did not want to be a "stumbling block" to her. I knew that many times in the past God had spoken to Terri before me about major changes that affected our family. If Terri was correct again, I did not want to answer to the Lord at the day of judgement for being a stumbling block to my wife in this matter. After many years of learning to discern Terri's heart, I really believed it was pure in this matter even though I did not understand why or want to convert myself. In addition to allowing her to convert, I gave our three older children their choice. Genece and Katie converted, while my oldest daughter Grace stayed with me and the four youngest children (Tully, Alyssa, Luke, and Bonny) in our old church.

During Terri's conversion period I struggled with many questions. At that time I was a deacon (to be ordained a priest) writing a catechism for our denomination, and felt responsible for the souls of the children I was teaching. Even though I felt this way, and wanted to believe my spiritual fathers when they told me that God wanted me to stay in their church, I began to have many doubts.

The primary cause for my doubt was the difficulty of meeting the spiritual and emotional needs of my family. My full time job at the local electric utility in addition to my "ministry" made time with the family difficult. I desired greatly to serve God as a full time minister, but did not want to sacrifice my children on the altar of ministry to obtain that goal. I knew other Protestant ministers whose kids were hanging out with very bad peer groups, knew very little about the Bible, and cared little for church because their parents felt that it was their duty to sacrifice time spent with their children for the ministry. God's grace had turned my heart to my children, and although I loved the ministry, I did not want my children to end up like that.

Although my children were nowhere near this danger, I knew they could be if I continued with my ministry. I also knew that the grace of God which had turned my heart to my children was continually hindered because I was too busy with ministry to be a father to them. I was beginning to agree with the Roman Catholic requirement for priests to remain celibate.

Although I felt I could serve God in the Catholic Church, I was confused as to why he would want me to leave "the ministry." This confusion was due to a combination of pride mixed with a child-like trust in what my spiritual fathers and many charismatic prophets had told me about my call to the ministry. This confusion was the great chasm I had to leap by faith. Only by a tremendous outpouring of God's grace was I able to take this leap of faith.

A large deposit of this grace came through an eight-week course on the new *Catechism of the Catholic Church* that I attended. As I read the Catechism many of my own questions about the Catholic Church were answered so that I had the grace I needed to make the "leap of faith."

God gave a mental image of this leap of faith, like Indiana Jones in the movie "*The Last Crusade*" taking a leap of faith off the lion's head. What was truly amazing was that at the same time God gave me this mental image, He gave Terri the same one! So when I shared with Terri my decision to convert, she shared that she had received the same picture in her mind when I did. God did this to prepare our faith, for we were about to receive "*various trials, that the genuineness of your faith, more precious than gold which though perishable is tested by fire, may redound to the praise and glory and honor at the revelation of Jesus Christ.*" All praise be to God!

Immediately after my reception into the Church the various trials began. One was being laid off from my job of fifteen years. After considering the options, Terri and I decided to move to Steubenville, Ohio. This was our primary choice for several reasons. One reason was to provide a family support network to our married daughter and son-in-law who lived in Richmond, Indiana. They had moved there just after my son-in-law converted to the Catholic Church from the same Protestant church I did.

A few of the other factors in favor of Steubenville included having a home schooling group of 100 Catholic families there to provide additional "extended family" support which we did not have for our home school in California. We also knew that Steubenville was a center for both Catholic orthodoxy and charismatic renewal which would help us grow spiritually. One other factor which we considered as a low priority was having a job already lined up. We knew from past experience that if we "sought first the kingdom of God" He would get me a job.

"Your 2,400 mile move is penance enough!" our Monsignor told us when he heard our confessions at our home the day before we moved. After selling or giving away anything we could not fit into a U-Haul van, we started our move immediately after receiving our Lord at communion for morning Mass on Ash Wednesday,

1995. Since then, God has showered me with many graces so that I might experience the truth of the Catholic Church that my wife knew with her mind and her heart.

One of the truths I have experienced that has confirmed my leap of faith as God's perfect will is the guarantee of grace I receive through the sacraments of the Catholic Church. As a Protestant, the grace I received was only as a result of my own fervor to serve God. When I receive the sacraments in the Catholic Church, I know that I am guaranteed to receive grace every time. Over the last two years I have increased my reception of the sacraments to the point that now I attend Mass every day and go to confession weekly. The grace I have received as a result of this has caused me to grow closer to the Lord in the last two years than in the entire twenty two years before.

The greatest truth I have experienced, however, is that of the sacrament of marriage. The sacramental graces I have received through choosing to place my marriage ahead of my Protestant ministry have been abundant. If I want to be involved in other ministry, there are numerous lay ministries I can be involved in. However, it is clear to me that my call as priest of the "domestic church" is the most important. Again, I may get involved in another ministry some day, but most important for now is working with my wife to guide my children into a love relationship with Jesus. My ability to do this as a Protestant minister was severely hindered because of the time need to fulfill my duties outside the family.

My conversion has made one of my favorite scriptures come true: "Delight yourself in the Lord, and he will give you the desire of your heart." My heart's desire has always been to be able to know with certainty that I could stand before our Lord at judgement day and hear him say: "Well done good and faithful servant, enter into the joy of the Lord." As a husband and father, I know that being a channel of God's grace to my family is the most important thing he will judge me on. Now that I am in the Catholic Church, I know now that God has granted me my heart's desire.

Still on the Journey

by Sharon M. Mann

I was baptized and raised United Methodist but did not receive a great deal of Biblical training. Around the age of ten I attended an Evangelical Free Church for a few months where I remember accepting Jesus as my personal Lord and Savior, but I returned to the Methodist Church for the remainder of my high school days.

Though not on fire for God, I had definite strong moral convictions, a sense of God's presence and a desire to do what was right. Then during my senior year in high school, I began reading Scripture with an open heart and became very excited. One verse that truly softened and converted my heart and which is still my favorite comes from Philippians 4.13: "I can do all things through Him who gives me strength."

At college I was blessed with 2 roommates—one Christian, one atheist. The Christian and I became instant friends (the atheist is now a Christian—Praise God!!) and I began attending a non-denominational Christian group on Campus. Through my interaction with groups like InterVarsity, I began seeing the passion of others serious about their faith. Becoming more entrenched in the Word, I took off!

After a mission trip the following summer, I discovered I had gifts for evangelism, leadership and also for discipling one-on-one. Relationships were a strength and by my junior year I was leading Bible Studies, worship, and discipling. I considered going on staff with the campus group upon graduation but I knew I needed to be a Christian in the "real world" for awhile before being in the comfortable, safe setting of other Christians. So, off I went to embark on my chosen profession.

God blessed me quickly with a local Evangelical Free Church. Within weeks I was plugged into high school students and discovered that they were my real passion and that my gifts excelled in that atmosphere. The youth pastor and his wife became my dearest and closest friends.

I share this past so you understand that my investigation into Catholicism is not a nonchalant experience but one that significantly impacts my life and will have an impact on the people around me. Many have assumed that I would one day marry a pastor since my heart is so committed to ministry. My passion is in helping others know Jesus and come into a living and active relationship with Him; to know His great love for them. My hope would be to somehow see this desire find fruition in full-time ministry.

My Catholic questioning began during the summer of 1995 when I began dating a young man. To let you know that I don't enter into dating lightly (!), I bombarded him with questions about his faith and where he stood with God before I considered dating him. In his honesty, he stated that he had not been making God the center of his life but that he wanted this to change. There was (and still is) a deep honesty with himself, God, and me, and an integrity in his character that became very evident over the period of a few months. As a result, I decided to begin the dating relationship.

Much of our early dating experience focused on sharing deeply about ourselves and religion. A cradle-catholic, he did not know much of Scripture (he was surprised to learn that the Assumption of Mary was not in the Bible!!) but had a desire to learn more. I waited and watched. His passion and love for the Lord was blossoming and his desire for the Scripture flourished. Our relationship did too! We saw that our emotional connection was intense, our gifts and personalities blended and I think we both began thinking of the future. (Thank God that our physical relationship remained pure!)

One night as he brought up a general discussion about marriage, I told him that I could never marry a Catholic. Though obviously upset, we did not break up at the time because in the newness of his studies and discoveries he was not calling himself a Catholic anymore. He had begun coming to the Evangelical-Free Church I attended and was fellowshipping with my friends.

Conversations continued but in my heart I figured he would finally see the *truth* and come to my side! We listened one day to an audiotape by Scott Hahn on the Eucharist that my boss had given me. In December, he reluctantly broke up with me because he had found himself trying to defend the Catholic Church instead of just looking for truth. He felt he couldn't pursue truth with the two of us dating seriously.

Devastated, I picked up a copy of the Catechism and began reading it to find out what he really believed. I was struck by the devotional nature of the first half and terrified at the things I read in the second half—the distinctively Catholic rules, doctrines, etc. I filled it with post-a-notes to have my questions answered. If I was going to lose the man I loved, I at least wanted to find out what I was losing him to!!

The first break-up lasted 10 days. Since we both wanted to be together, we decided that with the Holidays coming up and wanting to meet each other's families, we would work through these issues together. In Mid-January, he told me that he believed the Eucharist to be true and that based on prayer and study, he had to be Catholic. He had chosen God over me! How could I complain. I wouldn't want to be with a man who would choose otherwise! In February, the second break-up was official since I knew the doctrinal differences were too much for us to continue going forward.

That week I read *Surprised by Truth* and saw that evangelicals could become Catholic! I called him up late one Saturday and told him not to give up on us—that maybe I could be Catholic, too. I was intrigued how these people who loved the Lord could be persuaded into the Church. How could they? But, I decided that I would continue to pursue the teachings of the Church. It became an obsession. I couldn't eat (lost 15 pounds in 6 weeks), didn't sleep but a few hours a night. Every free moment was spent reading Catholic theology. I was sick at the idea of losing him so I wanted to be like one of those in the book. I was trying every possible option of having the two of us be together and remain Protestant, but more tolerable to the Catholic faith. "What could I believe that was Protestant but still be Catholic?" was the question I found myself asking! We continued having conversations every few weeks and the emotional connection remained intact.

Meanwhile, he reconciled with the Catholic Church after the February break up and expressed that he had never wept so hard nor experienced such grace as he did on that evening. Though feeling pain in the separation, he was buoyed by the grace of the sacraments and the confidence that he was where he belonged.

After several months of study, I realized that in honesty before the Lord, I couldn't be Catholic because of him but had to be Catholic because it was true. I had shared my desire to be Catholic with friends and they were open to the idea because they saw it as a tremendous mission field. I hadn't told them that I was beginning to wonder if it was true, because frankly, I was petrified that I could even have a thought like that. Apparently, John Henry Newman experienced similar feelings as he delved more deeply into Catholicism! It cuts at the core of everything you believe as a Protestant Christian and rips it to shreds. A definite paradigm shift.

I started reading the early Church Fathers and realized that whatever they believed, they surely were not Protestant. Catholic themes peppered the landscape of Church history. I couldn't deny it—nor could I accept it. Surely they were just misguided!! The Church was floundering in the first centuries and tons of crazy ideas were floating around—so I thought! When I began reading St. Augustine, however, I was stunned at how Catholic he was. I thought that if I became Catholic, then at least I wasn't any worse off than him!

The Lord led me to some very strong Catholics, and an on-fire priest who began answering my questions. I began to arrive at a point where I felt like the Catholic Church either was the fullness of faith or it was a farce. I was still petrified, though, because to think of the Eucharist as truly being the body and blood of Christ, and to think that absolution is truly given by the Lord through a priest to one who is repentant, and to think that we can ask for the saints to intercede, and to think that Mary was immaculate was all too much! I had grown to the point where I now respected the Church and those who were faithful to Her teachings, but to admit that I was actually one of them was ludicrous!!

I attended a Catholic seminar hoping to get a revelation as to truth. I want truth so badly and was fearful of one day standing before the throne of God realizing that I believed lies for the rest of my life. And then an incident in the beginning of the seminar took my spiritual breath away. The first speaker had just given his talk on angels and with a little bit of time leftover, he asked for questions. The first question of the seminar was from a gentleman who wanted advice for a friend who was seriously dating an evangelical female. Together they had begun listening to tapes by Scott Hahn. The speaker just responded that if they would pray, he was sure his friend's evangelical girlfriend would become Catholic. I felt like an arrow was struck right in my heart. How could someone know I was there? Was that for me?

Finally, Saturday night, at the Eucharistic adoration, as I saw 1000+ people kneeling on a hard, concrete floor giving adoration to the Sacrament, I found tears streaming down my face. I knelt, too, not knowing if this was real or whether these people were just crazy!! But every time the Sacrament came near me, my throat tightened and I couldn't swallow. I was being torn apart by my convictions. If the Lord was truly passing by, then I wanted to adore and worship Him, but if He wasn't, I was afraid to be idolatrous. The weekend left a very powerful imprint on my heart, and I found myself running out of good arguments to stay Protestant. My heart was longing to be Catholic and to be restored to the unity of all Christendom.

Knowing that I hadn't clearly expressed the real conversion that seemed to be occurring in my heart, I wrote my friends, the youth minister and his wife, Lisa (my best friend), telling them that I was feeling called to become Catholic. When she and I were finally able to have a long talk, I spilled my guts of all that I was thinking and that had happened. She was in disbelief. She couldn't believe that I could actually be thinking like a Catholic—especially about praying to dead saints! When she found out that the Catholic Church teaches that it is the true Church established by Jesus, she was especially concerned since it now began to sound like a cult! Her husband tried to change my mind since he believed that if a teaching like this was not specifically spelled out in Scripture, it therefore must not be for us (2 Tim 3:16).

So for over a month, we went back and forth on various issues. Both of them insisted that my boyfriend was the real reason I wanted to be Catholic; that I wanted so strongly for the Catholic Church to be true so we could be together, that I was willing to close my ears to reason and just accept it. Lisa especially could not believe that I would even be questioning the issue if my boyfriend were not in the picture.

Though I know in my heart that he was only the instigator and not the reason for the wrestling, I couldn't deny that the urgency behind my desire to resolve the issue has been a direct consequence of our relationship. So, one evening as I was praying, I became convicted by the Lord that I needed to eliminate the sense of urgency in the decision. I told my boyfriend that I could not see him or even talk to him again. I had to free him to move on in his life and ministry in the Church, and I had to be free to allow the Lord to direct the timing of the conversion, without our relationship as an outside influence. I had to allow myself to completely place my future, dreams, desires into the hands of the loving, merciful, holy God and trust. Only then would I know that if I became Catholic it truly was because the Lord, by His infinite grace, was leading me.

Much has happened in Sharon's life since this letter was originally published. She continued in both her prayer and study of Catholic doctrine, and in her separation from her boyfriend. She spent several weeks in India visiting several Catholic and Protestant missions, and came home more convinced in the truth of the Catholic Church and yet discouraged by the actual state of the Catholic witness at home and abroad.

However, particularly through continuing dialogue with friends she has made through the CHNetwork and over the Internet, she finally accepted the authority of the Catholic Church and with great joy was received into full communion on Sunday, March 9, 1997.

She writes "As expected, many were shocked by my decision. But I am grateful to the Lord that I have been blessed beyond expectation. I have lost a few friends over this decision but the majority of my friends remain by my side despite the differences that we now know exist. However, I believe they take comfort in seeing that I am not running away from Jesus, but that I believe I am runing towards Him. To God be all praise and glory forever."

From Canterbury to Rome

by Peter and Regina Cram

The membership of the Coming Home Network consists of men and women at all stages of the journey and from all spectrums and spiritualities of Christianity. The following testimony comes from a couple whose journey has brought them from mainline Protestantism through the Charismatic movement to the Catholic Church.

Peter and I joined the Episcopal church in 1978 right after our wedding. Since Peter's background was mainline Protestant and mine was Catholic, the Episcopal Church seemed to be a good compromise: liturgical enough for me and Protestant enough for Peter. At our church in Darien, Connecticut, we found good Bible teaching, a place where our faith was challenged and nurtured, and a national and international ministry of renewal in the Episcopal Church. We were aware of problems in the Episcopal Church of America (ECUSA) and in our diocese, but we paid little heed because our ministry was bearing fruit.

When we moved to the Hartford area in 1988, we immediately involved ourselves in another Episcopal Church. It was a smaller parish, however, so there was less awareness of the national and diocesan scene. In addition, by 1991 we had four children under the age of seven and hence were otherwise occupied.

Gradually, however, Peter became disturbed by the liberal agenda of ECUSA leaders and recurring moral issues being voted on at the triennial conventions. This led us to wonder if the theology, the fundamental beliefs in the Episcopal Church, is based upon a democracy rather than a theocracy. (One exasperated Christian recently joked that the reason liberals enjoy the Episcopal Church so much is that they get to vote on what they believe.)

As our discomfort over the unbiblical leadership grew, the Cooke embezzlement erupted, which was the largest financial scandal in American church history. In addition, the Bishop Righter trial began, pitting bishop against bishop in a public attempt to determine whether God meant what He had plainly said; and there was discussion with our diocesan bishop about his refusal to take a public stance on matters of moral obedience. It also became apparent that the pipeline for clergy and bishops was becoming increasingly liberal.

Despite the formation of the AAC, a new consortium of orthodox Episcopalians designed to bring about reform in the Episcopal church, we became concerned that, ultimately, the ECUSA will become yet another denomination that undergoes schism when differences within its ranks become too great. As Peter pondered these matters, he found himself wondering if perhaps Martin Luther and his peers made a mistake by breaking away altogether, rather than working for reform within the Church. Peter found himself no longer willing to participate in the financing of ungodly behaviors in the ECUSA, but instead, wanting to work toward a gathering of all of God's people into one Church.

In light of these concerns, Peter began to study other denominations in early 1995. He wanted a liturgical, hierarchical church with biblical teaching and some charismatic expression. Most Protestant denominations quickly dropped out on the liturgical issue; the Methodists are fighting over the same stuff as the Episcopalians; the Lutherans are too splintered and have too many issues with which we disagree; and Vineyard Fellowship, while excellent in many ways, concerns us due to the independence of the pastor and the lack of liturgy.

Eventually, against all odds, Peter looked at the Catholic Church. As a dyed-in-the-wool Protestant, he expected to quickly find serious failings that would allow him to reject it. Raised in a subtly anti-Catholic home and church, his early exposure to the Catholic Church through my family's home parish only served to reinforce his negative stereotypes. His first positive experience occurred through infrequent visits to hear the contemplative music of the monks of the Weston Priory in Weston, Vermont during the early 1980's. Also during those years, Peter first became acquainted with the life and ministry of John Michael Talbot, a convert to Catholicism with a powerful music ministry.

John Michael's autobiography captured Peter's attention, and his music captivated Peter's heart.

Five or six years ago, we became acquainted with the Catholic "Fire Rally" program, a large-group, two-day gathering of Scriptural teachings and praise designed to introduce people to the power of the Holy Spirit. I think Peter was rather offended to discover that Catholics know how to praise; it is not something reserved for Protestants. But these seemed to be isolated cases of life within the Catholic Church. Certainly Catholicism was not something to which he gave serious consideration.

So during 1995 when Peter began to more seriously investigate the Catholic Church, he was surprised and horrified to find himself studying a Church whose theology is steeped in biblical principles. He began dialogues with a number of Catholic charismatics. He continued his readings of the early Church Fathers and conducted in-depth studies of the Catholic catechism. He visited a local "Life in the Spirit" seminar designed to introduce a parish to the baptism of the Holy Spirit and visited the Brothers and Sisters of Charity hermitage in Arkansas where John Michael Talbot conducts his ministry. (I think he was looking for loopholes).

He read two encyclical letters by Pope John Paul II: "On Life" was a brilliant Bible study, and "That They May Be One" spoke to Peter about church unity. He also spent time with an evangelist from the Chicago area where the charismatic renewal of the Catholic diocese is in full force, including tent meetings in conjunction with Vineyard Fellowship. God has granted them enormous success, and they hope to hold Seeker Services as soon as they can train more small group leaders to accommodate all the new believers. Yes, in the Catholic Church! Peter also discovered an active Charismatic Renewal ministry in the Catholic Diocese of Hartford.

As Peter investigated the Catholic Church, both in theology and in practice, he was amazed to find that many of his long-held views were false. Other concerns turned out to be simply matters of semantics rather than substantive differences.

In the meantime, I have undergone a process of my own. What began as merely questioning the current problems in our diocese and national church has led much farther than I ever expected: I am now questioning the foundational truths of the Episcopal church and the very nature of Protestantism. (Big stuff for someone who has trouble remembering that the kids are out of socks).

For many years I have been uncomfortable with the divisions in the Christian Church. A variety of styles may be good, but a variety of foundational beliefs are not. This has often led me to ask: are so many differing beliefs really acceptable before God? Is it truly God's plan for there to be thousands of denominations? How can a set of beliefs for one church on one corner be in direct conflict with the beliefs held by another church across the street?

In independent churches, it sometimes seems that each church does what is right in its own eyes (or, more accurately, in the eyes of the pastor). In denominations, factions may eventually lead to the precise situation that the Episcopal Church now faces: in order to prevent open schism, we embrace such a wide disparity of practice and belief that we find ourselves embracing things contrary to Scripture. Such is the problem in a place where there is no absolute authority on matters of theology.

I have begun to think that, in its essence, the issue is what Scripture has to say about rebellion. My thinking has gone back hundreds of years to the time of the Reformation when corruption existed in the Church. But thinking back even further, I am reminded of when the children of Israel in the desert grumbled that they were tired of eating manna, and demanded that God give them meat. God dealt with their sinfulness by essentially saying, "You want meat? I'll give you meat. In fact, I'll give you so much meat that it will spoil and many will die from eating the spoiled meat." Later, the Israelites demanded to have a king so they could be like other nations. God knew they were rejecting Him and so, as punishment, He gave them what they asked for and they had centuries of wicked earthly kings.

As I consider the divisiveness of the Church today, I find myself wondering if, during the Reformation, God essentially said, "You want a different church? I'll give you a different church. In fact, I'll give you so many different churches that you won't be able to count them all." And now, hundreds of years later, we are reaping the legacy of Protestantism. It seems that God has given the protesters exactly what they wanted and much more: one long, continuous line of protesters protesting against their fellow protesters, generating thousands of denominations, para-churches, and "free churches," which are simply one-church denominations. Schisms occur when factions arise within denominations; rather than seeking absolute truth, the American appetite for individualism leads to yet another denomination.

I am aware that my thinking flies in the face of every tenet of the faith taught by Bible-believing Christians. Basically, we've been taught that when the Catholic Church became mired in corruption, God's favor was removed from it and has never returned, and that evangelical Protestantism is a much purer, truer form of the faith. But when I actually studied what the Catholic Church has to say, I found that its teachings are not mired in blind tradition or mindless drivel designed to concentrate the power in the clergy. Rather, there are well-researched, Scriptural approaches to every issue: salvation by grace, reliance on Scripture, the Eucharist, and a strong moral integrity. In addition, there is a movement of the Holy Spirit in the Catholic Church that is incredibly exciting. It's not unlike the renewal movement in the Episcopal Church, and just as needed. The fact that not all Catholics live out their faith, or that some excesses occur despite Church teachings, does not change the tenets of the Catholic Church itself.

Years ago, Peter came across a prophecy set to music in a John Michael Talbot tape, "The Regathering." In it, God said,

> *I've gathered one fold in one faith. I have built My Church on apostles and prophets who shepherd My people in My place. But some of the shepherds have pastured themselves on the sheep so I have come out against them and scattered My people of faith. Yet there still is one faith, one hope, one baptism, one God and Father of all. There is one Church, one Body, one life in the Spirit, given so freely to all.*

For some time, hearing this prophecy and sensing God's call upon his heart, Peter found himself longing for the unity of the universal Church to actually be one organizationally, or at least be heading in that direction. Then, in early 1996, he found the passage from I Samuel 16 playing over and over in his mind, with slight changes. It seemed that God was speaking to us, saying, "How long will you grieve, seeing I have rejected them as leaders over My people? Now get up ..." But get up and do what? Get up and leave the Episcopal Church? Get up and take a stand against ungodly leaders?

In the ensuing weeks, God simply said, "Seek Me."

All during this time, we were finding that the desire of our hearts, increasingly, was to be God's instruments in the Catholic Church. In April as we grappled with this, a parishioner came to us with a prophecy regarding us. In it God said, "You are to be a voice crying in the wilderness; the wilderness is the Church." The man assumed that God meant the Episcopal Church; we both wondered if He meant the Catholic Church. Certainly both places need it.

By this spring, we could no longer deny a rising sense of call to the Catholic Church. We made contact with a godly deacon at St. Paul Catholic Church in Glastonbury, Connecticut and we visited fantastic charismatic Masses that gave us the opportunity to worship alongside hundreds of charismatic Catholics who love the Lord just as we do.

In mid-May, we set aside a week for fasting and prayer as we made a final decision. Late that week, our hearts were set on fire by a passage in Jeremiah 32, in which God drew His people back together after ungodly leadership had scattered them. God said,

> *I will gather My people from all the countries from which I drove them in My anger and My wrath and in great indignation; I will bring them back to this place, and I will make them dwell in safety. And they shall be My people, and I will be their God. I will give them one heart and one way, that they may fear Me for ever, for their own good and the good of their children after them.*

After centuries of dispersion and separation within the Church of God, we have a desire to see reconciliation and restoration of God's Church, just as God reconciled and restored His people Israel.

At this point, we sense a call TO the Catholic Church, rather than AWAY from the Episcopal Church. Perhaps God just used the problems in the ECUSA in order to get our attention. So, at the end of the church school year in June, my resignation from the vestry took effect and we left the Episcopal Church to be joined to the Catholic Church.

We had on-going discussions with our rector, Tom White, throughout this process. He was highly sympathetic to our concerns about the Episcopal Church although he was aghast at our interest in the Catholic Church. After we announced our decision Tom called a special meeting of the vestry in order to pray with us for discernment. One vestry person shared that God had laid Matthew 10 upon her heart, in which Jesus calls the twelve to Himself and sends them forth as apostles. She said that she had a sense that God was calling us out as apostles to the Catholic Church. Interesting, because we have had the same sense.

On our final Sunday in the Episcopal Church in June, 1996, Fr. Tom called all six of us forward so people could lay hands on us and pray for us as we headed forth. He acted in a godly manner throughout the entire process, even when the decision of two of his key leaders caused him personal loss. We will always be grateful for his graciousness during a difficult time.

Many unknowns lie ahead. While we are excited about where God is leading us, we also know that becoming Catholic is very different from being Catholic. A local Catholic parish has some good things going on in terms of Bible studies, folk mass, and a core of orthodox believers, and there is also an active diocesan Charismatic Renewal Office. Still, it is a huge change for us, which only God's generous grace can see us through.

Three issues continue to emerge in discussions with Episcopal friends who have heard of our move. First, we have tried to stress that our departure is due to concerns over SUBSTANCE, not style. People have gotten all hot and bothered over the years about wanting a more charismatic style of worship, or a less charismatic style; more music, no music, more contemporary aspects, more traditional, and so forth. But these are merely matters of style, which is nothing more than personal preference. For us, style is not of concern; substance is. We are concerned about unorthodox teachings within the Episcopal Church, moral issues, liberal agendas of many high-ranking leaders of the ECUSA, and financial matters.

Secondly, many people are baffled as to why we would leave a perfectly good local parish simply because we object to national leadership. In essence, the suggestion is that the local parish is all that truly matters. And yet if Episcopal leaders increasingly question the validity of what the Bible says, or whether God really meant what He said, or whether there is absolute truth, (which leads to questioning whether there is such thing as sin,) then the Good News of the Gospel quickly deteriorates into a gospel of relativism. We are already seeing Episcopal leaders who want to alter language in the Bible to make it feel more comfortable; insist that our money be spent for projects that we find morally objectionable; and unmarried companions living in parish houses with the implied consent of bishops. The next step might include a new supplement to the prayer book filled with politically correct, unbiblical language; or a new hymnal with altered lyrics that mold God into man's image (oh, excuse me—humankind's image). Vestry and clergy may be required to sign statements of tolerance (read "support") of alternative lifestyles, as well as training in how to conduct a blessing of same-sex unions.

Sound far-fetched? I don't think so, if one is familiar with the rhetoric of liberal Episcopal leaders. And yet in Isaiah, God said to His people, "'Woe to those who call evil good, and good evil.' . . . Therefore, the anger of the Lord was kindled against His people." Unfortunately, there is reason to consider leaving a perfectly good local parish, even 'though it breaks our hearts to do so.

Thirdly, the question continues to arise as to how we can justify joining ourselves to the Roman Catholic Church, which is the church of origin for many Episcopalians. As we have described above, the Catholic Church bears little resemblance to the caricature held by most evangelicals. The late Archbishop Fulton Sheen once wrote, "There are not over a hundred people in the United States who hate the Roman Catholic Church; there are millions, however, who hate what they wrongly believe to be the Catholic Church."

All we can say in response to such friends who question our move is, take a look for yourself in order to understand accurately the Catholic Church. You may be surprised at the truth you find there.

May God bless us all.

The Gentle Persuasion of
Scripture and My Wife
by Paul Key

I was a child of the manse. My father was a Presbyterian Minister and my mother the Director of Christian Education. I had a good Christian upbringing and after college served as a Lay Presbyterian Missionary in Caracas, Venezuela. When I returned at the age of 26, I was ready to get married. While studying in an institute in Chicago, I was also actively chasing four Protestant women, all of whom looked eligible. But there was one fascinating young lady, Patricia, whom I considered safe to talk with since she was Catholic and therefore obviously not an option.

I still remember the night seated on old chairs in an old building on the west side of Chicago. As we were carrying on one of our delightful conversations, I realized all of a sudden that the level of conversation was at a totally different level than I had expected. We began evaluating very rigorously our personalities, our theologies, and particularly the fact that I was planning to be a Presbyterian Minister. I could not imagine her wanting to marry a Presbyterian Minister to be. But she replied that the Lord had told her this on the very first night we met. (Later our spiritual director concluded that the Lord had sent Pat to get me. The worst part of this whole process is having to admit to your wife that she was right, but I have a pretty good wife to admit that to.)

After a brief time of testing our convictions, we were married and three days later we were both enrolled in the Masters of Divinity Program at McCormick Theological Seminary. Patricia completed the whole program, Greek, Hebrew and all, while also completing 36 hours of her undergraduate residency requirements as well as being pregnant the second year. We raised our first son during the third year, and she graduated second in the class. And since I was not first, I obviously married up.

My wife is very gentle, but when she sees untruth she goes after it. She gently began explaining to me the biblical foundations for the Catholic Church. She even corrected our Protestant professors in seminary, but we survived and went on into the pastorate.

I very soon got into trouble for all the right reasons: as a good Protestant I started preaching from the Bible. It had been recommended in our seminary training to use the ecumenical lectionary which brought me into contact will all kinds of passages which otherwise I may have avoided. As a result, I found myself slowly realizing that my wife's claim that the Catholic Church was the biblical Church might be true. Emotionally this was very hard to say let alone admit to my wife.

Baptists generally consider Presbyterians to be almost pagan and ignorant of Scripture. Since our congregation was near to both an Evangelical Free and a Baptist seminary, we often had seminarians attending worship and Bible studies. I don't like to lose arguments, so to stay one step ahead of their biblical challenges, I kept busy studying Scripture. I rarely lost a biblical argument to these Baptist seminarians, but in the process I found myself accepting more and more the Catholic understanding of Scripture. Let me give you just a couple of quick examples.

To a Reformed Protestant, the distinctions of sola fide, sola gratia, and sola scriptura are almost the equivalent of the Blessed Virgin to a Catholic. Protestants seemingly worship these three pillars. I once attended a conference where these three great distinctives were posted on an enormous banner up in front. When the conference was over, I wondered where salvation by faith *alone* was found in Scripture. So I began searching, and to my dismay discovered that the origins of this phrase came out of Martin Luther's mistranslation of Romans 3:28. The word "alone" is not in the Greek text; Luther added it possibly because he felt it was to be presumed but more likely because it was needed to defend his radical reforms.

I also began to study the relationship of faith and works. My evangelical friends said that if you allow works any role in salvation you are becoming Roman Catholic. But I knew a couple of Scripture passages that seemed to imply this, like Matthew 25:41-46, where the vision of the last judgment includes the separation of the sheep from the goats. Here Jesus says nothing about faith and everything about works of love and compassion. I also knew of James 2:14-26, which explicitly teaches that faith without works, is dead. I decided to read the entire New Testament and found a plethora of verses emphasizing the importance of works, including: Matthew 7:21-23 and 16.27, Luke 10:25-37 and 12:9, John 3:10, Romans 2:1-16, 1Corinthians 3:8 and 6:9, 2 Corinthians 5:10, Galatians 5.21, Ephesians 6.8, Revelations 2:23, 20:12, and 22:12 and many others.

I was sensing deeply that I was in trouble. I began keeping a list of the places in Scripture where I felt the Catholic Church seemed to be right. When this list reached 20, I knew I was in trouble. When it eventually reached 30, I converted. Then with the eyes of faith since becoming Catholic, that list has grown to over 70 and it's embarrassing to admit how blind I was. But then I'm getting ahead of myself.

Another area that became overwhelming was the Sacraments. Protestants generally teach that Sacraments are but empty symbols and do not communicate power. Yet I kept finding Scripture passages that indicated they were intended to contain power. For example, in 1 Corinthians 11:27 and John 6 it is very clear we are talking about the reality of Jesus' body and blood in the Eucharist not just symbolic ideas. I eventually found passages for each of the seven Sacraments that indicated the same thing. From my Protestant prospective, these weren't supposed to be in there.

Another associated issue that is particularly difficult for a Protestant to deal with is Eucharistic Adoration. As I was getting closer to becoming Catholic, our Catholic Spiritual Director, who was also our referee in marriage, strongly encouraged me to spend some time in Eucharistic Adoration. Having never done this, let alone consider doing it, I asked him what one *did* in Eucharistic Adoration and he said, "Just talk to Jesus."

Most cradle Catholics may not understand how difficult it is for Protestant converts to do Eucharistic Adoration. In a Protestant's eyes this is out and out idolatry. But with a man of my spiritual director's stature, I couldn't escape. So I went into the chapel with my Bible really irritated but obedient. I decided if this has any validity what so ever there must be something about it in Scripture.

Turning to the explicit Eucharistic passages I started reading John 6 and was shocked. Just before the section where Jesus talks blatantly about eating his flesh and drinking his blood, there is a passage that just explicitly calls out to Eucharistic Adoration. John 6:40 reads: "For this is the will of my father, that every one who sees the Son and believes in him should have eternal life; and I will raise him up on the last day." Now when do you and I see Jesus? And I have to testify to you that I have found my times of Eucharistic Adoration to be incredibly fruitful, insightful and times of grace. The entire aspect of the Sacraments and the power of the Eucharist in Catholic Tradition have been personally overwhelming.

Maybe one of the strongest areas very central to my own heart that led to my conversion was in the area of marriage and sexuality. We worked hard in my Protestant congregation to build strong Christian marriages. From the pulpit and the classroom we offered lots of Christian Formation, Bible study, marriage Formation, and marriage enrichment. But I became increasingly uneasy as I realized that the resources and foundational concepts I was promoting though they were Scriptural tended to be Catholic.

Things like the understanding by St. Thomas Aquinas that the family is an incomplete society needing the State for its support in temporal matters and the Church for its support in spiritual matters. One of the implications of this teaching is that a husband and wife should not expect to carry all the emotional and spiritual weight of a marriage. There is too much going on between a husband and wife—and there was too much going on between Pat and me.

Pat has a strong personality although she looks very gentle. You just don't want to get her angry. One evening we were having one of our serious disagreements. I had been preaching this stuff on marriage, saying that every couple needs to have a spiritual director or someone they can have as an impartial informed third party for difficult times. That night she looked at me and said, "Why don't you do what you preach?!" Recognizing that she had me, I said O.K. and that's how our Jesuit spiritual advisor entered our life.

I found myself casting about looking for wherever I could find truth. Of course Scripture was most generally present, but when you're living with a Catholic you look at every other option first.

And though Pat was gracious and patient, she also had a good strategy. About once every six months when I was having a difficult pastoral or maybe counseling problem, she would say "You know Paul, if you would be Catholic with all the resources of the Catholic Church—spiritual direction, confession, explicit practice of the Sacraments, all the Catholic theology—you would be so much more effective." Now if a wife says that just once every six months that is not too much, but over 18 years that is 36 interventions. I finally avoided the whole issue by getting into a building program.

I thought I could justify to Pat and to myself ignoring all these issues while I was immersed in a building program. Around this time Scott Hahn's conversion tape was released, and my wife who never misses an opportunity obtained it. But with architectural drawings in hand I said, "I'm not interested" and avoided listening to the tapes for almost three years. After the building program was complete, I truly found myself Catholic and decided I needed a day of personal reflection and retreat.

On October 15, 1991, I drove off to my favorite hiding place along the Mississippi River fortified with a book of Catholic doctrine by Frank Sheed and two sets of Scott Hahn's tapes. After reading a few chapters and listening again to Scott's tapes on *Common Objections* and his series on Mary, I fully realized that all of my biblical arguments had disappeared. It became clear that day that if I remained where I was I would be compromising, I would be stagnating spiritually, and I would be facing spiritual death. When you can see the consequences of your behavior clearly you have a better chance of making a decision.

So I drove home and said to Pat, "I'm either going to stagnate and die or change," and together we decided that we needed to make some radical changes. I resigned from my pastorate and moved to Steubenville, Ohio to study Catholic theology and to become immersed in the very strong Catholic community. For the entire first week at Franciscan University after listening to Fr. Mike Scanlan orient the new students I was in tears because I realized how stubbornly I had been avoiding what I had clearly seen for eleven years. Then at the Easter Vigil Mass, 1992, with my wife and children and friends from the Masters program standing up and cheering in the back, I was received into the Catholic Church.

The Lord has truly blessed us. Through gentle leadings as well as with supernatural signs and wonders he has guided and provided whenever and whatever we have needed. Yes, in this journey we have learned in unexpected ways the importance of the evangelical councils of poverty, chastity and obedience. He has humbled me repeatedly, asking that I give up everything, money, position, power, even for long periods my wife and family, all to help me rediscover how much you and I can totally depend upon Him.

After a number of years of study and intense struggles, trying to discern how I might be able to continue to serve the Lord in the Catholic Church, I was recently hired by the diocese of Lubbock, Texas as Director of Evangelization and of their Spiritual Renewal Center.

In the Catholic Church, we have the richness and the fullness of the Tradition, the wisdom of pastoral practice, the wholeness of biblical theology. Now we must prayerfully and charitably help each other learn it and apply it. It continues to be an incredible journey and I give the good Lord thanks for everything he has done for us.

Home Again, Thanks be to God!

by Lynn Nordhagen

On January 24th, the feast of St. Francis de Sales, I was received back into the arms of the Holy Catholic Church. Since I had made a profession of faith in the Presbyterian church, I now made a renewed profession of faith in all the Catholic Church teaches. For this I chose to read the profession of the Council of Trent, since it spoke the truth in regard to specific errors I had embraced. Then I received the sacraments of Penance, Anointing of the Sick, and Holy Eucharist. As I wrote to my friends in the *Coming Home Network*, "What can I say? It's all beyond words somehow. I feel **plunged** anew into sacramental graces. *Drenched!* Penance, Anointing of the Sick and Holy Communion—all within the hour, and then a peaceful prayer time alone with Our Lord in the Blessed Sacrament. Visible, audible, touchable! 'This is what we proclaim to you: what was from the beginning, what we have heard, what we have seen with our eyes, what we have looked upon and our hands have touched—we speak of the Word of life.' (1 John1:1) Amen! I'll write more later. Right now I'm more or less melted by Love and speechless in the light of His Grace." Thank you dearest Lord, thank you St. Francis de Sales, thank you dear friends. And now please pray for me, that God may grant me perseverance.

Almost five years earlier, on April 5, 1992, after a full year of diligent study and faithful attendance, I stood before a Presbyterian congregation to make a profession of faith along with membership promises that included submitting myself to "the discipline and governance of the church." I joyfully wrote the date in my Bible. I was at the same time dedicating myself to serious study of God's revealed Word, in the classical Reformed tradition, embracing all the "Solas" of the Protestant Reformation: Faith Alone, Grace Alone, Scripture Alone, Christ Alone, and Glory to

God Alone. I had studied and read until I became convinced of the truth of "TULIP," an acronym for the distinctives of Reformed theology.[4]

At that point, I had left the Catholic Church not just once, but twice. I had grown up Catholic, before and during Vatican II. I enjoyed sixteen years of Catholic schooling, living close enough to walk to school all the way through college. Our parish was known in town, deservedly or not, as the "Holy Land," because of having the grade school, two convents, a high school, a Jesuit university, and a very high percentage of Catholic families in the neighborhood. I loved the Latin Mass, and in high school and college attended daily Mass and Communion. I was young enough to accept gracefully the changes of Vatican II, but not without some sadness. A wonderful Jesuit pastor formed a group for a few of us interested high-school students to study the Documents of Vatican II. We loved our Church.

So how could I ever have left the Church I loved? Only for what I thought was more of God. The charismatic renewal came to our Catholic college campus, led by a Bible-belt Pentecostal preacher. Many of us were caught up in the emotional appeal of belonging to a group of Christians who were really excited about Jesus. Eventually the charismatic group split along Catholic/Protestant lines.

About the same time, I married one of the Protestant young men. For three years of our marriage, I remained Catholic, but finally allowed myself to become disillusioned by the lukewarmness of so many cradle Catholics, compared to the Pentecostal ardor in my husband's church. So, in 1974, I gave up on Catholicism, and naively hoping that the Holy Spirit would soon unite all Christians anyway, I became very active in this independent charismatic church, attending at least five meetings a week.

Over the next ten years of raising our kids in this enthusiastic atmosphere, I nonetheless became very restless and increasingly sensitive to the frequent misrepresentations of what the Catholic Church actually taught. I perceived more and more differences

---

4   *TULIP stands for Total depravity, Unconditional election, Limited atonement, Irresistible grace, and the Perseverance of the saints.*

between the teachings of the independent church and orthodox Christianity, and so in 1984, under the guidance of a loving priest, a former teacher of mine, I returned to the sacraments. This was a difficult time for my husband, who was concerned about my confusing the kids and about his responsibility as spiritual head of the family. The fundamentalist teaching on submission left no room for a wife to worship elsewhere. The pastor counseled me to submit by staying "under the umbrella" of my husband's spiritual protection, but I insisted that I must "obey God rather than men." Although my husband and I felt the pain of not being able to worship together, I also experienced the peace and joy of being home again in the Catholic Church.

I wish I could say that was the end of my wanderings. But there followed several very distressing years, including the serious illness of both my parents, my father's death, and a difficult year of classroom teaching in a Catholic school. I sought counseling and became involved in a "Catholic" meditation group, which taught "Christian Zen" and other mixtures of Eastern philosophy and religion.

I had been devotedly practicing this for some time when, through my kids' involvement in pro-life activities, I began conversing with a Protestant co-worker whose kids had also been arrested. We soon discovered a mutual interest in theology. I felt quite up to the task of arguing doctrine with a Calvinist, since I had actually paid attention during my sixteen years of Catholic schooling, and had already had my "fling" with Protestantism. I felt secure in my Catholic faith, so I took on the apologetic challenge. Our lunchroom-table debate went on for a year and a half but I, the Catholic, didn't win. I was not as prepared as I had thought. I had not really come up against the strong intellectual side of the Protestant Reformation before.

Now I was reading Luther's *Bondage of the Will*, Calvin on the Lord's Supper, G.C. Berkouwer on faith and perseverance, and many other Reformed authors. In addition, I listened to hundreds of theology tapes by R.C. Sproul and others. I was outnumbered and should have asked for help, but instead, I looked critically at the New Age stuff I was involved in, saw the sheer volume of intellectual ammunition on the Protestant bookshelves, and became convinced that they had Scripture on their side.

I felt compelled to submit to the truth, and I started attending the Presbyterian Church in America where I would later become a member. This involved more stress for my family, because I was rocking our boat again. I became very seriously concerned and argumentative about the doctrinal errors in the independent church where my husband and kids still attended. But over the next few years, my husband became satisfied that I was at least Protestant again, and we both made good friends in my Presbyterian church.

Even then, I grieved over giving up my belief in the Real Presence in the Eucharist, and I harassed my friend at work about talking me into the Real Absence. Eventually I made peace with the real presence being spiritually communicated to believers by the Holy Spirit in a special way during the Lord's Supper. But there was always that tug in my heart for the Real Thing. Still, if the Catholic belief was idolatrous, I had to reject it.

For five more years I delved into Calvinism. It was very comforting to know that God was Absolutely Sovereign over human decisions, and to believe that as one of the Elect I was perfectly sure of going to heaven, no matter what I did, since it ALL depends on God. I believed in predestination by God's decrees before the foundation of the world, and that Christ died only for His chosen ones, because to think otherwise was to admit He was not in control of salvation. I was a deeply convinced Calvinist, and was working on convincing everybody else.

In April 1996, I read *Surprised by Truth* (Patrick Madrid, ed.), the collected stories of eleven converts to Catholicism. I found myself saying, "You know that's probably true. You've ALWAYS known it." Another part of me would say, "Then how did you change your beliefs so thoroughly?" And "How can you even trust yourself to 'choose' any one belief system over another?"

I started reading and studying with renewed intensity. I read again John Henry Newman's *Apologia Pro Vita Sua*. I read books on the Eucharist, and on the papacy. I corresponded by e-mail with *CHNetwork* members and other Catholic apologists.

A turning point came the day I finally realized I did not accept the principle of sola scriptura any longer and told my pastor so, because then my whole orientation to authority changed. It was also very depressing and unsettling, because I was still so unsure of many Catholic teachings. I became very fearful that this change would mean losing friends and upsetting family. I could not see how I was going to be sure of anything ever again, especially my own trustworthiness in decision making. I identified with Newman saying, "I had been deceived greatly once; how could I be sure I was not deceived a second time? I then thought myself right; how was I to be certain that I was right now?"(*Apologia*, p. 310)

Another crisis arrived a couple of months later when I started visiting the Blessed Sacrament to pray for enlightenment. I was unable in conscience to genuflect, because I didn't believe in the Real Presence. But one day, I realized I didn't believe in His Presence in the Lord's Supper at the Presbyterian church, either. Immediately I felt an anguished doubt—He was nowhere on earth! Neither in the Catholic Mass, nor in the Protestant Lord's Supper. I was ALONE. I felt cut off from ANY communion. That Sunday, I passed up the elements at the Lord's Supper, then I called and made an appointment with a Catholic pastor.

Doesn't it seem that the Catholic Church is never in a hurry? It seems the more impatient I was to know and decide, the more the priest advised me to slow down, to "make haste slowly." He assured me that things would all fall into place for me at the right time. It wouldn't necessarily be easy, he said, but I would know that it was right and that the time was right. How could I believe that all this exhausting effort was leading to something that was just going to "fall into place"? But after many months, when I was making a last ditch effort to find a livable compromise, one that would please my husband, myself, my family and friends, things did fall into place. One day prompted by the priest's gentle challenge about compromising, I knew what was right, and a great sense of relief came over me. I was ready for it not to be easy, just to be right.

It has been far from easy. I have felt overwhelmed and fearful, I have spent hours in desperate prayer, and finally said many tearful good-byes at my Presbyterian church.

One especially tough time was my meeting with the elders. I felt I had to honor the promises I had made to submit myself to their "discipline and governance," and had tried to stay open and candid with the pastor all during the many months of study, indecision, and conflict. When I told him I had finally made the decision to reunite with the Catholic Church, he said the elders wished to meet with me to hear my thinking and to admonish me from Scripture.

I had told the pastor about St. Francis de Sales, who was Bishop of Geneva soon after the Reformation. As a young man, before he was made bishop, he was responsible for the conversion of thousands of Calvinists back to the Catholic Church. He won their hearts with his gentleness and persistence in teaching the truth. When they would not listen to his preaching, he wrote leaflets and slid them under their doors. He lived among them at great personal risk, and won them by his love. I told the elders that I had decided to return to the sacraments on the day the Catholic Church celebrates the feast of this apostle to the Calvinists, January 24th. I felt that this Saint had reached down personally through space and time, through the communion of saints, to rescue one more little Calvinist. My meeting with the elders lasted almost two hours. After we had gone over most of the issues, the pastor read me their admonition.

On my way home, although it was late, I stopped to pray in the Blessed Sacrament chapel, and Newman's words expressed my feelings again:

> *Oh, my Lord and Savior, support me ... in the strong arms of Thy sacraments, and by the fresh fragrance of Thy consolations. Let the absolving words be said over me, and the holy oil sign and seal me, and Thy own Body be my food, and Thy blood my sprinkling; and let my sweet Mother, Mary, breathe on me, and my Angel whisper peace to me, and my glorious Saints ... smile upon me; that in them all, and through them all, I may receive the gift of perseverance, and die, as I desire to live, in Thy faith, in Thy Church, in Thy service, and in Thy love. Amen.*

Through Divorce to the Catholic Church
by Brenda McCloud

In June 1992 my husband, John, walked out the door. Half of me went with him, and I felt as though my heart had been ripped out and stomped on. My worst nightmare of a divorce was becoming a reality.

I turned to God from the depths of my being and cried out a heart-wrenching prayer for help. Then I saw my children, Jessica and Martin, and me in a boat with a storm surrounding us. I looked straight at Jesus walking on the water and prayed, "Jesus, we have to walk on the water. No matter what happens, I am going to keep my eyes on you." I visualized me taking the hands of the children, getting out of the boat in the midst of the storm, and following Jesus.

Little did I know then that through this terrible journey across rough seas Jesus would lead us to the shelter of His Church and, in time, to the renewal of our marriage.

A Seed Is Planted

As a child, I was baptized in a Protestant denomination and grew up in a fundamentalist church that preached ardently against Catholicism, though my parents did not share in those sentiments. At the age of 12 I heard about nuns committing themselves to a life of serving Christ. I longed for that type of life and commitment but was afraid to even speak of that desire. It was at that point that I began the long search for God, His Church, and an intimate relationship with Jesus.

I went on to Houghton College where I majored in Bible and minored in missions. I remember a theology professor saying, "If I did not have so many entanglements in Protestantism I would be Roman Catholic." I greatly respected this professor and asked, "Is the Catholic Church a cult or is it under the umbrella of ortho-doxy?" The professor replied, "No, it is not a cult; it is the Church."

Although I didn't realize it, that was the start of my journey to the Catholic Church. On my own I began reading about the lives of the saints. While I longed for their spirituality and love, I could not quite reconcile becoming Catholic. From my Protestant perspec-tive, I did not understand how these saints, with their deep love for God, could stay Catholic.

I took a course on the life of Martin Luther and found myself wondering why, after the Counter-Reformation, the people did not return to the Catholic Church. Later I attended a Lutheran Church and took classes to convert. But that denomination did not have what I was looking for. I ended up joining the Wesleyan (Methodist) Church because of its emphasis on holiness and its history of social action. I then went to Asbury Theological Seminary to study church history and theology and earn a Master of Divinity degree. There I did more searching. I again studied Luther and his life and works, Methodism, John Wesley's life and works, and Catholic theology.

I noticed in my studies that certain "Catholic" scriptures were simply glossed over or explained away. One such passage was the Bible's teaching on the Eucharist in John 6. I debated with my professors that when Jesus said, "This is my body.... this is my blood," he meant it literally. They would say, "but the bread re-mains bread and the wine remains wine." I held to my position. And I thought, if the Catholic Church is right about sacramental theology, the triune God, and other doctrinal issues, maybe it was also right about Mary, purgatory, and praying to the saints.

Somewhere along the way, someone gave me a rosary, which I cherished. But I did not know how to pray with it. I knew that on the small beads I should say the "Hail Mary," but I did not know that it was prayer. I thought I should just say "Hail Mary" ten times for each decade. I also began wearing a crucifix but did not know why. I thought someday I wanted to be Catholic, but not knowing any Catholics personally, I could not make that change. Besides, it was difficult to imagine leaving family and friends who were strongly tied to Protestantism. And my ties to Protestantism were growing deeper as I made a commitment to become one of the ordained clergy.

It was also in seminary that I met John. After getting to know each other in the small group, he asked me out. We hit it off immediately, as we both were very concerned about social issues and were definitely products of the Old Testament prophets and the '60s. We liked the same type of music, were concerned about the same issues, and our hearts were in tune.

We were married on December 15, 1979. Though we did not admit it to ourselves, we were off to take our intellectual "gospel" into the church and the world to confront the social ills of poverty and prejudice. In all our research and constant intensive study, we never did read a book about marriage.

Serving Together

Before coming to seminary, John had been a lawyer in the Army and was still in the Reserves. During the summer of 1980 he was called to be the lawyer at the base in Fort Chaffee, Arkansas. Twenty thousand Cubans were being sent there because of the Cuban Flotilla. I got a job on the base for Church World Service to help the Cubans find sponsors and get processed into the United States. I loved working with the Cubans. This was truly an experience of social action on the front lines.

Two days before we graduated from seminary in 1981 our daughter, Jessica, was born. What a miracle! What a delight!

After seminary we ministered in the Wesleyan Church and lived in Portland, Oregon. There we got to know my Aunt Mary and Uncle Dale, devout Catholics who belonged to the Secular Order of the Franciscans. My love of St. Francis of Assisi and the Catholic Church led me to have a lot of common ground to share with them. They introduced us to Franciscan nuns and their priest. We sensed they had a depth of spirituality and love we did not know.

Years ago my Aunt Mary and Uncle Dale had lived in Beaverton, a well-to-do suburb of Portland. They began to question their lifestyle and the example they were providing to their children. So they decided to move to an African-American neighborhood and take on the simple lifestyle of the Franciscans. They had a simple joy about them we could not get away from.

We worked with the Hmong refugees in Portland but were disappointed in the church members because of their lack of involvement in social issues. We were not ready for the deep-seated prejudice against the poor and ethnic minorities. Nor were we prepared for the power struggles of certain individuals in the local church and in the hierarchy. The very world we thought we could make a difference had overpowered us. We were ministering in our own strength and not seeking the Divine Will.

Going Separate Ways

We decided to leave that denomination and since John had been raised United Methodist, we were both ordained in the United Methodist church and assigned to separate churches. We were going in separate directions seven days a week and both on call 24 hours a day.

As we tried our best to minister to our congregations, we learned that two things in Protestantism have to be "perfect"—the Bible and the preacher. We were constantly subject to criticism. It was the big and little things that wore us down. We could not be our human selves but felt we had to be something we weren't. Every month the church board would go over the parsonage utilities and investigate if bills were too high but would not say anything if they were low. The Pastor Parish Committee would troop through the parsonage once a year to see if the pastor and family were keeping up "their" parsonage. If there was a typographical error in the bulletin, that was criticized. If we didn't visit the parishioners as some thought we should, that was criticized, yet we were to have plenty of time to prepare a "good" sermon for Sunday.

Finally in 1986 I burned out and voluntarily left the ministry. At that point our marriage was put on "maintain" and we started going our separate ways emotionally. We did not have the resources within ourselves to deal with what was happening to our marriage.

We moved to Uhrichsville, Ohio, in 1986 where John pastored for three years. I volunteered in the church. Martin was born in 1987. John wanted more children but I said no because I did not have the strength to take care of any more children. I went on to earn a Master's degree in Library Science, and soon became a director of the Bowerston Public Library.

Searching for Something More

My deep searching continued and even intensified. Some of my reading included the lives of St. Teresa of Avila, St. John of the Cross, St. Francis, works by Henri Nouwen, Thomas Merton, Thomas a Kempis, along with related works. Meanwhile, the gulf between John and me was widening. John was critical of my devouring book after book. I was critical of John lying around watching sports in the evening and not talking to me. I had to work all day and come home to do laundry, fix supper, and tend to the children, while John read or watched TV. The dreams we had shared at the start of our married life were not being fulfilled. I felt that we no longer had a clear purpose as a married couple. We didn't even pray together anymore.

One day John came home and said he felt God leading him back into law. I didn't feel God leading us anywhere. What had happened to our commitment to ministry? He went into law in spite of my questions. Since I felt I did not know John the lawyer, I wondered how we would relate together now.

I worked harder and harder trying to hold the family together. I was critical of John in my thoughts and words, trying to get him to change and talk to me and love me. Anyone looking in on this situation could have told us criticism does not draw a couple closer. John was getting angrier all the time. When he went back into law, he took a year away from ministry. I thought we would be able to spend more time together, but he started a Bible Study on Sunday evenings. Then he joined the choir, so we couldn't even sit together in church. I continued to sit alone in church just as I had in ministry. Of course John and I did not discuss this situation.

The following year he took a small church on the weekends. I didn't even like to listen to him preach because our lives did not measure up to what he was preaching. Somewhere along the way, we had lost respect for one another.

One morning in May 1992, I went into the family room and there on the floor was a banana peel and an empty Twinkie wrapper. I barely could pick them up and throw them away. I did not have the energy anymore to pick up another thing after him. I could sense something terrible was happening to us, but I didn't know what to do.

The Beginning of the End

At some point John began drinking too much at parties. One night he did not come home until 1 a.m., and someone had to drive him home because he was drunk. Another night we went to a party where he drank too much and I had to drive home. The children were with us and I was so angry with him that words could not express my rage.

In June 1992, our marriage hit "crazy time." "Crazytime" is when marriage partners can no longer communicate, the marriage spirals out of control, and divorce seems inevitable. I had never read anything about such a thing and did not know what was going on. Someone, I thought, has to help us. I could not go to his church members with our marital problems. I didn't know any of his lawyer friends very well. The United Methodist pastoral counselor was on vacation. And we were told that the district superintendent was the "pastor's pastor." I called the DS and poured out my heart to her. She immediately called John in and raked him over. I quickly learned the DS's role was not to be the pastor's pastor. John came home and said he had made arrangements to live with his parents. He moved out that night.

Something inside me painfully and horribly died. Our lives were broken and the pieces scattered beyond repair. The rejection was so great. My heart felt like it had been ripped from my body and stomped on. Half of me felt as though it were gone. As he shut the door that day I sobbed and asked God, "What am I going to do?" He said as plain as day, "Keep your hands off and stop trying to fix things." I said "Jesus, the children and I are getting out of the boat now and we have to walk on the water. No matter what happens I am going to keep my eyes on you. If I begin to slip and fall I'll reach up and take your outstretched hand and you can pull us back up."

John and I met with the children and John told them we were getting a divorce. Jessica started to cry even though she had sensed it was coming. Martin, just five years old, was sitting in the recliner with some pizza on his plate. He took one piece of pizza and threw it on the floor. I reached out and touched him and said, "It's okay to be angry." He took the other piece of pizza and smeared it on his glasses and face. I wanted to take him into my arms and hold him but he wouldn't let me. He got up out of the chair crying and angry and said, "I'm not angry about that. Now no one will play checkers with me!" He stormed out of the room.

"Where My Heart Is Calling Me"

That Sunday I went to another United Methodist Church. As I sat there, I thought, I know everything in church history, theology, and the polity of the United Methodist church and what I am looking for is not here. All they will give me is a few pats on the back and tell me how sorry they are over the divorce. I need more. I need something more.

I thought now that I am on my own, I will go where my heart has been calling me for so long. The next Saturday night, John had the children so I went to Mass at Immaculate Conception in Dennison. As I stood looking at the sign outside the church to make sure I had the right time, Jessica's former third-grade teacher, Nancy Thompson and her mother, Mrs. Valentine, approached me. They inquired if I were looking for someone. (John and I were well known in the county as United Methodists and his law practice made us very public people.) In much pain I told them John and I were getting a divorce and I wanted to become Catholic. They took me in and showed me the Missalette and the order of the Mass. It was all strange to me but I loved it. It was so peaceful; there was a holy quiet there. After Mass they took me behind the rectory to show me some beautiful flowers that were planted around a grotto. The flowers seemed to be saying there is life and beauty in the midst of death. They had just fed me my first "sacramental." Mrs. Valentine turned to me and gently said, "I know you will find God here." My heart wept for love, hoping she was right.

In July our next door neighbor died and Father Engle, the parish priest, was at the house. I was working in the front yard when he came down the steps and over to speak to me. I told him John and I were getting a divorce. He told me how sorry he was. Then he said, "Brenda, you will have to discover the difference between loneliness and solitude." He prayed the following prayer of abandonment by Brother Charles of Jesus; it was the prayer of my heart as well:

"Father, I abandon myself into your hands; do with me what you will. Whatever you may do, I thank you: I am ready for all, I accept all. Let only your will be done in me, and in all your creatures—I wish no more than this, O Lord. Into your hands I commend my soul; I offer it to you with all the love of my heart, for I love you, Lord, and so need to give myself, to surrender myself into your hands, without reserve, and with boundless confidence, for you are my father."

Another prayer I identified with going through the divorce was by Thomas Merton:

"My Lord God, I have no idea where I am going. I do not see the road ahead of me. I cannot know for certain where it will end. Nor do I really know myself, and the fact that I think I am following your will does not mean that I am actually doing so. And I hope I have that desire in all I am doing. I hope that I will never do anything apart from that desire. And I know that if I do this you will lead me by the right road, though I may know nothing about it. Therefore I will trust you always though I may seem to be lost and in the shadow of death. I will not fear, for you are ever with me, and you will never leave me to face my perils alone."

One of the darkest days of my life was August 17, 1992, when I signed the dissolution papers against my will. From my perspective, the marriage covenant I had taken was now broken. I signed these papers because I needed the child support for Jessica and Martin. I did not know at the time that my signature was not a requirement to receive child support. I decided to let John go if that was what he wanted. I also decided not to go through divorce court because I wanted to leave the door open for reconciliation. I did not want our dirty laundry aired in public where it could degrade us.

The way I came into the Catholic Church was not the way I would have chosen. I would have chosen to come in strength and intellectual expertise. I came instead on my knees in brokenness, through the sin of divorce. I wasn't sure how church members would accept me. I felt as if I were now wearing the scarlet letter "D" on my chest. I felt I was marked as a failure, rejected, no good, the worst of sinners; yet the people at Immaculate Conception lovingly took me in. One woman told me, "Brenda, we are all sinners here; that is why we come to Mass. We need God's grace every day." I wanted to know their God. These Catholics had such a simple trust and love in this God. I did not want to grow bitter and angry but to choose to go the way they were pointing—to life and love. Here was the Church where I did not have to wear a mask anymore. I could just be myself, sin and all. I came just as I was.

RCIA—Coming Home

The Rite of Christian Initiation of Adults (RCIA) started in October. Mary Corso was the team director of RCIA. She said we all answered an inner call of God to come to the Catholic Church. I had never before looked at my desire for the Catholic Church as a call of God but I began to see how true that was. Each of us was asked to tell our names and a little about ourselves. I barely could say my name and I told everyone I had been wanting to come to the Catholic Church for more than 20 years and that I had two children. Then I broke into tears. "I've been recently divorced," I said. Karen, my sponsor, put her hand on my shoulder in love and support. I knew I had found a home.

When I came to the Catholic Church I was so broken and starving for human touch. The emptiness and deep pain within made me realize that a Christ who is only spiritual is not enough. At one of our first RCIA classes Mary Corso told us, "We have many gifts to give you. God has called you here in this time and place." I was so hungry and thirsty and the Family began to feed me. The Church, through her members and priests, began to give me the gifts of the Church and I began to receive them.

Through a book called *Centered Living* by Basil Pennington, I learned the difference between taking and receiving. One particular sentence he wrote described the change that occurred in me when I came into the Catholic Church. He wrote, "We stop taking and begin to receive." I contemplated the difference experientially between taking and receiving.

Webster says "to take" means "to get by conquering, to get possession of by force or skill." We take a nap, take a chair, take a walk, take a book from the library, take a wife or take a husband, we buy clothes and we take them home, take a vow, take the blame, take deductions on our income tax, take a bus, take all day, take a poll, take notes. When we take something it does not really meet our deep needs, so we find ourselves taking more.

I began to realize that as I was taking from John by demanding that he meet my needs. I wanted him to help with the housework, play with the children, pick up his socks, and the list could go on. I could not continue to work 40 hours a week and keep up with all these things and still be the loving cheerful wife with a lot of energy for John.

I did not know that years ago John had handed the controls over to me to "help" me. He had made me the head of the household and I had gladly taken over. When we were at one church we had to mow two acres of grass. To avoid more criticism from the church people I felt the grass had to be mowed perfectly. John did not care a bit how the grass was mowed just so it was generally done. I got so angry with him. Through the years I let go of the grass being perfect but John did not see that change in me and never forgave me for that incident. What John did not see was that my tremendous fear of the people's constant criticisms was wearing me down. As our marriage continued to fall apart, we were both depleted of emotional resources. I began to realize that John and I had given so much of our lives to the Protestant church and taking so much from each other that we had nothing left for each other. Now I wondered how I could learn to receive. But I was discovering that here was the Church that gave us gifts and did not just demand our gifts. Through this Church the family of God enabled us to receive God's life through these gifts.

"Receive" means to "enter," "to have room for," "to grant admittance to." When we receive a gift, we enter into the gift. We receive love. We receive the Eucharist. We receive God's healing. We receive the warmth of the sun as God's gift to us each day. We receive the light of the moon to guide us in the darkest night. We receive God's peace through the gift of music. We need to open our hearts to receive God's love and mercy and grace. The gifts of heaven and earth are full of God's glory.

We cannot demand and take love. When we return to the center of our being through repentance, Jesus is there. It is only at our center that we are open to receive. When we receive we enter into the gift. When we open our hearts to receive the gifts of heaven and earth, we find they are full of God's glory.

For so long I had been searching for God out there but could not quite reach him. Father Engle told us, "Christ is in you." I kept repeating this to myself driving to work and any spare moment. Father said, "Faith in God is a gift—you cannot do it yourself. We need to accept this gift. We'll make many mistakes, so don't get down on yourself or God. Many know about God but do not know God. You are now a member of a community. Your life will change this year." Here was an opportunity to grow in faith in this God I knew primarily intellectually and to grow with the help and in relation to a community of people. I wanted to learn how to be still and know God and the Church.

My experiences with God through the years were never enough for one-time sustenance. I needed the everyday. Conversion should be more than a one-time "born again" experience; conversion is a lifelong journey of hearing the Gospel in deeper and deeper ways and putting our faith into action to become Eucharist to one another. Every day I need to allow God to change and mold me into his image. I needed to learn from my heart of a God that was forgiving and merciful to a great sinner. Through my RCIA experience I was hearing the fullness of the Gospel in a new way. Could God take my broken life and breathe his life and healing into me? I remembered reading in the lives of the saints how various saints were confronted with the horror of their own sinfulness and how they cried out "Lord, be merciful to me a sinner." They received God's grace.

What did these saints find that I had not found in Protestantism?

Father Engle was talking one night in RCIA about the Incarnation and the sacraments. The divine and human nature of Jesus is what we experience through the sacraments and many sacramentals. Through the divorce I became very aware of my deep need for touching God through the physical as well as the spiritual. I needed the human and divine touch. This is the answer I was searching for. This is what the saints knew.

Pray the Rosary

Mary Corso had said, "Brenda, pray the Rosary." I thought, if I am going to become Catholic, the rosary is part of it. I listened to Scott Hahn, a Catholic theologian who had converted from Presbyterianism, speak about the Blessed Virgin Mary and he answered my Protestant obstacles to her. I began to look at the Blessed Mother as *my* Mother who loved me perfectly and wanted me to experience the love of the Holy Family and the Blessed Holy Trinity.

Mary Corso said, "Pray the Rosary *slowly*. Meditate on the mysteries. Focus on the love of Mary and Jesus." So I decided to pray the Rosary from my heart to see if there was anything to this. I gave myself plenty of time to pray. When I started my mind was like a wild storm that would not quit. By the time I finished I felt such a calm and peace. I felt loved by the Blessed Virgin Mary. She had taken me into the community and love of the Blessed Holy Trinity.

When tragedy strikes our lives through death, financial stresses, discord between family and friends, divorce, sickness or whatever, our emotional and spiritual lives are in chaos. We find it difficult to even verbalize our feelings to others and in prayer. We can recover our feelings of hurt and anguish only for them to come up later in anger and bitterness. Time does not automatically heal without God's touch and our reception of his love and grace. One of the many gifts of the Church that brings healing and peace through the storms of life is the Rosary. The repetitious prayers calm the mind. The mysteries lift one out of misery into hope of new life.

Through meditating on the mysteries of the Rosary I began to reflect on other Biblical stories and they began to come alive for me in a new way. This is when I saw that my Catholic friends knew Scripture in a different way than I did. They might not have known chapter and verse like the Protestants, but they *experienced* the stories. It was more than an intellectual knowledge, it was a heart-felt knowledge.

The Blessed Virgin

Does the Blessed Virgin Mary understand our sufferings to intercede for us? She said "yes" to God even when her bearing

God's Son would bring misunderstanding and humiliation among family and friends and the community. She experienced the dark cloud of divorce until an angel came and visited Joseph. When Jesus was twelve years old, for three days she thought she had lost her Son. What anguish she must have suffered. Every time John came to pick up the children for his visitation I felt a sword pierce my heart—would the children be properly watched and cared for? I prayed for their protection.

The Blessed Virgin Mary experienced the grief and death of her husband, Joseph. She walked the hill with Jesus while He was being jeered, beaten, rejected, and finally nailed to the Cross, yet she kept all these things in her heart and spoke not a word. In all these sufferings she trusted God and found peace and joy. How many times was her heart stabbed with pain? Just look into her eyes at the Cross. Then at the Resurrection, the Ascension, and at Pentecost, God caused her spirit to rejoice.

As St. Augustine once said, "Mary's quality as a mother would have been of no value to her if she had not borne Christ more intensely in her heart than in her body!"

I have Called You by Name

In December of 1992, we, as RCIA candidates, were to participate in the Rite of Acceptance into the Church period called the Catechumenate. As each of us went to the front of the church, the lector said, "I have called you by name." We said our name out loud and signed our name in a book. Oh, how good is was to hear those words.

John for several years before our divorce did not call me by my name. In fact, he did not call me anything. He used to call me "honey bunch" but that had ceased long ago. I used to ask him about this but he would never tell me. In my crying one night I heard a voice say, "Why are you crying?" I said, "My love left me. He divorced me. He doesn't love me anymore!" Then I heard the voice of Jesus say, "Brenda, I love you." I understood how Mary Magdalene must have felt in the garden outside Christ's empty tomb when he called to her. I turned to him clutching those loving words and clung to him and cried, enveloped by his pure love. In the midst of my Good Friday the resurrected Lord called my name! Those words, "Brenda, I love you" went over and over in my mind. This love is one of faith because I cannot touch Jesus physically as Mary Magdalene did or see him physically with my eyes as she did, but through faith I could feel his touch and love from the deepest sense of my being, my spirit.

Finding God's Love

At one RCIA class, a team member, Vicki Dominick, talked about prayer. She told the story of the Velveteen Rabbit. She said, "Realness comes in coming to know God. We must look to God to find what is 'really real.' The Velveteen Rabbit was thrown out on a dump when he thought he had found love. The fairy picked him up and put him a garden and made him real. It wasn't until he was just about destroyed that he found out what being real meant."

I reflected as she told this story and did not hear much more of what she said about how it related to prayer. Lost in my own thought I felt John had thrown me out on that trash heap, but I did not want to stay there. I wanted to live as the saints, who encounter the tragedies and problems of this life and yet live immersed in the presence of God.

Blessing, Not Cursing

Another dark night came for me on December 31, 1992. John came to pick up the children. He told me he had been dating a woman and was planning to marry her. I was hurt so deeply and was so angry I could hardly speak. After he left I took my truck out, slowly drove around the streets, and cried and cried. I prayed, "God, I thought you were going to get us back together and now he is marrying another woman. This is the ultimate rejection. I chose to trust in you, believing you know what you are doing. I have to live the rest of my life alone but I know whatever comes my way you are with me and in me. Pierce my heart even more deeply to rid me of my own anger and bitterness. May you give me more grace to keep my mouth shut and not say any more hurting words against John. "

My dear Catholic friend, Ann West, told me to bless John whenever he came to pick up the children. In my mind I thought, "How can I bless him when he has hurt me so much?" Then I thought of my own sinfulness in the negative and destructive criticism I had hurled at John. Jesus said, "Bless those that curse you." So when John came to pick up the children in January 1994, I began to bless him in my thoughts. The first few times it was very difficult and I bitterly said, "Bless you." Then something began to change within me. The walls of hatred, anger, and bitterness within me began to crumble. I began to see John as a human being whom God loved. John in his own way was looking for this love as well. I began to feel love in my heart once again for John as I reflected on him as a person created by God.

I even tried to think of a way I could bless John with Holy Water. I thought maybe I could secretly put Holy Water on the handle of the garbage and ask him to take the garbage out when he left with the children. But I was too afraid to ever do this.

After the divorce when I had a lot of time alone, I read a lot of books and found John's symptoms revealed that he was deeply depressed. I had been so insensitive to his needs. Here I thought it was only me and I kept trying to improve myself to make him love me once more. His anger against me was due to some unresolved issues in his past long before we even met. My low self-esteem had prevented me from understanding the "crazy-time" we were going through.

John used to be loyal and dependable and had a good sense of humor. He used to write songs and sing them to me, but now his guitar was silent. He used to be so sensitive to his family and me. I thought he had strong character when I married him. He was intelligent and very romantic and I thought he had high moral standards but now he stooped to divorce to solve our problems. Where was the John I once knew?

I came to realize my own sins were low-self esteem, fear, and criticism. I came to the Catholic Church not just with a list of lifetime sins and mistakes, but a whole way of life in marriage that was wrong. I prayed that God would forgive me for this most grievous sin of divorce and my contributions that led to the divorce. If Christ and the Church could ever forgive me, then it would be the greatest news in the world.

I would sit in Immaculate Conception Church and look at the large crucifix. Jesus said, "It is finished." What did that refer to? The Passover began in the book of Exodus when the death angel was coming to kill all the first born sons in Egypt. The Jews were instructed to kill a perfect lamb, put the blood on the doorposts and then as a family eat the whole lamb.

Jesus was beaten severely and nailed to the Cross. This was the New Covenant Passover complete. Unless we eat this new Passover, eat Christ's flesh and blood, we cannot partake of the fruit of the Spirit and the Bread of Life. The Holy Eucharist restores family communion with each other. I felt so unworthy to partake of the Eucharist, Christ's very body, blood, soul, and divinity, yet he still calls me to come and eat.

The Protestants put a big emphasis on the empty Cross and the resurrection. My Roman Catholic friends told me you will experience your own resurrection in God's time but you must go by way of the Cross.

Receiving the Sacraments

During Lent I went to my first Confession. This is the Sacrament of Reconciliation. I learned from experience that if we truly confess our sins there is power in absolution. When we confess alone in prayer, there is not the same sense of assurance that we have received God's forgiveness. Through the Sacrament of Reconciliation we enter the confessional weighed down by our sins but leave free from sin and experiencing the marvelous grace of God.

During the Easter Vigil of 1993 I received the Sacrament of Confirmation and my first Communion, the body and blood of Christ, and was welcomed into the Church. I found a new land of God's presence and love and dance! This is a mystery but I loved John, even through the deep hurts, and would wait for God's timing for reconciliation. At that time, I knew it was God's will that we be reconciled but did not know whether we ever would again be married. I just trusted God knew what he was doing even though my earthly vision of the circumstances was limited. Weekly I need the body and blood of Christ. What a privilege to receive Jesus—

body, blood, soul, and divinity. This is the Bread of Life, the ultimate gift of the Church!

In June of 1993, I was to pick up the children at John's parents' home. As I drove up I saw John's car there. As I walked up the sidewalk to their house I prayed for God's will alone. When I went in John said he had to talk to me. I knew by the tone of John's voice this was not good. Essentially he wanted to cut the child support in certain areas. I said, "no," because the children needed it. The very presence and peace of God was in and with me. When John was done talking, I said to him with tears in my eyes, "John, I am so sorry that I did…" I confessed to him my contribution to the divorce. Tears welled in his eyes. He then confessed what he had done and was so sorry. The very presence of God fell upon us and the walls between us crumbles. We hugged and wept in each other's arms.

He said, "After three months of marriage, I have left this woman. I have moved back in with my parents." I did not know any of this. He said, "You do not know what I have been through." I saw a broken and lost John. He said, "I don't know if we can ever be married again because you're Catholic now." I said, "That doesn't matter, but just let me share with you some of the gifts of the Church." In the weeks that followed I gave him the Rosary, the Stations of the Cross, Holy Water, the lighting of candles, and much more. He read book after book in Catholicism. He spent hours at Immaculate Conception before the tabernacle realizing the Real Presence of Jesus Christ and praying for mercy.

We went to Father Engle to ascertain the position of the Church in our particular circumstance. We wanted to be obedient to Christ and the Church. The Church's position was that John's second marriage was only a civil proceeding, not a sacramental marriage; actually, the Church considered it adultery. John moved into an apartment in Dennison until the other divorce was final. We were celibate during these months and committed ourselves to prayer and fasting to get us through. In January 1994, the divorce was final and five days later at Immaculate Conception with Father Engle and our friends, we reaffirmed our marriage vows and by the State of Ohio were considered remarried.

Over those months of waiting in prayer, John was fed by the Catholic Church. He took the RCIA classes. He finished out his commitment in the weekend church he was pastoring. In June 1994, he, too, was confirmed and received his First Communion. Father Engle also arranged it so our seven-year-old son, Martin, could receive his First Communion. (Jessica had received the Sacrament of Reconciliation, First Communion, and Confirmation in spring 1994.) That day our whole family partook of the Holy Eucharist together. We lift our hearts in praise to God for the great things he has done in our lives!

It is now 1996, and John and I are still deeply in love and greatly respect and trust one another. We are new people and have a new marriage. We have not "arrived," but the Church is teaching us how to live and love. The work of God was so great in our lives that we do not think about each other's past sins. We did not reconcile on our own but have forgiven each other by the grace of God. Father Engle, Mary Corso, and the many prayers and love of the people at Immaculate Conception helped us along with the powerful transforming work of God in our lives.

Grace upon Grace

by Jeffrey Ziegler

What shall I render to the LORD
for all his bounty to me?
I will lift up the cup of salvation
and call on the name of the LORD.

Psalm 116[115]:12-13

What shall I render to you, O Lord, for all your bounty to me? You created me out of nothing, you hold me in existence, you redeemed me by your Son's Precious Blood, you adopted me in the Sacrament of Baptism. You have given me an angel as a guide and protector and a Virgin Mother as an advocate and refuge. You have led me to the fullness of faith in the Catholic Church, and through her, you call me into an eternal communion of life and love with you. Truly I can justly thank you, O Lord, only by offering myself to you day by day in the Holy Sacrifice of the Mass, in union with the oblation of your Son.

I did not exist, and then I came into being, and this was your doing, O Lord. You loved me into existence when you infused an immortal soul into the body that my parents had procreated. And so I was conceived, a sinner who shared the taint of original sin merited by my first parents. You rescued me from the fate that befell so many hundreds of millions of my contemporaries—death from chemical or surgical abortion, death from the abortifacient Pill or IUD or Norplant or Depo-Provera, death from the burning of salt or the dismemberment of limbs. Through no merit of my own, you willed that I be born into a family where I was loved, in a place unafflicted by starvation or war. Six months after my birth, you baptized me, O Lord Christ, by means of a Presbyterian minister, and divine life flowed into my soul.

You allowed me to receive the rudiments of Christian formation at the Western Presbyterian Church (PCUSA) in Palmyra, New York. When I was in third grade, just before my family stopped attending church and I stopped attending Sunday School, I received from that church's minister an RSV Bible that would play such an important role in later years. Because of the graces that flowed from my baptism, I never doubted the inerrancy of Scripture, for which I thank you, Almighty God.

That year I attained the age of reason, and thus began the long train of sins, which you have forgiven in the Sacrament of Penance, and for which I must render an account at the moment of my death. And was there not something more involved than the world and the flesh—namely, the devil? Did I not tell a friend in fourth grade, in bizarre words that shock me as I recall them, that "Lucifer is the king of darkness, and I am the prince of darkness"?

Despite my sins, O Lord, you sought me out. At about the age of nine, I saw an advertisement in TV Guide for a television show devoted to the end times, and I watched that show. You inspired me to jot down the address at the end of that show and to write for further information. Thus I began to receive two pamphlets every month from the Radio Bible Class. I did not read the literature, but you moved me to keep it in a desk drawer.

As I passed through junior high school, I excelled in school, I excelled in athletics, and I became more deaf to my conscience. I thought only of myself and never of you. Once you spoke loudly to me through my conscience as I was about to commit a grievous sin against charity, but I chose to ignore your voice.

At the age of thirteen, I became infatuated with a girl, and she did not like me. You inspired my mother (who probably saw my distress and wanted me to become more active outside of the home) to ask me either to attend Sunday School or to join the Boy Scouts; you gave me the grace to choose Sunday School. The teachers, a married couple, were evangelicals. They told me how to become a Christian, and on the afternoon of Sunday, September 25, 1983, I followed their instructions and those of the text we were using in that class. I confessed my sinfulness, my inability to save myself, my faith in the substitutionary atonement of Christ on the Cross, and my belief in salvation by faith alone. I accepted your Son as my personal Lord and Savior.

You inspired in me, O Lord, an increasing hunger for Scripture and prayer. By your grace, I delighted to memorize the Scripture passages quoted in my Sunday School text. I went on long walks, prayed to you, and at times knew the peace that only you can give. You led me to open up the desk drawer and devour the material from Radio Bible Class. I would read the epistles of Saint Paul in that RSV Bible I had received years before, and how deeply moved I was by his description of Christian family life.

And so the years of high school continued, and you were there as a provident Father. I read Scripture (all 66 books of the Protestant Bible in 1986), I prayed for others, I attended Sunday School, I went to church, I tried to lead others to you. I continued to read the material from Radio Bible Class; I bought several Bibles, Strong's Exhaustive Concordance, and many books by evangelical authors. On occasion, I listened to Focus on the Family. I subscribed to Christian Herald and Christianity Today. I imbibed the anti-Catholicism of much of my reading.

When I was about to sin, my evangelical mind told me that I was saved no matter what I did, but my conscience told me that I should not sin; often I rationalized and sinned.

My father supervised the book review section of a secular newspaper, and you moved him to bring home books on religion for me to examine. One book he brought home was Preaching the New Common Lectionary (Abingdon), and by your grace I used it as a basis of prayer. As I meditated on the Scripture readings for Sundays and feast days, I understood the importance of the liturgical year and the biblical basis of feasts like the Annunciation, the Visitation, the Presentation, and Epiphany.

During my last two years in high school, you led me to pro-life books, and my revulsion for the Roman Catholic Church was changed to a grudging tolerance, for I respected her biblical positions on abortion, divorce, and sexual morality. You allowed to be moved by the attractive example of charity lived by a few large Catholic families that I knew. You permitted me to catch the flu during the winter of my junior year, and while ill I turned on the television one Saturday afternoon and discovered Malcolm Muggeridge on Firing Line. He was a Catholic, and yet I thought, "This man must be a Christian."

You led me to the Middle English of The Canterbury Tales, and I was struck by its Christian ethos, even though it was written by a Catholic. You led me to Aeterni Patris and the Prologue of the Summa Theologica, and I was struck both by the apparent arrogance of Leo XIII's authority and by the beauty and logic of the Summa's Prologue.

I was convinced I was fully a Christian, a member of the invisible Church of the saved; but you gave me the grace to try to discover which denomination was most biblical. (I could not in conscience join the PCUSA because of its tolerance of abortion.) By your grace, I would spend an hour or so each week in the church library reading about the various denominations; and there I also read parts of Eerdman's Handbook of Christianity. From that book, I copied a list of the major Christian authors throughout history—from Clement of Rome to Hans Küng(!)—and thought that perhaps they could help me in my search for the most biblical denomination.

I began my studies at Princeton University in September 1987. I joined Princeton Evangelical Fellowship; its leader told me that he would eventually introduce me to dispensationalist theology, which he said was more biblical than convenantal theology. I attended the Sunday services of the Presbyterian Church in America's congregation in town, and I loved the strong, biblical preaching of its pastor, an ex-Catholic. He told me that he would eventually introduce me to covenantal theology, which he said was more biblical than dispensationalist theology. You placed in my heart a hunger for the Eucharist, so I also attended Episcopal services on campus.

Father of mercies, by your grace I recalled quotes from Chesterton's Orthodoxy that I had read the spring before in Christianity Today, and I borrowed the book from the campus library. Every day after the conclusion of classes, I would read a chapter of it, and I loved it. Here, too, was a Catholic who seemed so Christian.

One day in September, I was sitting in a faculty department office waiting to speak to a professor. You led me to pick up the campus newspaper, which I did not usually read because of its liberal bias, and I saw an advertisement for an Introduction to Catholic Teaching class taught on Wednesday evenings by Father C. John McCloskey III, a priest of Opus Dei who was then a chaplain at the Aquinas Institute (the name of the University's Newman center); he is now the chaplain of Mercer House in Princeton. And so, by your grace, I began to attend these short weekly classes in Murray-Dodge Hall in October. After one class, a thought came into my head that one day I might be Catholic; I developed a palpable revulsion at the idea.

That month, you moved me to borrow Humanae Vitae from the Princeton library (I was the second person to take it out—the first since 1968); I read it, and it made sense to me.

On Wednesday evening, October 21, you led Father McCloskey to invite me to his office and give me a copy of Spiritual Journeys (edited by Robert Baram and published by the Daughters of Saint Paul) and a catechism written by, among others, then-Father Donald Wuerl. Like many evangelicals, I thought that the Church taught that all non-Catholics would go to hell; preoccupied with this issue of salvation and convinced that C.S. Lewis was the epitome of both intellect and sanctity, I asked Father McCloskey, "How could a C.S. Lewis be in hell?" Father McCloskey patiently explained the Church's understanding of extra Ecclesiam nulla salus (no salvation outside the Church).

Fall break approached, and I stayed on campus to study. I often prayed in the Princeton University Chapel, a lovely neo-Gothic structure with stained glass windows that portrayed figures as disparate as the archangels, St. Sebastian, Plato, Calvin, and St. Thomas Aquinas; only an Anglican could have designed it. On Friday evening, October 23, you gave me the courage to pray in the Marquandt Transept of the University Chapel, where the Catholics had their daily Mass; it was the only part of the chapel with kneelers. Though I often knelt when I prayed in my room, I found it hard to kneel in a public place—like the sign of the cross, the practice reeked of Catholicism, ritualism, and salvation by works. As I sat alone in the chapel that Friday evening, part of me wanted to kneel to pray, and part of me did not. Then the kneeler in front of me came crashing to the floor. I looked around to see if any disapproving evangelical might be in the chapel; I saw none, and then I knelt to pray.

During that fall break, I spent much time each day studying material for my four classes—classical Greek, Latin, linear algebra, and ancient Greek literature—and I was also able to spend more time in prayer and spiritual reading. I read much of Father Wuerl's question and answer catechism, and most of the Catholic doctrines made sense to me. I started to read or re-read the works from that Eerdman's list, beginning with the letters of St. Clement of Rome and St. Ignatius of Antioch. I was shocked to find the these two Apostolic Fathers not only mentioned but emphasized the Real Presence of Christ in the Eucharist and the necessity of submission to the hierarchy of bishops, priests, and deacons in order to maintain the unity of the Church. I was shocked because I thought these were post-Constantinian additions to the original Christian faith; now I saw that they were there at the close of the first century. And as I looked at the Greek text of St. Ignatius's letters, I saw that the bishops, priests (presbyters), and deacons of the Catholic hierarchy were nothing more than the development of the New Testament episkopoi, presbyteroi, and diakonoi.

During that break, I also began to consider what a wonderful thing it would be if all the Christians in Princeton could worship together in one church; for the first time, the divisions in Christianity disturbed me. Then a thought occurred to me that perhaps it might be God's will that all Christians worship together as Catholics—but I dismissed that thought, which I believe also caused me physical revulsion.

At the conclusion of the break, on Saturday evening, October 31, I did my laundry in the basement of Lourie-Love Hall, and you led me to pick up Spiritual Journeys. I became engrossed in the book, and story after story began to make a deep impression on me. Person after person converted to the Catholic Church after renouncing the private interpretation of Scripture and submitting his intellect to the Church's Magisterium. For the first time, I realized that when I read the Bible, I was interpreting it; previously, I had believed that I was merely absorbing its obvious meaning.

The clock of the tower of Nassau Hall tolled midnight, and I took a walk from my dorm room to St. Paul's Church on Nassau Street to the Aquinas Institute and back to Butler College. As I walked, you gave me the grace to think something like, "Here I am, Jeff Ziegler, seventeen years old, with my own propensities to sins X and Y, and breathing this Marxist, materialist, secularist air, conceiving that I can interpret Scripture; and there is the Catholic Church, with twenty centuries of never-changing but ever-developing interpretation of Scripture. Who am I to go against the Magisterium of the Catholic Church?" At that instant, you gave me the grace to know the truth of the Catholic faith. I also knew that I could choose to accept or reject this grace. By your grace, I chose to seek reception in the Catholic Church. I returned to campus as the clock struck one o'clock.

When I awoke the next morning, I did not go to the PCA service, but instead attended Mass at the Aquinas Institute. I attended daily Mass and continued my instructions with Father McCloskey. On December 8, 1987, I made my First Confession, was confirmed, and received my First Communion at the 7:30 PM Mass in the Princeton University Chapel.

"And from His fullness have we all received, grace upon grace." (John 1:16) Grace upon grace, O Blessed Trinity, grace upon grace! If any one of the events described above had not occurred, would I be a Catholic today? And you know, O Lord Christ, how utterly impoverished I would be without frequent encounters with you in Confession and Communion, how blind my intellect would be without the teaching of your vicar on earth, and how tepid my heart would be without the graces granted through Eucharistic adoration and devotion to Our Lady.

"What shall I render to the LORD for all his bounty to me? I will lift up the cup of salvation and call on the name of the LORD."

Jeff Ziegler, a graduate of Princeton University, works in the Development Office of Franciscan University of Steubenville. He serves on the Network's Board of Advisors.

Journeys Home

From Sectarianism to the
Communion of Saints
by William J. Cork

O n the morning of October 23, 1844, following a long night of eager anticipation, thousands of Americans experienced what has become known as the "Great Disappointment." They had believed that New York farmer William Miller had found the key to understanding and decoding the apocalyptic prophecies of Daniel and the Revelation, and had determined the precise date of the return of Christ to judge the living and the dead. Now, the sun shining harshly on their rude awakening, they took circuitous routes home through their cornfields to avoid the ridicule of their neighbors. Some could not accept their fate, and continued to accept dates. Others gave up all belief in God. Many turned towards spiritualism or the Shakers.

But one group saved face in an ingenious way. They reasoned that Miller had hit on the right date, but had misidentified the event. They persuaded themselves that on October 22, 1844, Jesus had entered the most holy place of the heavenly sanctuary, to begin a final work of investigative judgment, which would culminate in the blotting out of sins of believers immediately prior to his return. They did not mind that they alone had come to see this—the rest of the world was "Babylon," and was fallen. Further study led them to adopt the keeping of the seventh day of the week, Saturday, as the Sabbath, and to give up eating those meats declared "unclean" in Leviticus 11. They were encouraged in these conclusions by the visions of a young woman from Portland, Maine, Ellen G. Harmon, later married to James White.

The movement that James and Ellen White midwifed through the Great Disappointment became known as Seventh-day Adventism. They no longer set dates, but they still looked for the imminent return of Christ. They believed that great day would be preceded by a time of persecution, directed at them because of their sabbatarianism. The pope had led Christianity away from the Biblical faith, and had persuaded all Christians to accept Sunday as the Sabbath. Now, in these last days, these Adventists expected the Catholic Church would unite with Protestantism, and together the apostate churches would persuade civil authority to legislate Sunday observance. Those who kept Sunday at that time would receive the mark of the beast; those who kept the Sabbath would receive the seal of God. And the servants of the beast would do all they could to put the faithful to death.

This was the worldview in which I was raised. In 1980, I entered Atlantic Union College in South Lancaster, MA, to begin study for the Adventist ministry. It was a period of theological ferment within Adventism. Australians Desmond Ford and Robert Brinsmead questioned the Adventist views of salvation and the judgment, and California pastor Walter Rea was documenting Ellen White's plagiarism. Many Adventist pastors and seminarians left; some became evangelicals, others started independent "evangelical Adventist" churches. At the end of my junior year, I made the break myself. Having been raised in a legalistic and sectarian environment, I had two critical issues: the gospel and the Church. I liked what Ford and Brinsmead were saying about the gospel's message of unconditional forgiveness, but I didn't think forming a splinter movement of a splinter movement was the answer. My study of the Church's history opened to me the continuity of the faith of the ages; experiences with other Christians led me to seek out new and wider forms of fellowship. The gospel, I came to believe, must create a community of faith in continuity with the preaching of the apostles. It must draw us toward other believers, not away from them.

I could never have made this decision without the influence of my Adventist professors—even those who never would have dreamed of breaking with the church themselves. My scripture professors introduced me to form and redaction criticism; this led me to seek the authority of scripture not in a process of verbal inspiration, but in scripture's transmission in and through a community of faith. Theology professors took us to lectures in Boston to hear such theologians as Wolfhart Pannenberg, Charles Hartshorne, and

Langdon Gilkey. And my history professors pushed me continually back to the sources of Christian thought.

My doubts about the truth of the Adventist claims grew, and as a writer (and—briefly—editor) of the student newspaper I gave voice to those doubts publicly. In 1983 I finally made the decision to leave. A professor took us to the annual gathering of the Evangelism Association of New England. Francis Schaeffer was the main speaker. As I gazed upon that diverse crowd of Adventists, evangelicals, Catholics (in habit and collar), and charismatics (waving their hands), I was overwhelmed by a sense of our unity in Christ, and the need to seek fellowship with these brothers and sisters. At that moment, the Adventist sitting next to me poked me in the ribs with his elbow and muttered, "It's too bad these people don't know the Truth." That was all I needed. The next day I visited a Presbyterian Church in Clinton, MA, and shortly thereafter I wrote a letter of resignation to the Adventist church where I was a member.

At this time, however, I had been married for a year. Joy's father is a very conservative Adventist pastor, and my "apostasy" shattered him—and Joy found herself pulled between us. My own father had become a Christian when I was in high school, and he had become an Adventist himself about the time I went to college. In such emotionally charged surroundings, Joy was not about to even consider leaving—she has remained an active Adventist to this day. My marriage could have been shattered at that time had it not been for one of my professors, to whom I went for counseling. He helped me see that one who undergoes a conversion experience goes through the same sort of grief process as one who is watching a loved one die—and the convert's family and friends go through a parallel process. There will be anger, and denial, and depression, he warned. And so there was. But knowing its source helped us get through that period.

This emotional upset was one reason that I chose to stay close to Adventism for awhile; I felt Joy needed the extra support. I finished my B.A., and accepted a teaching assistantship at Loma Linda University, to begin graduate study in church history. My responsibilities there included giving occasional lectures in the undergraduate church history survey, and helping to edit a journal of Adventist history.

On Reformation Day, 1984, I first entered Trinity Lutheran Church in Riverside, CA, a congregation of the Lutheran Church in America. In the Lutheran confessions, I heard the New Testament gospel. In the Lutheran liturgy and especially the Eucharist, I recognized the Body and Blood of Christ, and felt connected to the church of all ages. Lutheranism united for me the evangelical and catholic dimensions of the Christian faith. At this point, however, there was no way I could have considered becoming a RO-MAN Catholic—I had too many years of anti-Catholic propaganda ringing in my ears. And yet I was clearly being led on a road to Rome—how else to explain my concern for the church, and for liturgy, and for the Eucharist? Ironically, it was once more Adventist professors who were instrumental in nudging me toward considering the Roman option. My department chair introduced me to Newman's *Essay on the Development of Doctrine*, had me read the documents of Vatican II, and required that I visit a Catholic Church as a class assignment.

Due to financial constraints, Loma Linda was not able to guarantee me scholarship funding for the next year. I began to think it was time to transfer to a seminary. My chair suggested I consider Gettysburg Lutheran Seminary; he said if I was going to continue in church history, Luther scholar Eric Gritsch would be a great mentor. He also introduced me to the book Gritsch wrote with Robert Jenson: *Lutheranism: The Theological Movement And Its Confessional Writings*. This book is a standard work for "evangelical catholics" within the Lutheran Churches, for it defines Lutheranism not as the start of Protestantism, but as a movement of evangelical reform within the Catholic Church. Its premise is that the Lutheran confessions are not a constitution to begin a new church, but that they assume Catholic dogma and practice wherever the same is not criticized. This resonated with my own growing understanding of Lutheranism as a VIA MEDIA between Rome and the excesses of the Reformed Protestantism of Calvin and Zwingli. But this raised other questions, questions inspired by Newman's *Essay*—is such a VIA MEDIA really possible? If one accepts the Catholic principle of the faithfulness of Christ to his Church through time, will not one be pushed eventually to seek communion with Rome?

I transferred to Gettysburg Seminary in the fall of 1985, endorsed by the Pacific Southwest Synod of the Lutheran Church in America. Joy was regarded with great skepticism by some in the administration. In one of our first conversations, Dean Gerhard Krodel (a former Luftwaffe pilot with a thick Bavarian accent we all loved to imitate) leaned back in his chair and said, "Now, I don't say this myself, but you are going to find yourself in a parish one day and they are going to say to you, 'If you can't convert your own wife, what the hell business do you have preaching to us!' So, what you should do is go down to the bookstore and get a copy of Werner Elert's book, *The Structure Of Lutheranism*—that will give you everything you need to convert your wife."

Even apart from such intimidation, the next few years were a busy period. I finished my M.A. in church history the following spring, with a thesis on the abolitionist and transcendentalist Theodore Parker. I continued working on my M.Div., taking some classes through the Washington Theological Consortium at Catholic seminaries. I joined the Army Reserve's Chaplain Candidate program, and completed a unit of Clinical Pastoral Education at Walter Reed Army Medical Center. I returned to Trinity Lutheran in Riverside, CA, for my internship. And my senior year, I became a member of the Brothers and Sisters of Charity, Domestic, an ecumenical Franciscan community founded by John Michael Talbot. Each of these experiences put me into contact with Catholics, with whom I began to form very close friendships. Knowing what took me to Lutheranism, they continually asked me, "Why not go all the way?"—and this was echoed in my own heart. But I still was not able to act.

I graduated from Gettysburg in May 1989. I was called to be pastor of the Thompsontown Lutheran Parish in Juniata County, PA, and was ordained on June 11. Ten days prior to this, my wife entered the hospital with severe hemorrhaging; our son Andrew was born late that night, two months premature, due to a placental abruption. I began my ministry with him in the hospital for two months.

During my time at Gettysburg, many of us had been concerned about the forthcoming merger, which would result in the formation of the Evangelical Lutheran Church in America. We were troubled by the fact that the merger process had decided to put off discussion of theological issues until after the merger. We felt it was becoming just another mainline Protestant church, with no commitment to either scripture or the Lutheran confessions. This confusion was clearly illustrated by my experiences at Thompsontown. This was a two church parish. Emmanuel, in town, had kneelers in the pews, and a hand-carved Tyrolean crucifix over the altar; it used wine for communion, but thought that communion should be held only once a month. Centre, in the country, was indistinguishable from a Methodist or Reformed church; it used grape juice for communion, sang evangelical Sunday school songs, but was a very close, supportive community of faith. Worse, I got sucked into a 30-year conflict between the two, and stirred up old jealousies. I exacerbated the situation by defending a more Catholic view of ordained ministry over against congregationalism.

I resigned after a year. That summer, to gain some healing, I attended a conference for Priests, Deacons and Seminarians at the Franciscan University of Steubenville. I was subscribing to *New Covenant* Magazine, and had seen in an advertisement that Fr. Francis Martin would be one of the speakers. Fr. Francis was one of the Catholics I had taken a class with when I was in Gettysburg—it was a class on "Romans" at the Dominican House of Studies, and I had been very impressed with the way he dealt with the hermeneutical disagreements between Lutherans and Catholics. The worship services and the talks were all inspiring, but it was the private conversations that I remember best.

One day I was talking to some priests about differences between Catholics and Lutherans over the Eucharist. Contrary to Catholic and Reformed misunderstandings, Lutherans have never believed in "consubstantiation." Luther simply denied that Aristotelian metaphysics were useful in discussing the miracle of the Eucharist. He was content to stick with the words of Scripture, as when at Marburg he wrote the words "Hoc est enim corpus meum" on the table, and when Zwingli attempted to rationalize their meaning, Luther ripped aside the table cloth and pounded on the words and said, "This is what the word of God says, and I won't try to get around it." One question that remains, however, is whether the presence of Christ perdures following the celebration of the liturgy.

Lutherans have either said it goes back to being mere bread (so that one Lutheran church I preached at had no problem throwing the leftover bread to the birds!), or they avoid the problem by consuming all the bread during the liturgy. And yet we had no problem taking communion to the sick without reconsecrating it!

One of the priests listened to all my objections and excuses and quietly said, "When God gives a gift, he doesn't take it back." That night, when the evening meeting ended, I found myself in a stampede of priests rushing downhill from the red and white tent to the chapel.

"What's going on?" I asked.

"Holy hour," said a priest.

"What...?" I started to ask. But he was long gone.

The chapel fell into hushed silence as the Body of Christ was exposed in the monstrance. Priests fell on their faces. I was speechless. The reality of the Presence of Christ overwhelmed me, and all my objections fell away as I found myself praying, "My Lord and my God!"

Another day that week I was walking with a priest and we came across another group of priests. After some casual conversation, one suggested praying the rosary. I tried to back out gracefully. A priest (the same one from the other day!) pressed the point. I nervously remembered a quote from Lutheran theologian Gerhard Forde about "not talking to dead people." The priest looked me in the eye and replied, "Don't you believe in the communion of saints?"

The climax of the week for me was a gut-wrenching experience of profound grief and alienation as I sat alone in the pew as the priests and deacons around me went forward to receive the Body and Blood of Our Lord—we fell on each others shoulders and cried.

From there, I went on to Arkansas to attend the "Chapter of Tents" of the Brothers and Sisters of Charity at Little Portion Hermitage. One night, they were going to have a "living rosary." I groaned, "Oh, no! Here we go again!" I tried to hide, but Sr. Viola saw me, grinned, stuck a candle in my hand, and led me to my spot and said, "You are in the creed." I thought, "Someone is trying to tell me something!"

The next few months passed in a blur. I did some more Army training, during which Saddam Hussein invaded Iraq. I spent that fall at Ft. Bragg, NC, helping out at the 82nd Airborne Division Memorial Chapel.

At Christmas, I was called to be pastor of Shepherd of the Hills Lutheran Church in Montpelier, VT. If I could have been a "Catholic" sort of Lutheran anywhere, it would have been here: we reserved the Blessed Sacrament, had weekly Eucharist, "smells and bells"—even a touch of charismatic praise. One of the church's traditions was to use Luther's *Formula Missae* as the order of service on Reformation Day. This was Luther's 1521 revision of the Mass—he kept it in Latin, with German scriptures and hymns and a German sermon, but this parish did it all in English. One year, I suggested doing it in Latin, as Luther had intended (contrary to myth, he never had a problem with the Latin mass as such, but thought it should be retained as an option). We used 16th century Lutheran hymns in English, and scriptures and sermon in English, but the rest was in Latin, in a simple chant setting. This was one of the best received liturgies I ever did anywhere.

And yet, in spite of all this romantic Romanism, this church was congregationalist in the extreme—in fifteen years it had been a member of the Wisconsin Synod, Missouri Synod, AELC, and ELCA. It saw no need to participate in the gatherings of the larger church, or to send money to the Synod. Not that I blamed them entirely. In 1990 the ELCA published a study on human sexuality that declared that scripture and church tradition had no answers to contemporary questions on sexuality, and that the church must seek its message in an ahistorical "radical imperative." I found myself giving up hope that a "Catholic" version of Lutheranism would ever amount to anything other than a sectarian option within a generic old-line Protestant denomination.

I continued dialogue with many Catholic priest friends, especially those I worked with as a chaplain in the Vermont National Guard, and began meeting regularly with the local Catholic pastor "for coffee." I made my permanent profession in the Brothers and Sisters of Charity. I attended other Priests Conferences at Steubenville. In 1992, a financial crisis forced Shepherd of the Hills to cut me to half time, and this provided me with the opportunity to take the action I had been trying to avoid, Hamlet-like, for so long. I entered into dialogue with a Catholic archbishop and with my Lutheran bishop; they felt it best for me to resign at the end of October. My last sermon was Reformation Day. On November 11, 1992, in a private ceremony attended by some priest, deacons, and Franciscan friends, I was received into the Catholic Church.

For the next eighteen months I was unemployed, with a wife and two children (Aimee was born in March 1992, also premature!). Many Catholic friends obtained financial help for us. A couple of bishops helped me with networking in looking for jobs. I continued to work part time for the Vermont National Guard, I wrote regularly for the diocesan paper, I got a position preaching Catholic parish missions. And I got food stamps and was on welfare for a period. And I wondered whether I had done the right thing. On top of it all, my daughter was diagnosed with a congenital hip dislocation, and we spent $3^{1}/_{2}$ years undergoing repeated hospitalizations to attempt to correct it.

That was a trying time. It gave me a lasting love for St. John of the Cross.

The worst thing, perhaps, was the difficulty of finding a job in a Catholic Church. I sent out hundreds of inquiries, got handfuls of responses, and three or four interviews, at which I kept coming in second. I grew angry with the patronizing excuses that people gave for not wanting to hire me: "We don't think it would be just to pay you only $20,000 a year"; "We don't think it would be fair to your family to move so far"; "Would you accept a janitorial position at $6 an hour, an hour's drive from your house?"

In July 1994 I finally got a full time position as a Director of Religious Education. I had a couple of experiences there (which included many broken promises and some indescribable treatment of my wife and children by a nun) that were so bad I decided to go back to Lutheranism. I felt I had really made a stupid mistake. I contacted my old bishop and began the process for reinstatement. I took tests, and psychological evaluations, and submitted to all sorts of humiliating interrogations, and the committee decided to place me in a kind of second internship to feel me out. I met with the pastor they wanted to put me with—and he was exactly the kind of pastor I had been, with the same questions and concerns that had sent me to Rome in the first place. I attended a regional retreat of the Brothers and Sisters of Charity in Connecticut, and on my way there it struck me what a stupid decision I was on the verge of making. I had stayed faithful to Christ and his Church through eighteen months of unemployment, and now, after a bad experience in one parish I was ready to throw the towel in and go back. I thought of several scriptures that touch on that theme. And I realized there is no going back. Christ never calls us backward; he only calls us forward. "Further up and further in!" The crisis was past, and a couple of months later, I was offered a position doing campus ministry at the University of California at Santa Barbara—I could not help but feel the heavens were smiling!

If I were summarize the primary reason I became a Catholic and why I remain one, I think the best answer comes from Cardinal Newman's *Essay on the Development of Doctrine*:

> *Whatever history teaches, whatever it omits, whatever it exaggerates or extenuates, whatever it says and unsays, at least the Christianity of history is not Protestantism. If ever there were a safe truth, it is this.*

> *And Protestantism has ever felt it so... This is shown in the determination already referred to of dispensing with historical Christianity altogether, and of forming a Christianity from the Bible alone... Our popular religion scarcely recognizes the fact of the twelve long ages which lie between the Councils of Nicaea and Trent, except as affording one or two passages to illustrate its wild interpretations of certain prophesies of St. Paul and St. John... To be deep in history is to cease to be a Protestant.*

I was a novice church historian when I first read those words, and yet even then I felt their truth. I had already experienced the pull of the faith of the fathers of the church; I had experienced the sense of mystical union through the Eucharist and Baptism; I had learned to say "Amen" to the truth in Augustine, the Cappadocians, Francis and Dominic, Aquinas and Bonaventure, Vatican II and John Paul II. When that priest asked if I believed in the communion of saints, I had to say, "Yes! Of course I do!"

To this day, I believe that Newman's remains the best reason for a Protestant to become a Catholic. As long as Catholic converts try to argue from scripture to scripture in a fundamentalist fashion, the Protestant will win the war, if not the battle. For if apologetics is simply a matter of proof-texting, who is to say whether the Protestant or the Catholic twist is the right one? But step back, and look at the Church of the post-apostolic generation, the period of Clement and Ignatius—a period in which some of the books in the New Testament were being written—and the Protestant must recognize that this is clearly a Catholic Church. Christ promised Peter that upon a rock he would build his church, and the gates of hell would not prevail against it. We've spent so much time arguing about the rock that we've let the main thrust of the text get away from us! Christ promised that the Church would be maintained in faith and purity to the end; every Protestant ecclesiology demands that we deny this, and posit a global apostasy.

Since I became a Catholic, my wife has remained an Adventist. I have come to realize it is not in my power nor is it my place to try to force her to convert. After all, Catholicism, against Luther and Calvin, has always stressed freedom of the will. The Catholic tradition also insists on the primacy of conscience. Back when the Dean made his comments about Joy, I had no answer. Later, I thought of one; the fifth article of the Augsburg Confession says that "in order that we may obtain the faith that justifies, God gave the word and sacraments; through these, as through means, God gives the Holy Spirit, who works faith, when and where he pleases, in those who hear the gospel." I still like that. It says that I am called to be faithful in my witness to the gospel, and the rest is up to God.

And God can give us a surprise or two when we do that. A couple of years back, I got a letter from my brother Jim, a student at the Univ. of Massachusetts. He had joined the Air Force out of high school, spent some time in Japan, dabbled with Buddhism, and then entered UMass to study Japanese. The letter before me began, "You might want to sit down before reading this." I've never gotten a letter like that with good news in it. I sat down. "I've met a Catholic girl. I started going to Mass with her during Advent. I've entered the RCIA. I'm going to be received into the Catholic Church at Easter."

The next year, I got a letter from my brother Dan. He had gone to Israel with Youth with a Mission (YWAM), where he had gotten interested in Islam and Orthodoxy. Then he, too, transferred to UMass. He, too, started going to Mass. He entered the RCIA and was received into the Church last Easter. He's thinking about the priesthood.

My brothers and I have had many chuckles about how we all left Adventism in different directions, and found ourselves in the same place. I remarked once, "It just goes to show that 'All Roads Lead to Rome.'"

Thank you, CHNetwork!
by Janine and Chris LaRose

First, let me thank you for the job leads you sent us. I do have skills in these areas, but we have been that route and got burnt so to speak (moving to an unknown church and area). We are very happy in the church we attend here and are both involved in music ministry, RCIA, youth/family ministry, adult education, etc.(all unpaid). Our pastor is very spirit-filled and has undertaken a 're-newal' program and we are in on the ground floor.

I truly appreciate what you have done for us and what the *CHNetwork* continues to do for us. Our journey in the Catholic Church still is filled with great joy and sadness—we still have not regained our Protestant friends and have not made many strong Catholic friends. I kind of know how the lepers must have felt.

When I fell off my horse and encountered Jesus in 1990, I left my old life behind including my professional career and only wanted to serve Him in the church. But then He beckoned us again, this time to His one, holy, Catholic, and apostolic church. I then left the Methodist Church and my opportunity to serve Him as a local pastor. I had a couple of short jobs in the human-service field, before taking a youth/family minister position in a 'progres-sive' diocese in Michigan. This we thought was the ministry "I" wanted in the Catholic Church—we did what we felt the Lord wanted us to do there, but had to shake the dust from our feet and came back home. Jesus was not too well received at home either now that I think about it!

What is my point here? I am not sure, maybe I just need an-other shoulder to cry on. Kind of like Jesus needing prayer support in His hour of need.

As anyone can see from a secular standpoint, my resume does not look very stable. Many moves, short jobs. All of this coupled with an unemployment rate of 8% in our county and many, many qualified people looking for the same jobs, is most discouraging. And yet He has never let us down. He has been there for us always. Why can't I trust in Him? He tells us not to worry about anything, for what good does it do. All I can do is cling to His cross, while bearing my own.

I would only ask for the prayers of support from our brothers and sisters in the *CHNetwork* who know these feelings only too well. We look to our spiritual father St. Francis of Assisi, who lived in simplicity and poverty, to walk with us on this narrow path. We ask our Mother, most blessed Virgin Mary, to help us to keep our eyes and hearts focused on her Holy Son Jesus. And allowing the Holy Spirit to pour out His graces on us, we can be sure Jesus will bring us to His Father.

We only want to bring Jesus in the fullness of His Church to all who do not know Him. How we are to do this only He knows. We only hope that our lives and love for Him may be a light to all we meet. He owes us nothing. He gave all He had on the cross for you and me. What an awesome loving God we serve!! I shall love Him always, as I love you my brothers and sisters in Christ. We must keep this network going to lift up our fellow holy brothers and sisters who too have dropped their nets, to follow Jesus wherever He calls.

I thank you for listening to another hurting soul, for the sake of Christ. Your reward shall indeed be great! Please continue to keep us posted with the happenings in your life, and that of all the *CHNetwork* folks. Know that you are all in our prayers to the Lord God. I still remember Fr. Scanlan's comment at the Defending the Faith Conference after we sang "Raise Up An Army," he said ... "We are the army ... The battle continues."

The Joy of the Lord is our Strength!

Part Two
The Journey of the CHNetwork: A Response to Needs

The *Coming Home Network International* didn't appear over night like a surprise winter snow, nor did it emerge as a finished product from the bantering calculations of a carefully selected committee of highly trained spiritual guides. It began solely as a response to specific needs and cries for help. We never intended that it become an organization. It began as a fellowship of Protestant clergy who had basically two things in common: they loved Jesus Christ enough to go wherever He called them, and then discovered that He was calling them home to the Catholic Church.

Central to the beginning and growth of the *CHNetwork* has been its newsletter. This homespun rag has served as the primary means of communicating words of encouragement and courage to the membership. Each issue generally begins with the *"Convener's Corner,"* a reflective report from Marcus Grodi, the *CHNetwork's* co-founder and "Convener," on how the membership was growing, and what was being planned or dreamed.

The following collection of these and related articles, therefore, tells the story of how this fellowship has prayerfully tried to follow God's leading in helping the constantly growing fellowship of men and women, clergy and laity, on their journeys home.

Journeys Home

July 1993

Convener's Corner

I am a Protestant minister with a family of five. However, after many years of searching, study, prayer, and at times painful disagreement, my wife and I now know that I must resign from my pastorate so that our family can come home to the Catholic Church. We are not scared. We have been completely broken down and now have nothing to do but trust Him. We are certain of His call to become Catholics. We just need support.

This cry for support and encouragement from a Protestant pastor is one of many I have been receiving over the last few months. Ever since we let the word out that we were starting a fellowship for clergy converts and their families, the floodgates have been overflowing. We thought there might be just a few, but the Holy Spirit has overwhelmed us by the work He is doing in the hearts of our separated brethren.

For my part, the idea for this type of fellowship came about as the result of my own struggles along the faith journey from ordained Protestant ministry to the Catholic Church. I felt like I was making my way along a scarcely walked path, only to be pleasantly surprised to discover the great number of others also being called by God to make similar journeys. It is like driving a long distance to a meeting only to find upon arrival that dozens of others from your same town had also made the same journey, each driving alone, oblivious to the others. We could have car-pooled! We could have chartered a bus and fellowshipped along the way!

The purpose of this newsletter and the *Network* fellowship is to help those who, once called to ministry in the Protestant faith, are now on the road to the Catholic Church or have already become a member and who want to continue serving Christ in ministry in the Church. This desire brings up many questions concerning vocation, protocol, finances, educational needs, opportunities, etc., in an ecclesial structure and system that is strange and foreign to many of us. We hope that the *Network* will serve as the charter bus, or at least the car pool, so that you and I don't have to face these challenges alone.

"How Should We Then Serve?"

On Sunday, June 27, 1993 the *Network* had its first gathering in conjunction with the *DEFENDING THE FAITH IV CONFERENCE* at Franciscan University of Steubenville, Ohio. After a full weekend of inspiring presentations, more than twenty former or inquiring Protestant clergy and their wives gathered for the luncheon and fellowship.

After becoming acquainted over a well-stocked cold-cut luncheon, Fr. Mike Scanlan, the president of this fine Catholic University, welcomed us with words of encouragement and support. We then spent more than an hour with each person sharing briefly his or her own journey to the Catholic Church. This was a very powerful time as we heard how faithful God has been to each of us even during the tough times. We also learned of some difficult imminent situations that required prayer and continued counsel.

After a break, Fr. Ray Ryland addressed us, reflecting on a number of the concerns expressed in our sharing. For those of you who do not know, Fr. Ryland was an Anglican pastor who converted to the Catholic Church with his wife Ruth in 1963 (read their story on pages 33-44). He was instrumental in opening the door for the celibacy dispensation so that American Anglican pastors who enter the Catholic Church could petition for priesthood. In 1983, he himself was ordained to the priesthood under the then new Pastoral Provision. Fr. Ryland has consented to be our Chaplain.

The luncheon ended with a business meeting as we discussed the future of our fellowship. It was unanimous that the *"Network"* be formed. That we have an interactive newsletter and that we plan annual weekend retreats so that members, both converts and inquirers, can gather for mutual support. It was also decided that we continue the "How should We then Serve?" luncheon/Seminars each summer in conjunction with the Defending the Faith Conferences, as our annual meeting, annual checkup. The meeting ended with prayer, with great joy and a sense of excitement, as we knew our common experiences had confirmed the true touch of the hand of God's Spirit.

Stand Firm and Hold to the Traditions

As a Protestant pastor, I was committed to presenting the truth of Jesus Christ and His Gospel. I took this seriously and building my teaching and preaching upon the foundation of Scripture alone, I believed that what I was feeding my congregation was safely palatable. As I look back, I am amazed at how blind I was. There are so many Scripture texts I either unconsciously missed, conveniently avoided, or consciously explained away.

Some of these, such as Matthew 16.18-19, John 6.51-69, 20.23, 1 Timothy 3.15 and others are fairly obvious to me now, since I've become more apologetically informed. However, one particular text has become very significant to me: 2 Thessalonians 2.15:

> *So then, brethren, stand firm and hold to the traditions which you were taught by us, either by word of mouth or by letter.*

To Paul and the Christians to whom he wrote, the touchstone for theological, doctrinal and ecclesial truth was the words and teachings being passed, preserved and revered, orally and sometimes by hand. Similar texts, such as 1 Corinthians 11.2 and others, actually indicate that the readers were to accept the written testimonies BECAUSE they were in agreement with the oral testimonies—the oral traditions were the authoritative template.

Most modern biblical scholarship has thrown out not only the trustworthiness of early traditions but also the validity of any original "deposit of faith." This of course is the expected trajectory of the Protestant emphasis on Scripture alone as the only trustworthy testimony of early Christianity.

However, what makes me pause is that Paul and the other New testament writers were moved to write almost entirely because they needed to address specific imminent problems which they could not correct in person. This has several very important implications: (1) there were probably many problems the New Testament authors took care of personally which they never wrote about; (2) there were also many things that were going well which they never mentioned; and (3) if they COULD have handled all the problems in person, we may have had a very short New Testament! When we Protestants limited ourselves to only the testimony of the written word, we made ourselves naively susceptible to the problems and stubbornly resistant to the solutions that in fact ecclesial tradition alone has preserved and addressed.

The reality is that Sola Scriptura exists no where in any Protestant denomination. In every case we encounter new traditions erected to fill the void left by the rejection of Sacred Tradition. And when the validity of an authoritative deposit of faith is rejected, the basis for establishing any authority even in Scripture is short-circuited, leaving us where modern scholarship has left us, slaves to individual or scholarly opinion.

I have come to joyfully accept the reality that the tradition that Paul so often commanded the early Christians to hold fast to was the inspired truth Jesus promised that the Church would receive through the guiding, protecting presence of the Holy Spirit (John 14-15). I believe a portion of this became recorded in the written Word, but most remained present in the oral tradition. This has remained one of the primary reasons for the existence of the Church throughout the ages: the protection and preservation of this Truth. May we remain faithful to Paul's command, and actively do our part to "stand firm and hold to the traditions." And may we also protect and defend the institution Christ established as the steward of these truths.

September 1993

Difficulties and Opportunities of the Journey

I begin this edition of the newsletter with great excitement. Since the first *Network* Newsletter, we have received many letters of encouragement as well as many new names. Many of you are on very similar pilgrimages, facing similar circumstances, concerns and needs, while others are facing very unique challenges and feel quite alone, even to the point of despair. But the common thread running through all your letters is a love for Jesus Christ, a commitment to His Church, and a desire to follow and teach the truth.

I was moved and humbled to hear of the great variety of ways God has been leading you, even through the trials you have been facing. One man, for instance, was a cradle Catholic from Ireland. He came to Canada, left the Catholic Church, and eventually became very active in a conservative Protestant church. He earned his Master of Divinity degree from an evangelical Protestant seminary and was ordained to the pulpit ministry. However, in his seminary studies, seeds were planted that opened his heart to the Church of his birth. Now after four years of ministry, his wife and family are united with him in wanting to return to the Catholic Church.

They attend Mass on Saturday evenings but only in secret. On Sundays, he still leads his Protestant congregation in worship. If they knew of his Catholic leanings, they would be shocked and certainly ask for his dismissal. But if he resigns from the ministry, he would not only be left without income and very little savings, but also his visa requires that he be immediately deported to Ireland.

He would be open to ministry in the Catholic Church but has no training nor credentials to teach, for example, the Right of Christian Initiation of Adults (RCIA). He wonders if a correspondence course on basic Catholic doctrine could be developed to provide some form of credentials service, which might help converts pursue parish or diocesan teaching positions. He is stuck but hopeful.

Others of you find yourselves in marriages that are divided over your movement towards the Catholic Church. In some instances, the division is so intense that the marriage itself is in jeopardy. What should you do? What does God expect you to do? Some have asked for a support group specifically for marriages divided over this issue, so that both sides can share their frustrations and concerns.

On the other hand, some of us have had pretty clear sailing. Why is God dealing with us each so differently and how can we encourage one another when the sandals we wear are so diverse?

One thought I have had lately goes out to you who are still in active pulpit ministries. I look back with aching, yearning hindsight to the last months of my own pastoral ministry, a ministry I no longer have nor may ever have again. I remember being convicted of Catholic truth but not sure to what extent I should share this with my Presbyterian congregation.

With hindsight, knowing now the theological distinctions better than I did then, I wish I had utilized those last few months of preaching and teaching to slowly and sensitively bring them to understand what I had discovered in the Catholic Church. I wish I had helped them discover the true biblical relationship between faith and works, challenging their presumption of guaranteed salvation. I wish I had preached on those texts that emphasized the parallel authority of both written and oral tradition and the teaching authority of the Church.

I'm ashamed to admit that my ten years of sermon files contain no sermons on Matthew 16.18-19, Luke 1.39-56, John 6.53f or 1 Timothy 3.15. I also regret that I did not take the time to correct the Protestant spin I had used to explain away the clearly Catholic meaning of so many texts, especially those in Christ's sermon on the mount and his parables of the kingdom, as well as the Epistles of Romans and James.

I would like to encourage those of you who still have active pulpit ministries to recognize the great privilege you have right now. You may yearn to be actively involved in Catholic worship, sharing in the great joys of the Eucharist. But until that is possible you have in your hands a wonderful opportunity to witness for Jesus Christ and His Church. You have under your care men and women who have been given only a portion of the truth. God may have you where you are to complete their joy. You may be in the middle of one of this world's most potential mission fields. If there is any way we can help you in your discernment, please let us know.

One Brave Conversion; Generations of Faithful

If you are like me, you may also wonder whether your personal life witness, especially the bold step in faith you may have taken from Protestant ministry into the Catholic Church, has any positive influence on your friends or relatives. In my case, few of my old friends ever call and if they do, they never broach uncomfortable inquiries. Our immediate relatives also do not bring up the issue; they act like our journey was no big deal.

However, last weekend I met a priest whose personal testimony was very encouraging. Three generations ago, his ancestors were all Presbyterians. On his mother's side, his great, great grandfather's family was a thoroughly Protestant family, with ten church going children. One of these children, the youngest girl, married a Catholic against the wishes of her parents. She wholeheartedly converted to Catholicism, and was harshly criticized by her family as a result. But she remained lovingly faithful both to her new Catholic faith and to her family. In time, one after another began considering her new found faith until eventually all of her family, including her parents converted! Now three generations later, this priest is the product of their bold faithfulness. But there's more!

This priest told me that he had grown very discouraged and complacent in his priesthood. He even considered leaving it. Then someone gave him a copy of Scott Hahn's conversion tape. He didn't listen to it at first, but stuck it in his glove compartment. Then, a few months later while on a long drive, he played the tape out of curiosity. By the end of the tape he was in tears. He was deeply moved by Scott's brave desire to give up all he had so that he could gain what this priest had begun to take for granted. He repented, recommitted himself and "reentered" his ministry. But there is even more!

He said that last year his aunt wanted to express her appreciation to all her relatives who had devoted their lives to the Church as religious or priests by sending them to Rome at her expense. When the research was complete, there were 19 priests and religious in their family! All from the testimony of this one brave girl three generations ago. Praise God! Only He knows whom the testimony of your life may touch!

October - December 1993

An Empty Altar but Full Confessionals

Recently, I visited my seminary alma mater. I wasn't certain whether anyone there was aware of my conversion to the Catholic Church, so I felt free to stroll the hallowed halls without question or confrontation.

I was amazed at how differently so many things appeared now that I perceive them through Catholic eyes. The newly constructed chapel, in which everything was arranged to revolve around a central pulpit, was starkly bare. The old chapel had once actually been a Catholic chapel, since this evangelical Protestant seminary had previously been a Carmelite seminary. When I had attended, the icons and statues had all been removed, but the large stone altar and the confessionals were still in place. Today the old unused chapel stands practically vacant. The altar area, now covered with Ping-Pong tables, and the confessionals, crammed with folding chairs, are vivid reminders of the disdain that is still held in this place for its Catholic roots.

Later in the morning, I attended an installation service for a prominent Old Testament theologian. Many of the professors seated around the front of the pulpit area were old acquaintances who should have recognized me, but none gave any sign of recognition.

But then I couldn't believe what I heard! During this celebrated theologian's reception sermon, he mentioned in an aside that of course we all know that the Catholic Church still teaches that we are saved by our works. He then backed this up with several quotes from contemporary Catholic theologians, all of which were taken out of context and without the necessary explanation of Catholic terminology. I was saddened, not just because of the falsehood that was proclaimed, but because this prominent theologian apparently felt it unnecessary to check his misinformation before he disseminated it.

My visit was capped off by a two hour, sometimes heated discussion with another Old Testament professor over the authority of Scripture vs. Tradition. I asked this learned and lettered scholar if he had ever taken the time to read the teachings of the Catholic Church in books written by a Catholic author espcially the documents of Vatican II. He responded matter of factly, "No, I don't have the time for that."

This encounter reminded me of how ignorant I once was of what the Catholic Church really teaches. I too had blindly accepted and spread myths about the Church and as a result had misinformed hundreds of people. I am thankful that this was done in ignorance and not with malice, and pray that somehow, in some way, I can help my old friends come to know the truth about the Catholic Church. I also pray that I will be able to do this with love.

January - February 1994

Our First Network Retreat

On Friday, December 10, we began our first Fall *Network* retreat. Graciously willing to leave their warm South Carolinian climate for cold and snowy Ohio, Fr. James Parker and his wife Mary flew into Pittsburgh airport, anxiously wondering what was in store for them at this gathering of Protestant clergy converts (or almost converts). Fr. James Parker was the first American Episcopal pastor to receive dispensation from celibacy through the Pastoral Provision to become a Catholic priest in 1982. Cardinal Law expressed his regret that his calendar prevented his attendance, but he gave his enthusiastic support to the *Network* and for our speaker, who serves as Cardinal Law's right-hand man in working with Anglican converts.

After refreshments, we gathered for opening devotions and immediately discovered a warm camaraderie built around our similar journeys. Of the 24 people present, six Protestant traditions were represented, including Episcopal, Methodist, Lutheran, Presbyterian, Baptist, and Church of Christ. The group was split about 2:1 between those who were already Catholics and those who were somewhere along the journey. After each presentation and during breaks, the interaction was lively and stimulating. As we shared, it was amazing to discover how similarly God has guided our lives. Yes, our journeys have all been different—God has given us different gifts for different tasks in different circumstances in the Kingdom, but His mercy and love have been the same for all of us!

Fr. Parker's presentations followed the schedule: after setting the direction of the retreat with his opening devotions, he led us through reflections on why we must be Catholics, how we can use our gifts for ministry once we've swum the Tiber, and especially how we can help renew the Church. He was completely supportive of our pilgrimages into the Church. There was no hesitation or discouragement, as some of us have experienced from overly ecumenically minded priests. He did, however, remind us that the Church offers no guarantees, either for opportunities for professional ministry, or even for openness to our ideas for renewal. His strong encouragement was to come humbly into the Church with an undemanding openness; to become Catholics without expectations; to become faithful lay men and women before we seek to become spiritual leaders. In the end, after a weekend of fellowship and interaction, Fr. and Mrs. Parker were both very excited about the positive potential of the *Network*, and promised to promote it not only to Cardinal Law, but to the President of the National Conference of American bishops.

I apologize for the cursive nature of this summary. The retreat was truly a grace filled experience. It not only provided support and encouragement for those of us who have completed the journey into the Catholic Church but gave those who are still on the journey a sense of hope and an opportunity to express doubts and fears in a loving, receptive atmosphere.

A Celebration of Fulfillment by Rev. Benjamin Luther

I discovered the *Network* Retreat through a friend, a minister in the Church of Christ, who was at that time on a spiritual journey toward consideration of the Catholic Faith. "I'll go if you'll go," was the deal. I was interested in the sound of things and wanted to support him as well.

The experience was a most positive one. I would like to share with you just why it was so positive, what I sensed while there, and try to convey in some sense the meaning it had for me.

I am a convert to the Catholic Faith from the Church of Christ in the early days of my life—I had never been a minister in that or any other church. In fact, I was the sole man present at the meeting who had not been in the active ministry in some denomination.

Present at our meeting-retreat were former ministers who had converted to the Catholic Church from the Episcopal, Presbyterian, Lutheran, and (northern) Baptist Churches. Two of the former Episcopal priests are now ordained in the Catholic priesthood. Almost all of these former ministers also had their wives present with them, and they made great contributions to all the discussions.

Our prayer times, the Masses in the student chapel, the talks, the many group discussions, were all marked by a deep sense of reverence, courtesy, and charity. An outstanding element in all the discussions was respect for the spiritual traditions of former homes of prayer and ministry.

What I came away with from the meeting was the most distinct impression that generally we could all agree on one point among many others and that was the achievement of fulfillment on the part of former ministers and their wives in the Catholic Church. The phrase from Karl Adam's outstanding work *Catholicism* kept coming to my mind: "We repose in Catholic fullness."

In other words, all these great and so sincere folks, each with a particular spiritual journey-story to tell, with all the joy and pain, all converged on one central focus: we are home, we have come home to our Father's house, which is literally chock full of spiritual goodies and untold riches. What we had was good and fulfilling but elements were missing too. Now we have it all. We are home.

One impression I came home with and pondered here in my little Kentucky parish was the realization that there are more men and women in ministry out there in various denominations who are tending toward the Catholic Church. There are many more than I ever realized.

As a fellow convert, even though I could not from my personal history share what conversion means in terms of leaving not only a home church but also a ministry, I can still have empathy for those who have made the journey and feel for those who are underway in the various stages. Our concern, love, and prayers go with each one, whoever and wherever you are.

I just want to add my two cents worth to the great testimony of the wonderful group on the *Network* Retreat at the Franciscan University of Steubenville and say to any minister or other person who has begun exploring the Catholic Faith, that G.K. Chesterton's warning should be well taken. It went something like this. You begin to delve into the riches of Catholicism. It is something like opening the door and walking into an incredibly variegated, immense building filled with all kinds of spiritual delights and wonderful surprises, enough to last for a lifetime, nay, for an eternity. "After a while," he wrote, "it all begins to take on the nature of a menacing love affair." When you fall in love, you know how maddening that can be, but it is a divine madness which comes from the Holy Spirit. I say as a fellow convert to the Catholic Church: let go, and let God.

If and when you do come to repose in Catholic fullness, you will fill in the missing pieces in your thinking and life and embark on a new journey that will never end in this life and in fact will continue in and through the Blessed Trinity for all eternity!

A Convert's Carol

The Christmas Season is to be the most joyful season of the year. Our culture knows this and has taken financial advantage of it, trying to convince us that the source of this joy is buying, giving and receiving. It has even turned a great saint into nothing more than a fat jolly toy producer.

Of course, we really can't point fingers. My two boys, my wife Marilyn, and I had our own fair share of joy producing gifts. And at least half of the gifts came from Santa.

But the joy wasn't there for me this Christmas. Not because we had missed the point of Christmas; we did many things as a family to make sure we kept before us the true meaning of Christ's Mass. But I couldn't shake a lingering sense of depression, an aching, empty feeling. It seemed to invade my soul like a creeping cloud of dread.

And then I had a dream ...

An Angel of Christmas Past woke me and put before my eyes Christmases of the past, and I remembered. I remembered the long and frenzied days of planning and preparing for the highly pressured Christmas Eve services—those services where half of my congregation would make one of their twice-a-year appearances. The pressure was on to produce, to inspire, to impress. The sermon had to be the best; the music had to be truly inspirational; the candle lit environs had to be life changing. And then the long lines of cheek-aching smiles and the creative fumbling through long forgotten names. This was repeated two or three times each Christmas. When it was all over and the lights had been darkened and the doors closed, I would return home with a sense of joy that God had been so gracious.

But then the Angel helped me to remember that on the next mornings, after the presents had been opened, the breakfasts prepared with some new kitchen utensil, and I had begun driving the family on their annual Christmas pilgrimage to grandparents, a similar depression would enter my soul. It was partially the result of being physically, emotionally, even spiritually drained. Preaching had always drained me—that's why God gave us Sunday afternoon NFL ("Now Feel Lazy"). But the Angel also helped me to admit that I had tried to be the people's savior. I had tried so hard to make everything so right, so perfect, so that their lives would be changed; so that when it was all done, they would return home different people, exclaiming "Wasn't that the best Christmas Eve service ever?! And that sermon!!!" I would feel depressed because I would wonder whether through all the pageantry, the preaching, and self-promotion, they had ever found Jesus.

Later, another Angel came. This Angel of Christmas Present let me stand back and re-examine the Christmas I had just completed: no longer shouldering all the responsibility, no longer pontificating from the pulpit, no longer greeting long lines of well-wishers, but sitting with my family in the pew, a member of the congregation. I looked at myself and saw this depression; it had affected my expression, infected my attitude, embittered my love, it had even shortened my fuse. And as I looked, I saw that I missed being the savior. I missed the preparation, the planning, the frenzy, the aching cheeks, I missed the attention. And I wondered if through all this, I had seen Jesus at all. I wondered if my self-centered depression had prevented my family from seeing Him.

Then, of course, a third Angel came: the Angel of Christmases Yet To Come. But what the Angel placed before me was not a gloomy graveyard scene with a looming tombstone carrying my epitaph, nor a surrealistic future Christmas Eve service with my growing Catholic family overflowing a pew and cowering about me, a depressed, self-centered, angry old Scrooge. Rather the Angel merely took me for a quiet walk. And as we walked my attention was drawn to a distant pillar of salt, a reminder of someone whose yearnings for the past had blinded her to the blessings of the present. And then the Angel pointed to a distant mass of people, wandering in a desert wasteland, who had so thanklessly yearned for the past that their present was an aimless confusion.* And then I saw a plowman.** The tires and blades of his tractor were buried deep in the muddy middle of a partially plowed field, whose furrows were anything but straight; they were twisted and crossed. And while the air was pierced with the deafening noise of the repeating back-up alarm, I saw him sitting there, grasping the steering wheel with one white-knuckled hand, while with the other he searched hopelessly behind him. And as I looked I saw his face. And it was me!

Immediately I awoke and found myself sprawled headlong over my computer keyboard, with the cursor signal bleating in my ear. And a joy filled my heart, lifting me ecstatically out of my cushy office chair for I knew the state of my future Christmases were not coldly predestined! I could change! I didn't have to be enslaved by my yearnings for past pulpits! I could be free to enjoy the present opportunities God had given me! With trusting submission I could enjoy Mass sitting contentedly beside my wife and children. I could relinquish the unresolved, irrational resentment that I harbored against God and his Church for not letting me continue in pastoral ministry. I could let go of my past and with joy trust God with my present and future! What a joy it is to find oneself safe in the hands of a loving Father!

"God bless us everyone!"

---

* See Numbers 14.

** "Jesus said to him, 'No one who puts his hand to the plow and looks back is fit for the kingdom of God.'" (Luke 9:62)

March - April 1994

From Listening, through Following, to Receiving

> *"Thus says the Lord: These were my orders:*
> *Listen to my voice,*
> *Then I will be your God and you shall be my people.*
> *Follow right to the end the way that I mark out for you,*
> *And you will prosper.*
> *But they did not listen,*
> *They did not pay attention;*
> *They followed the dictates of their own evil hearts,*
> *Refused to face me,*
> *And turned their backs on me."*
>
> Jeremiah 7:23-24

This was the first reading for Thursday, the third week of Lent. I was alone on retreat at a local state park lodge, trying to discern peacefully and patiently God's direction for my long-term future. I love my work as Director of the *Light and Life Foundation*, but the duration of this project is limited by its funding. What should I be planning towards? Ph.D. and teaching? Writing? Ministry management? Music?!

It seemed that as I reopened the door for occupational choices, all the previous dreams I had considered over the years began to resurface. I swung emotionally from wondering whether there was anything at all open for me—anything at all that I could even do, to whether there was anything closed to me—anything that I couldn't do if I bravely tried (somewhere in my 42-year old, adolescent brain, I still envisioned myself a folk-singing balladeer, strumming my faithful guitar to the standing applause of weeping, melancholy baby-boomers).

I spent nearly an entire day trying to get myself in focus, but my mind and body kept finding distractions: another book I "needed" to read, a jaunt down to the book table at a Nazarene Pastors Convention that was also meeting in the lodge (boy, if THEY knew what kind of infidel was sharing their lodging!), a quick jog around the park in freezing rain followed by a welcome dip in the jacuzzi, some catch-up tasks from work, and a few games of solitaire on my laptop. By evening, I was much more relaxed but no closer to reflecting on the reason for my retreat. I considered at that late hour diving into it, glancing at my untouched journal on the table, but instead chose to escape back into a Dorothy Sayers' mystery.

In the morning, I found myself afraid to begin, afraid that I may not hear a still small voice or discern the dew on the fleece. But, I figured I must at least start the morning with devotions.

For years, my normal procedure has been to read scripture until some paragraph, some verse or word grabs me, inspires me. After recording this text in my journal, I address Jesus directly as my Lord and caring elder brother, and then prayerfully record my reflections and petitions.

On this particular morning, the above text from the *Daily Missal* unexpectedly glowed with conviction. It seemed that a virtual pillar of fire and smoke rose from the pages, enveloping me, carrying me away from my self-centered confusion and finally bringing me with eyes free of scales to a new yet old understanding of God's Call for my life.

These prophetic words from Jeremiah spoke of the spiritual journey we all must take:

> From listening...
> through following...
> to receiving.

God promises a close covenantal relationship, corporate and personal, if we would only listen to his voice: "I will be your God, you will be my people." I will be your Father, you will be my child. He promises that if we will then do to the end what we have heard, He will bless us: "if you keep my commandments, you will abide in my love (John 15.10)." Normally, I tend to focus more on the "if" side of "if-then" propositions. I tend to focus, for example, on how well I have or have not been listening and following. And in this case, I did begin this way. I recorded:

I've spent a lot of time and mental energy over the years, maybe most of my life, trying to nail down what I will do once I "grow up." I must admit that I have failed to be faithful in the obvious—I have not always "listened" and "followed" in the way You have clearly marked out for me in Your Word ... Therefore, it is understandable that I may be less sure about vocational direction: why should I prosper? Why should You help me? Why should You direct my paths? (Remember Proverbs 3.5,6!)

But then the pillar of fire seemed to flare up, and through the din of my self-absorption, I heard the still small voice. I wrote:

Yet, You have done so; You have always directed my paths! You have been so good to my family and me over the years. No matter how much I have failed you, You have never failed me!! Maybe sometime long ago You delegated my case to a very patient yet persistent guardian angel!

It became very clear that my future was really not my concern. I was in fact living in the future I had once fretted over; I was having a wonderful ministry that I could have neither imagined nor planned for! As a Protestant seminarian or pastor, I never dreamed I would one day be the North American Director of an international Catholic evangelistic outreach to teenagers! Nor that this ministry would bring me into contact with deeply committed Catholic Christians all over the world! And I received this spiritual "prosperity" not because of any insightful career planning on my part, but solely because of God's faithfulness.

There is no question in my mind—no doubt in my heart—that if God has called Marilyn and me to leave Ur (the Protestant ministry) and follow Him by faith into a strange land (the Catholic Church), He will have something for me to do. He will be faithful! What He expects of me now is to listen and follow faithfully, "right to the end of the way that I mark out for you." (And this is of course true for every one of you that have heard and still hear the still small voice of God in your heart. Remember: He will never leave you nor forsake you.)

As the pillar of fire burned down to an ember and the smoke cleared, I sat in stillness, motionless. And my mind began to wander. Once again I found myself dreaming. I was there singing ballads before a crowd of attentive, reflective groupies. And as I strummed my guitar, allowing *Amazing Grace* to explain my self-insufficiency, I saw before me seated at a coffee table right up front, Jesus, smiling.

My GREAT Grandfather Shaw! by Marilyn Grodi

Being and becoming a Catholic is so exciting and challenging. I'm not sure we will ever feel as if we have arrived. We became a part of the Church about a year ago, so we are experiencing many firsts through now Catholic eyes. Even the burial of my last remaining grandparent brought much to be treasured as we faced contemplating what happens after our earthly lives are over.

But naturally, I must reflect first about that earthly life of this very special grandfather and what he represented. My grandparents were third generation owners/operators of a large, fully functioning farm. When I was a youngster, I spent many a day roaming the hillsides, exploring forests, haylofts and what have you with my brother or cousins. My grandparent's home seemed to be such an anchor: a place for hugs, long evenings being read to in front of the fire, or just cuddling in one of the many beds in the huge upstairs. And always a reverence for God.

It has been such a privilege to share a little of these experiences with my husband and two sons. With the help of my younger sister, my 91-year old grandfather, still living in his childhood home, produced and sold apples from his orchards until 1992. There's nothing like having "your own" place to go and pick apples each fall.

At Christmas time, 1994, when we were all home—my brother, two sisters, myself, and our families—my grandfather was rushed to the hospital. The sister who has been the closest to him insisted that her ex-pastor brother-in-law make a pastoral-type visit to his bedside before we left town. In sharing scripture and praying together, it became very apparent to my husband that grandpa was prepared for God's will to be done. Then, while my husband watched the kids, I was able to tell grandpa for a final time that I loved him—O, how his eyes sparkled, his sense of humor remained constant, even there in the emergency room.

Well, less than two weeks later, we got the call. How could it be—he had seemed so good to me when I last saw him. Well, the children (6 and 2 1/2) quickly reconciled themselves to their great grandpa's passing. He's going to be with Jesus. What could be better?!

When we arrived at the traditional family viewing hour at the funeral home—who knew (well, God probably did) what our 6-year old would do. In typical Jon Marc fashion, he immediately embarked upon a project. Somehow he had slipped in with a 3 x 5-inch pad of paper and pencil, and upon a sheet he drew Jesus on the cross and wrote "grandpa" in capital letters. Then he laid this on his great-grandfather's chest.

Imagine my instant horror at the realization that my son hadn't just placed a cross in the casket, but a crucifix! Well, all of you one time Protestants know the significant difference, and I assumed that my Protestant family members might object to such an outrageous symbol. I managed to mumble my apologies sometime during the course of the evening, but was informed that the consensus had been taken and the object was to remain.

Just one more precious memory of my grandpa. Somehow it seems significant that he was buried wearing a crucifix, for many reasons. The most obvious one being his response to our 1992 Christmas letter informing the world of our conversion to the Catholic Church. We thought it quite remarkable that he was the only person who gave us any type of reaction to our life changing news. In fact, we considered it quite astute that he wrote to tell us, "I was probably a Presbyterian only because my grandparents were Presbyterians." And then he boldly said how much he respected us for following Christ.

Yes, each major respective turn in the life cycle makes us ever more appreciative of our new reconciliation with Jesus' Church. Birth, baptism, marriage, and funerals all point us to the richness of our faith and traditions. It is such comfort to know that grandpa is in the process of becoming completely pure in preparation for being with our Heavenly Father forever. And that he is still very much a part of our lives as he prays for us and we for him. God bless you grandfather John! We still love you dearly!

May - June 1994

How Do We Discern How FAST God Is Calling Us to Step Out in Faith?

Sometimes Scripture calls us to wait ...

> *Wait for the Lord;*
> *Be strong, and let your heart take courage;*
> *Yes, wait for the Lord.*

Psalm 27.14

While other times it seems to encourage acting without hesitation ...

> *Jesus said to them, "Follow Me ... ;"*
> *And they immediately left their nets and followed Him."*

Mark 1.17-18

Often it's very difficult to discern which one God is calling us to do. How do we discern how fast or how soon God wants us to move in ministry? What criteria should we use? What if our spouse or family isn't in agreement? What if the fleece isn't wet on either side, and the still small voice is inaudible?!

I'm drawn back again to this difficult issue of making the courageous jump out of Protestant ministry into the Catholic Church, because every week I continue to encounter men and women somewhere along this journey struggling with this decision. I've talked with many who are convinced that the Catholic Church is the true Church of Jesus Christ, but the juxtaposition of difficult knowns and unknowns in their lives causes them to stand poised with their hand on the plow wondering which way to proceed and when.

I of course must be careful not to push too strongly. We each must discern God's Call for ourselves. However, I have no hesitation whatsoever in affirming the faithfulness and providence of God for my family and me.

Within a month of joining the Church, I realized that the income I thought I could depend upon to support my family while I pursued a Ph.D. was gone. However, once I let my need be known and pursued what doors opened before me, I found myself the North American Director of the *Light and Life Foundation*. This project has brought me into contact with hundreds of faithful Catholic brethren and leaders all over the world. And even though this project has now encountered a difficult funding crisis which has necessitated a drastic reduction in staff and a major change in direction, God still continues to open doors. Our experience has proven to us as a family that trusting God means being boldly obedient to what God is calling us to do right now, while leaving the needs and responsibilities of tomorrow to Him. It has required us to be flexible, to accept a different standard of living, to leave friends and familiar places. But God has always out given us! Our cup now overflows with new loving and supportive friends.

In the September Newsletter, I described the difficult situation of a Protestant pastor in Canada who was also struggling with this decision. He had been a cradle Catholic from Ireland who had left the Church, traveled to Canada with his family, and eventually became active in a conservative Protestant denomination.

Last month, this pastor sent me an exciting update that I want to share:

> *Hello again from Canada. Some good news. Today I have finally been able to resign my position as associate pastor at _____ Church, and will finish up there on May 31st. On June 1st, I start a new job as Director of Adult Faith Formation at St. Joseph the Worker Parish. The job title has been chosen with care. Adult education implies the impartation and reception of knowledge. But in a Christian context, what is learned must result in the transformation of life, hence the title.*
>
> *St. Joseph's is just five minutes walk from where we live, and that part of my double life has kept me sane over the last several months. I'm grateful for _____, the director of the Catechumenate, who trusted me and invited me to be part of the RCIA team so that I could get my feet wet again in min-*

istry in a Catholic setting. It led to invitations to teach to the charismatic group, and they believe I'm the answer to their two-year long prayer for someone to teach them. To oversee the group is part of my job description. Truly the Lord is wonderful!! I feel like I am home at last. There is such a sense of comfort for us in St. Joe's that my ministry is a pleasure rather than labor as it so often was.

The task before me is not an easy one, and I will need much wisdom and grace. There are 2,800 families in the parish with only about 20% who have a meaningful relationship with the Lord. The staff has defined my task to be evangelizing the sacramentalized. May the Lord make me equal to the task. As sojourners in a strange land our circumstances have been different from most, but the Lord has shown that He Himself does what He commanded of Israel in the First Testament—show kindness to the stranger. Blessed be His name. Thank you so much for your prayerful support.

A month ago, another pastor paid us a visit from Arizona. After many years in the Presbyterian ministry, he was finally ready to consider following his convictions into the Catholic Church. Yet over dinner he shared his concerns and the many unanswered questions. Then, a week later I received a note that said he was making the move; he was ready to accept whatever God had in store for him.

Two days ago I sat across from a Lutheran pastor who after 32 years of ministry desires with great joy to enter the Catholic Church. Yet, he faces the difficult question that so many of you face: what will he do now? Does he wait three more years until retirement? Does he remain in a situation where he must keep his inner convictions private—where he questions whether the sacramental ministry he now performs is even valid? His Bishop may offer him a position as Pastoral Administrator but he is not sure. He first must face a difficult hip replacement on June 13 (pray for James), and then will decide when to make his move

There are others whose experiences have been very difficult, who have gone long periods without employment or income, whose marriages have suffered, even disintegrated.

The decision is not easy. As Paul states, "Let each man be fully convinced in his own mind" (Rom. 14.5b). But this is why the *Network* exists. So that we can hold each other up in prayer. So that we can use our telephones and mail to encourage one another. So that we can share information about job opportunities. So that we can share our blessings, our victories and our resources with one another. So that together we can pray for the Church and its leaders, that they might be continually more open to the gifts and experiences we bring and desire to share in the ministry of the gospel.

July - September 1994

"How Shall We Then SURVIVE?!"

Grace and peace to you at the end of a long summer! I pray that all has gone well for you and your families.

The summers at Franciscan University are always full of great weekend conferences. Our second annual *"How Should We Then Serve, Too"* Luncheon/Seminar was a great success! Over thirty attended for the fellowship and sharing of journeys. Our keynote speaker was Steve Wood, a former Presbyterian pastor who converted to the Catholic Church in 1990. In his talk, *"How Shall We Then SURVIVE?!,"* he addressed the difficult issues we encounter as individuals and families along the journey from the Protestant pastorate into the Catholic Church.

After a brief summary of the trials and blessings of his own family's journey, Steve gave the following **Ten Survival Suggestions for Catholic Converts, and Those Desiring to Help Them Survive:**

1. **Be Willing to Rediscover Your Call and Calling**: We must recognize that our Calling is not static, but a constant, continuous walk with Christ. Therefore, during this period of rediscovery, we must be willing to accept that "whatever your hand finds to do, do it with all your might" (Eccl. 9.10). It may be that in the most unsuspecting place, you will discover what God has always intended you to do.

2. **Spread Suggestions for Hiring Converts:** Tell others about the gifts converts have to give to the Church. Tell others about converts needing work, and tell converts about job opportunities.

3. **Be creative in your search for assistance:** Dioceses and parishes sometimes have residences or convents sitting vacant. An empty convent may be a perfect solution to housing a convert and family. Remember that secular employment of over 30-hours may bring health coverage.

4. **Seek to overcome "avoidance" and help others do so:** People tend to avoid those to whom they do not know how to relate. Face it, to many Catholics, both lay and clergy, converts are strange! With the Holy Spirit's help, seek to avoid bitterness and frustration. Patiently get to know your local diocese and parish, and give them time to know you. Let the Holy Spirit work in and through your relationships to open doors for service.

5. **Take Time to Reprogram Your Theology and Worldview:** In comparison to where most of us have come from, the Catholic Church and her customs appear at first to be a combination of landing on Mars and "Fiddler on the Roof." Before you charge in ready to correct every problem you uncover, take time to discover what really needs to be changed, and what you need to leave behind. You may discover that most of what needs to be changed is within yourself.

6. **Network with others:** Support and help each other. Look for and create opportunities for others to engage their gifts and talents, as well as support their families.

7. **Begin in "Jerusalem":** When Jesus sent forth his apostles to conquer the world, he yet told them to begin right where they were standing. With the help of your local parish priest, look for ways you can volunteer in your local parish. Creative teaching opportunities abound everywhere! In your giving, you may discover that your local parish also has much to give you.

8. **Discover the Holy Hour:** Seek the guidance of your parish priest or a Spiritual Director who can help you discover and grow in Catholic spirituality. The depth and breadth of Catholic spiritual traditions can be overwhelming, so take small steps. A daily or weekly Holy Hour before the Blessed Sacrament is a great way to find strength for the journey.

9. **Be Willing to Make a Sacrifice:** In many ways, modern clergy converts are pioneers of a new movement of the Holy Spirit. As a result, we must be willing to accept whatever cross and pay whatever price as we seek to follow Christ. The price we pay and the sacrifices we make to become Catholics will win a hearing. We must also learn to appreciate the power of redemptive suffering. What we give up and suffer is all for the unity of the Church. Offer it up!

10. **Keep the Long Term Perspective:** Jesus gave some very challenging, yet encouraging instructions to his apostles in John 15. He said:

    > *You did not choose me but I chose you and appointed you that your fruit should abide, so that whatever you ask the Father in my name, he may give it to you. This I command you, to love one another.*

    We can become discouraged and bogged down when we focus on the problems of the moment. However, we must constantly trust God's much larger perspective and plan, and then seek to produce with love the fruit that lasts to eternity: our family, our friends, and the needy around us.

God's Hopes in You: Ignatian Thoughts on Guidance by Dr. Kenneth J. Howell

Spiritual guidance is a difficult matter about which we can discover a great many differences of opinion. Some approach it rationally as if finding God's will were a decision like comparing cars when shopping for transportation. Some approach it mystically as if God's will could only be found in the moment of illumination or frenzied adulation. The history of the Church presents us with a variety of approaches to guidance with the underlying common belief in the need of the Church to approve such methods. One approved and highly influential method is the spirituality of the Jesuits whose famous thirty-day retreats have helped millions come into a deeper experience of the life of Jesus Christ.

Ignatius of Loyola founded the Society of Jesus in the sixteenth century on the practice of giving his *Spiritual Exercises* to novices in the order. An essential part of Ignatian spirituality is the search for God's will by discerning the hopes which God is hoping in you. This method is sometimes called Authentic Desiring. God places his hopes deep in your heart so that you might find his will. Your search for God's will begins by eliminating all those desires which are distorted by the world, the flesh and the devil. Each Christian is likely to have a configuration of such desires which repeatedly hinder him or her from finding God's desire. These desires may be good in and of themselves but they always endanger you from finding your true inner self where God has placed his hopes for you. The authentic desires are those which God has placed in you at a deeper level and which are fitted to your disposition and personality. Only you can discern whether those desires are truly in accord with God's hopes in you, but there are several guidelines to fence off those that are not God's hopes from those that are.

Ignatius distinguishes those matters that are proper subjects for discernment from those that are not. Matters of truth and morality are not matters of discernment. Any practice or avenue of service which involves falsehood or immorality are already matters of revealed truth and are not properly subjects of discernment. Any action which is against the truth defined by the Church is likewise not optional. A Christian need not ask God for guidance about having an abortion; you already know that it is a vicious crime against God and nature. God's desires in you will never be immoral nor will they ever lead you to violate the law of love to God and neighbor.

Having distinguished matters of truth and morality from issues of discernment, Ignatius advises the Christian to begin a process of elimination by digging deep down into the inner recesses of the heart to find those desires ordered by God. A key step is to know God's desires rather than those that others want for you even though he may make you aware of his desires through other people. God's authentic desires for you will be truly comfortable in your inner person so that discovering them always brings a sense of peace and calm.

The process of finding God's desires is not haphazard. We find God's will for our lives by entering more fully into the sacred heart of Jesus. As Jesus' life and heart becomes ours, we discover how he wants us to perform his will in the world. Ignatius urges us to contemplate and reflect on the life of Jesus for he believes that somewhere in this process Christ's desires become ours and God's hopes in us rise to the surface where we become conscious of God's will for our lives. Nothing more satisfies the heart of the Christian than knowing that we can say, "Thy Will Be Done."

Let me give you a personal illustration. In 1993, I directed my wife and myself in a *Do-It-At-Home Retreat* (Ignatius Press) using a book with the same title by the French Jesuit Andre Ravier S.J. Another book, Ignatius of Loyola's *Spiritual Exercises*, was arranged and commented upon by Fr. Joseph Tetlow S.J. Over a period of about a month and a half, I found myself much more aware of the presence of Jesus in my life than I ever had before. This, I think, was due to the Exercises being not simply a reading of Scripture but a reliving of them. I was able to enter into Jesus' life and heart, to hear his words, to feel his touch and the sweat that dropped from his brow. The *Spiritual Exercises* brought me into a deeper awareness of my sin, of Christ's mercy and of how living Christ's passion is a daily reality.

Progressing through the life of Jesus, I came to a place of Active Indifference where I was ready to do whatever Jesus wanted me to do. This is the place where my heart was so completely united with Jesus that I was actively seeking to follow him but was indifferent as to where following him may lead. I told Jesus that I was ready to follow him into the Catholic Church if that was his plan for me. I was also ready to remain where I was if that were his will.

Then my wife reminded me of an earlier principle that Ignatius taught us, namely, that matters of truth are not subjects for discernment because discernment is a human subjective process that involves personal judgment. The truth of the faith, however, is a matter of revelation. If we believed something was true, we had to follow it. So, Ignatius taught us that the question of whether we should enter the Catholic Church was a matter of truth, not discernment. If we were convinced that the Catholic Church is the true Church of Jesus Christ, we had no choice but to enter it. Coincidentally, I read around this time in *Lumen Gentium* (no.15) that those who know the Catholic Church to be founded by Christ as necessary but who refuse to enter cannot be saved. At the time of our retreat in the summer of 1993, neither my wife nor I believed that the Catholic Church was the true Church of Jesus Christ. I especially had learned a lot and was grateful to the Catholic tradition but I had not yet come to the most important conviction of all.

Over the next two years a completely unforeseen occurrence transpired. I continued to come closer to the Church while my wife remained unconvinced of any necessity to enter the Catholic Church. This put us in a position that we never dreamed we would face in our twenty years of marriage, to have a religiously divided home. Yet here too Ignatius was my guide in matters of discernment. By 1994, I was certain that I would someday enter the Catholic Church but my wife was still not convinced. The question of whether I would enter the Church was not at issue. It was only a matter of when. That was truly a matter of discernment. Should I wait on my wife or should I go ahead?

Two years later, in the spring of 1996, I came to a position that demanded a decision. Over those two years my wife and I had studied, discussed and prayed about our decision. We wanted to be together in the same church. We both knew it would be best for our children but at the end of those two years, we still could not resolve our differences of belief. However, the process had proven fruitful in an unexpected way. We had moved through a period of estrangement to a new tolerance and even deeper communion because of all the time we had spent discussing our beliefs.

It was a mixture of sadness and acceptance. Sadness because we knew this was less than a perfect solution. Acceptance because we had learned to live in a world that was less than perfect. But we both knew that we were at a standstill. I had to move forward but she could not. So, in the spring of 1996 I spent another month in prayer and discernment, this time not an Ignatian retreat but using Ignatian principles. During this month of prayer, I concluded that to put off entry into the Catholic Church would be disobedience. There comes a time when we know, not from passing emotion but from deep-seated conviction, that to remain in our current state would be sinful.

Discernment involves subjective judgment about how to implement truth in our lives. Truth can never be compromised but how we live God's truth out in the decisions of our lives does require plumbing the depths of our hearts finding there God's desires for us. The only way to find God's desires is by having the heart of Jesus.

Journeys Home

October 1994

We're in this Together!

My seven-year-old son, Jon Marc, just began studying the cello. Initially, my wife and I gave him a few instruments to choose from, even though we preferred the cello and nudged him in that direction. With great enthusiasm, he began. He was especially excited when he brought his rented cello home for the first time and heard the sound of the strings as he plucked and ran the bow across them.

Now, several weeks later, we've already encountered the normal resistance to practice that all parents face with children and music lessons. The initial enthusiasm has waned, the drudgery of repetition has grown, and the grind of the discipline has set in. Last night I was tempted to say, "Jon Marc, if you want to learn the cello, you have to practice. If you don't want to learn the cello, that's fine." I was tempted—but I didn't say it. I suspected that given his seven-year-old priority system and lack of discipline, he might make a choice he would regret twenty years down the line. So, instead, I encouraged him with words of praise.

Putting myself in the shoes of my son Jon Marc, I'm reminded how easily one can become discouraged, unfocused, undisciplined—second guessing choices and giving up once the initial enthusiasm has waned. I also try to mentally fit myself into your shoes—especially those of you who have written or called, expressing a difficult struggle with making the final decision about entering the Church or who are doubting the timing of your decision.

The purpose of the *Network* is to support you as you count the cost, sift through vocational issues and discern the timing. We're not here to push you or pull you, although we might occasionally send you a little nudge. All of us have been through the journey in one way, and we can benefit from discussing the struggles and joys of embracing Christ and His Church. I gladly proclaim the Catholic Church as the true Church of Jesus Christ, built on the teachings and traditions faithfully handed on and defended by the Magisterium centered around the seat of Peter. But I also know that four years ago, I never would have dreamed that I would be saying, believing or fighting for this. For me, the essential work of the *Network* is to appreciate the struggle and to be sympathetic and empathetic as you continue on the journey.

Recently, articles about the *Network* have appeared in the *National and International Religious News*, the *Pittsburgh Post-Gazette*, and soon in *Christianity Today*. I've already received many calls and letters from Protestant pastors who feel completely isolated in their interest in the Catholic Church and are very excited to hear about the *Network* fellowship. My prayer is that this media coverage will help inform both Catholics and Protestants about the *Network*, and its desire to help sincere searchers for truth who are considering the Catholic Church.

Every other month, we sift through the articles you send for the *Network* newsletter. So many of these are touching as you explain through your eyes the struggles and joys of your pilgrimage towards and then into the Catholic Church.

Many of you communicate how helpful and encouraging this newsletter has been. Whenever I receive a call from a Protestant pastor who is considering the Catholic Church, I send him the back issues of the newsletter. For this reason, and for so many others, I implore you to send articles, short or long, to continue making the *Network* newsletter a helpful and encouraging resource. One of the greatest concerns expressed by ministers who've entered the church, is the emptiness they feel because they no longer have congregations with which they can share the gospel. The *Network* newsletter is an opportunity to share ideas, scriptural insights or theological reflections that can encourage others on this journey we share together.

Please pray for the continued work of the *Network* as we pray for you and your heartfelt desire to follow Jesus Christ. As we enter Advent, may the Holy Spirit bless you and your family in every way in the coming Church year.

November - December 1994

Go, Sell, Give, and Follow

L ast Tuesday, I was sitting in the chapel at the Franciscan University during daily mass, awaiting the proclamation of the Gospel, and I must admit that I was not feeling the joy that Jesus had promised would accompany my walk with him. Instead, I was feeling a tremendous amount of stress and anxiety over decisions and situations piling up in my life. There had been drastic changes in the direction of projects and programs I am responsible for and now there were plans and demands for moving ahead into new areas and projects for which I have no previous personal experience. There were countless details and red tape involved with moving out and then into a new home. And through all of this, I was feeling frustrated because I missed being actively involved in the pastoral ministry.

I sat watching the priest lead us in worship and felt strangely disconnected and isolated. And in my dreamlike distraction, I arrogantly picked out a few things that I thought might be done a little differently or even better as I reflected on my own past experiences leading worship.

As I sat awaiting the Gospel, I heard in my memory the words of the psalmist cry out, "Why are you cast down my soul" or maybe even more strongly, "Why have you forgotten me, O my God?" Then I stood for the Gospel, blessed myself with the triple signs of the cross and heard, not coincidentally but providentially, my favorite story from the life of Christ: that powerful incident when Jesus is confronted by the rich, young man (Mark 10:17-27).

This story has always spoken to me, challenging me to re-examine what is the center of my life. At different places along the journey of faith, this story has confronted me to cast off different things. When I was an engineer considering a full time ministry, this story encouraged me to lean not on the financial security of my engineering career, but to be willing to let it go to follow Christ. Years later, this story challenged me to be willing to let go of the security and familiarity of my Protestant ministry to again follow the word of Jesus, "You lack one thing; go, sell what you have, and give it to the poor, and you will have treasures in heaven and come, follow me."

When I heard those words again last Tuesday, I asked, "What is the thing that I lack this time? What is it, besides Christ, that I'm tightly clinging to, that I must be willing to let go, sell, give away, and then follow with abandon my Lord Jesus?' As I considered this, it struck me that maybe it was time for me to quit being a convert, and be a Catholic.

So often, I still view and portray myself primarily in the context of being a convert, an ex-Protestant Pastor rather then moving on and accepting the fact that I am now a Catholic. Yes, I will always be a convert, and I may never lose the perception that my 40 years as a Protestant and 9 years as a Protestant pastor bring. But yet every Catholic is a convert from sin to a new creation in Christ.

As I sat there repeating the words from the Mass, "Lord I am not worthy to receive you...," I sensed Christ challenging me to accept that this place, where he has me at this time, at this moment, is exactly where he wants me to be. He wants me to be doing these projects, emphasizing these priorities, doing and implementing these plans, which may have very little connection whatsoever with the Protestant pastoral ministry I was doing five years ago. He has merely by his wisdom placed me in a new place with a new assignment in the ministry of his kingdom. To this assignment I bring more than 40 years of a great variety of experiences, but it is to this assignment, at this point in my life, in this place in my life, in these relationships, and in this wonderful Church that he has called me to "go, sell, give, and follow."

The stress I was feeling was mostly worry about tomorrow, but He has called me to "go, sell, give, and follow," today. My wife Marilyn and I have just moved into a beautiful new home. If I allow myself to become anxious about how I will finance this house and support my family in the future, I again find my soul growing weary within me. But Jesus' words remind me that all the resources, even the very job I now have, were all gifts of God's grace which five years ago I could never have dreamed of having. Once again I am reminded that the future rests completely in his hands.

I recognize that some of you who have written or called are concerned about how you will handle not only the financial needs of your future, but how you will fulfill the ministerial calling you have heard and followed. How you will faithfully fulfill Paul's exhortation to Timothy, "Do not neglect the gift that you have, which was conferred on you through the prophetic word with the imposition of hands of the presbyterate. Be diligent in these matters, be absorbed in them, so that your progress may be evident to everyone" (1 Tim 4:14,15).

From my own family experience, all I can say is to "go, sell, give, and follow." Where you are right now and all that you have accomplished up to this point has come through the grace of Jesus Christ. Where you will be tomorrow and all that you will accomplish then will come from the same source. To follow Jesus means being willing to carry whatever cross he gives you.

I suppose Jesus could have told that rich, young man, "You have done a superb job in your diligence at keeping the commandments. Keep up the good work," and then let him go. The young man had probably been more faithful than most. But Jesus wanted more for him, and of him, and probably saw that through his individual sacrifice not only would he, but many others would be drawn to the kingdom. Therefore, Jesus placed before him a very demanding choice and then let the young man choose freely. I sense that God is challenging many of you with the same kind of choice.

In this advent season, we are reminded of other difficult decisions that involved great sacrifice: the decision of Mary to be willing to do whatever God called her to do and the willingness of the very Son of God, who as Paul says in Philippians " ... although he was in the form of God, did not count equality with God a thing to be grasped, but emptied himself, taking the form of a servant, being born in the likeness of men."

My prayer for you during this Advent and Christmas season is that you will be encouraged by these models as you struggle in your decisions along your pilgrimage to the Catholic Church. There is great joy to be found here, and an assuring sense of freedom on the rock foundation of Catholic truth. May this season be the time when the spirit of Christ empowers many of you to boldly take the step to "go, sell, give, and follow" Jesus Christ into the Catholic Church.

Journeys Home

January - April 1995

Our First Survey: "Why all these Conversions?!"

During the first years of the *Network*, we received an amazing number of phone calls and letters from people inside and outside of the *Network* asking "What is going on? Why are Protestant pastors and their families coming into the Catholic Church and seemingly in such large numbers? Why at this time? What is the Holy Spirit doing?"

Being one of those pilgrims, my response to these questions was admittedly shaped by my own personal pilgrimage and opinions. My wife, Marilyn, and I had very real and strong reasons for embarking on a journey which was nary a glimmer in our minds when we had committed our lives to Christ years before. However, it was also evident that each of the *Network* members had embarked on their own journeys "home" for sometimes very drastically different reasons, coming out of very different needs and situations. We, therefore, were curious to see how the membership might answer these questions.

We posed ten questions to the membership, with the promise that all personal data was to be kept completely confidential. However, for this publication some of the authors have agreed to reveal their identities. These excerpts from some of the many responses are essentially like the preceding testimonies in *Part One*, but presented in a more itemized, orderly format. Our hope is that as we read and reflect on these together and compare them to our own journeys, we will more clearly discern what the Holy Spirit is doing or saying in this movement at this time in the Church. We also hope these excerpts will help us understand how to more winsomely dialogue with our separated brethren, especially those who might be open to discussions about the truth of the Catholic faith.

"Since the Bible came to us from God inseparable from its context in the life of the people, it was in that context that the Bible should be heard, lived, and taught. From that realization, I was essentially a Catholic."

by Karl Cooper

Give a quick outline of your pilgrimage, what faith you were brought up in, how your faith was formed through the years, what led to your call to ministry, where did you train, where did you serve, etc.

As an agnostic young person growing up in a Unitarian home, my vague view of religion was distributed and somewhat reorganized when I read James Michener's *The Source*. Fascinated by the images there of uncompromising obedience to the word of God, I was yet more deeply fascinated when I met evangelical Christians my own age who shared their faith in the saving work of Christ. They seemed to be living a generally happier and healthier life than mine.

I became a Christian and was baptized as a senior in high school, largely in response to the love and witness of young evangelicals and the dedicated adult leaders who worked with them. The heart commitment to justification by faith and the inerrancy of Scripture which grew naturally from conversion in such a context also kept me focused as opportunities for leadership unfolded during college years. The InterVarsity Christian Fellowship chapter I helped found and lead was a remarkably close and prayerful body of believers, including Protestants and Catholics, charismatics and non-charismatics, theological conservatives and theological liberals. The true unity we experienced on account of our common commitment to Jesus Christ as Savior and Lord, and to the good news of salvation by grace, was a vivid lesson in ecumenism.

Encouragement from others to consider continuing in Christian leadership resulted in my enrolling at a Presbyterian theological seminary after college, and the many opportunities for fellowship, learning, teaching, and service arising in that context led to my willingness to serve as a ruling elder in a local church, with special responsibilities for Bible teaching, ministry to young adults, and round-the-clock hospitality for searching visitors.

A thirst for more intensely intellectual appropriation of biblical truth drew me to doctoral studies in New Testament, during the course of which I was invited to teach at another Presbyterian Seminary. I taught New Testament there for three and a half years, enjoying immensely the privilege of contributing to the intellectual and spiritual development of young Presbyterians.

How open were you to the Catholic faith because of your tradition?

Since the religious tradition of my childhood was relatively thin and lacking in biblical symbolism, my exposure to the Catholic faith awakened an immediately positive response. If there was a community where God's love was felt, God's Word was received, and God's people recognized each other as members of a family stretching out through history to eternity, I wanted to be part of it. The palpable beauties of the Catholic Church were clearly part of this picture. The less palpable intellectual and hierarchical framework of the Catholic denomination was less clearly part of it.

What were the primary issues that opened you to the Catholic faith?

Of the many issues that helped crystallize for me the essential accuracy of the Catholic theological account of the Christian faith, the central one was the issue summarized in the Reformation slogan Sola Scriptura. The apologetics of Cornelius Van Til and the gospel proclamation of Martin Luther were two examples of the application of this principle that fired my imagination in college and seminary. Whenever I became discouraged by the intractability of theological debate and by a tendency of conservative Protestants to split into smaller and smaller ecclesiastical units, I took solace in the confidence that a more consistent commitment to Sola Scriptura would surely bring about healing.

Excellent seminary instruction in church history afforded a strongly optimistic view of the Reformed faith as nothing more nor less than the Christian faith of all ages. An intense, biblical focus on the attributes of the church as one, holy, catholic, and apostolic, reinforced this optimistic view. In my work as a teacher of New Testament, I sought to exemplify Sola Scriptura in the manner and content of my teaching, and to draw as widely as possible from the riches of the Christian tradition. I quickly learned that there were unwritten Presbyterian traditions that many viewed as essential bounds on the exploration of biblical truth, and repeated admonitions to mute my message made those bounds hard to ignore.

It finally dawned on me that Presbyterians did not in fact apply Sola Scriptura—they held rather to a more organically constituted body of traditional belief and practice, in which a certain stratum of biblical interpretation had great influence, but over which the Bible alone would not prevail. Perceiving this, I had to ask, "Is this right?" And then ask, "Where does the Bible teach Sola Scriptura?" And finally to admit that God always intended the message of the prophets and apostles, yes even of the Apostle and Prophet, to be mediated through the common life and celebration of the people of God. Since the Bible could not be coerced into teaching Sola Scriptura, it was a fundamental contradiction to hold it. Since the Bible came to us from God inseparable from its context in the life of the people, it was in that context that the Bible should be heard, lived, and taught. From that realization, I was essentially a Catholic.

What were the barriers and main issues?

One barrier to accepting the Catholic view of authority, tradition, and scripture was (in my view at the time) the lack of serious engagement by Catholic teachers and thinkers with evangelical Protestant theological contentions. It seemed that carefully thought-out systematic objections to the theology of Trent, of Vatican I, and of Vatican II did not receive carefully thought-out replies. I hungered for a Catholic discussion partner who perceived the appeal of the evangelical and Reformed systematic theologies.

Where are you now in your journey? What are your plans for the future?

At this time in my journey, I am a joyful member of a Catholic parish and happy to be shepherded by Catholic priests and bishops. Mass is the high point of the week for me, and though I cannot see the turns in the road, I am happy to walk it in the fellowship of many millions from all generations and nations.

Plans for the future are especially murky. Intensely involved with my wife and five children in our common life, I expect God to continue to feed my heart from that source. Helping my wife homeschool the five, and watching with fascination as each of the children grasps hold of key insights into life, I feel especially privileged to be able to share with my family the same basic orientation to biblical truth, Catholic worship, and Christian unity. We would like to go to Europe; we would like to be able to share scripture study with others of similar intensity; we would like to be deeply and directly involved in the Church's liturgy. I have at various times been attracted to the Secular Franciscans and to the office of deacon; but neither of these ideas has really seemed to provide a focus for my desires to learn, teach, serve, love, and be loved. The family is where it's at, for me, for the foreseeable future.

How do you interpret what is happening and why?

There is one church, as Ephesians 4 teaches. Any who seek to live the Christian life as though there were several churches, and as though they could have what they need in one of them, will inescapably find themselves hungering and thirsting for more. In particular, as evangelical Christians become less aware or less appreciative of their roots in western Christendom, they sense a corresponding lack of depth in their intellectual and liturgical experience. There are healing waters by the lakefull in Catholic life, as many are finding. The Holy Spirit is doing what He always does: fostering unity in the bond of peace.

What has your experience been since coming into the Catholic Church? Do you think the Network and its members should be pro-active in reaching out to Protestant ministers and congregations?

In the Roman Catholic Church I have found a warm welcome, unconditional love which reflects the unconditional grace of God, and a steady involvement with a liturgical tradition that has grown organically from its beginnings in the apostolic age. Surely we of the *Network* should be pro-active in reaching out to those outside the Church. Love reaches out, the gospel is a proclamation, and there is room for all Christians in Peter's boat. We should freely give as we have freely received; and we should continue to be as willing to receive from others as our neediness warrants.

Journeys Home

"Long familiarity with and respect for great Catholic philosophers and theologians opened me up to the Catholic faith."

Give a quick outline of your pilgrimage ...

I was brought up a Mennonite missionary kid in an evangelical interdenominational environment. I met my Dutch-Reformed wife in a mission high school. We later married during college years at a Calvinist college, where I was influenced by the Neo-Kuyperian Dutch Reformed tradition. After spending a year studying with Francis Shaeffer at his L'Abri retreat center in Switzerland, I finished my BA in Far Eastern Studies at Sophia University in Tokyo (Jesuit), and then took a Master of Arts in Religion at a Presbyterian seminary in the states (I sensed no ministerial vocation, but wanted theological training). My academic hunger not yet quenched, I then completed an MA and Ph.D. at two Catholic universities—both in philosophy, which was my chief interest. I taught briefly at one of these universities until I took my first full-time philosophy-teaching position at a Lutheran (ELCA) liberal arts institution.

How open were you to the Catholic faith because of your tradition?

My Mennonite missionary parents were never anti-Catholic. They were very open-minded about inter-faith matters, taking us to Eastern Orthodox Easter services, boarding us in Lutheran homes, and having us taught by Episcopalian priests. But my high school years brought me into contact with many anti-Catholic fundamentalist ideas, though they always remained for me a puzzling curiosity. The Catholic Church always loomed in the background of my consciousness as a massive, imposing, mysterious, and somewhat forbidding edifice. I had Catholic friends who struck me as sincerely Christian, so I never entirely bought into the anti-Catholic prejudices, although I know they influenced me. Catholicism seemed confused, formalistic, and legalistic at best but not un-Christian.

What were the primary issues that opened you to the Catholic faith?

A number of key issues opened me up to the Catholic faith. First was my family's inability to find a church home after our move to my first teaching position. We were dissatisfied with the fundamentalist or liberal alternatives. Second was my exposure to the Lutheran liturgical tradition and practices, and a more Catholic understanding of the Eucharist and Baptism.

Third, extensive reading, beginning with a footnote in a textbook on the history of the Western legal tradition, which led me to question Protestant anti-Catholic prejudices, and then on to John Henry Newman, Louis Bouyer, Thomas Merton, the patristics, and the conversion stories of Tom Howard and others.

Fourth was my long familiarity with and respect for great Catholic philosophers and theologians, especially St. Augustine and St. Thomas Aquinas, as well as an abiding respect for the learning represented by the three Catholic institutions of higher learning I had attended.

Fifth was my personal experience of the beauty of the Eucharistic liturgy, first in Lutheran, then in Anglican, and finally in Catholic communions. In the latter I had several vivid experiences of the "authenticity" of Christ's Real Presence in ways that escape verbalization.

Sixth were personal contact with a few Catholic individuals who radiated a warm "evangelical" piety, as well as existential confirmation of the authenticity of the Catholicism I had been studying.

Seventh was the growing conviction of the authenticity of the Catholic tradition and of the truth and integrity of Church teaching on faith and morals.

In retrospect, the main issues were and still are two—the real historical-temporal authority of the Church and the real Presence of Christ in the Mass.

What were the barriers and main issues?

The main barriers were intellectual and psychological. First, I struggled intellectually with the justifiability of extra Scriptural tradition, the Marian dogmas of the Immaculate Conception and Assumption, the veneration of and prayer to saints, the role of obedience in justification vs. faith alone, and the historical and theological warrant for papal primacy, succession, and infallibility. Psychologically, I began to question the Protestant image of Luther as a white knight in shining armor against all the devils of Hell at Worms.

I, also, struggled with the justifiability of private revelations and Marian apparitions, such as those at Fatima and Lourdes, the counterintuitive nature of transubstantiation and Eucharistic adoration (which has since become an unspeakable blessing), and personal devotions involving the saints. (I had been asked by a bishop to consider praying to John Henry Newman, and to take up the rosary—again, both these matters have become very dear to me in time.)

But maybe most initially and quite seriously, I wrestled with the fear that Catholicism's plausibility might be a part of some great Satanic scheme to deceive even the elect! More practically, though, I was concerned about marital disharmony over the Roman option, familiar considerations—how to raise the children in a mixed marriage, and uncomprehending relatives and friends who might all become alienated by my decision.

Where are you now in your journey? What are your plans for the future?

I was received into the Church in Easter of 1993. Because of marital and family discord over the Roman option, I have not felt entirely free to practice my Catholic faith as I might wish to under other circumstances. The result has been trying for all of us. Yet the Lord seems mercifully to be bringing some healing on this front.

I am not in church ministry, but in college teaching, so my case may be different from those of the majority of *Network* constituents. Because of our mixed marriage and family situation, I am involved in more than one church congregation. This poses both challenges and opportunities.

I plan to continue college/university teaching, writing, and publishing, as I am doing now. I'm also involved, de facto, in ongoing ecumenical discussions among my Lutheran (ELCA) friends at the Lutheran college where I am employed.

My greatest hope, of course, is that my wife and family might come to know the blessings of membership in the Catholic Church; but I can't freely share even this sentiment with them just now.

What are the effects this has had on your family, your extended family, and friends?

Among my best Lutheran friends, the response has been uniformly supportive. Some of them wish they felt free enough to follow suit, but are tied down in parish ministry and other such connections, which make the prospect difficult for them to envision. Among my theologically liberal friends—both Catholic and Lutheran—the response has been polite incomprehension.

Among family members and other friends, the response has been mixed—from horror to warm support. Most of our closest evangelical former friends have chosen to avoid the issue and to avoid me. Some have struggled with the fear that I may have lost my faith. Others have warned my non-Catholic wife to keep our children from me, for fear of Catholic influence.

There are many former acquaintances with which I have not felt free yet to share my conversion, due to circumstances on the home front.

How do you interpret what is happening and why?

What is happening to us personally I take to be a kind of spiritual trial and purging. What is happening in the Church at large I take to be, similarly, a kind of spiritual trial and purging or winnowing. Both are frightening. Both are utterly indispensable.

The return of the "separated brethren" cannot occur without holiness—in them and in us. What I see happening in the Church in the world is both frightening and exciting—frightening, because of the apostasy among so many clergy and theological faculties; exciting, because precedents exist in Church history which give hope, as do the remarkable phenomena of conversions among people like those in the *Network*.

What has your experience been since coming into the Catholic Church?

I've found a mixed bag. Catholics can't sing. The liturgy needs to be reformed now more than ever. Some priests follow the winds of trendy-lefty developments, making innovations where they shouldn't in the liturgy, teaching things that are questionable, and avoiding subjects that could be read as politically "incorrect." But there are many faithful clergy, Lord love them. And even if the Eucharist were celebrated under a patched tent in a vacant lot, it would still be the Holy Sacrifice of the Mass, where Christ Himself comes to be present with us.

So who can complain, in the final analysis. The sacrament of confession, or reconciliation, is absolutely essential and a splendid thing. Perhaps it's been one of my most glorious discoveries in the Church. There is a great hunger for truth and Scriptural substance. We need more biblical literacy, more literacy in Church history, more celebration of the great traditions in the Church. Not pathetic attempts to make ourselves more "Protestant." We do need to remove as much as possible needless ethnic and extraneous cultic "offenses" to those separated brethren thinking about coming home. But the great treasures of Church history should never be thrown out: Marian devotion, crucifixes, St. Thomas Aquinas, days of holy obligation, fasting, etc.

Do you think the Network and its members should be pro-active in reaching out to Protestant ministers and congregations?

This is a hard one to answer. I can see good arguments on both sides. Initially, my response was to say: keep the *Network* a support-group. Yet I can see how running articles of a more apologetic nature may be of help to those outside the *Network* constituency. I'm not sure.

I do think we need to address the challenging issues of marital discord, etc., as you have been doing. I also think we need to run articles displaying the splendor of the Church, to show the winsome side of Catholicism, and to avoid the appearance of gloom and doom.

Again, I appreciate your confidentiality, and I covet your prayers.

This convert has asked to remain anonymous since up to this point he is the only one of his family that has made the journey to the Catholic Church. The entire process has caused great stress on his marriage. With great joy, though, he has announced that his oldest son will be received into the Catholic Church this Easter Vigil, 1997. He asks for our continued prayers.

"We understood Lutheranism as a reform movement in the Catholic Church, and were taught that Lutheranism was never intended as a permanent arrangement."

Give a quick outline of your pilgrimage ...

My wife and I were both brought up in conservative, traditional, ethnic Swedish Lutheran parishes. That meant a stress on personal piety and a rather Catholic liturgy. My call to the ministry was very clear since childhood. I trained in a Lutheran Theological Seminary. Harvey Cox and secular, relevant, liberal Christianity was the order for the day for four years. I suffered a great deal because of this. I served two parishes in New England before converting to Catholicism. The first pastorate lasted for five years, and the second for fourteen. We entered the Catholic Church on Reformation Day, 1990.

How open were you to the Catholic faith because of your tradition?

My wife and I were quite open to Catholicism even from our teenage years. We understood Lutheranism as a reform movement in the Catholic Church, and were taught that Lutheranism was never intended as a permanent arrangement. I was quite "Catholic" in my Lutheran ministry—Eucharistic vestments, clerical collar, hymnody, and even theology, like Mary and the sacrificial nature of the Eucharist.

What were the primary issues that opened you to the Catholic faith?

We were propelled out of Lutheranism because of its ever-growing acceptance of liberalism, specifically, watering down the true presence of Christ in the Eucharist, a pro-choice stance on abortion, and the acceptance of the integrity of the homosexual lifestyle. Catholicism was already open to us theologically.

Where are you now in your journey? What are your plans for the future?

Right now we are five years and four months into the journey. We have built our own house, had another child, and found an excellent parish. I'm in the process of seeking a bishop who will sponsor my petition to Rome for ordination to the priesthood, but even if ordination never comes, we're extremely glad to be in the fold of the Church founded by Jesus, and would never go back.

In the immediate future I will continue to work as a pastoral associate. This is actually quite fulfilling, and I enjoy the freedom of not having to worry about parish administration. Hopefully I will be ordained sometime in the next eighteen months. If ordination does not come to pass, I will not take up secular work. I would hope to build a chapel here on our property. We have 15 beautiful acres on the Connecticut River, and I would devote myself to prayer and teaching of the Word as I could.

What has your experience been since coming into the Catholic Church?

My wife and I have found two extremes in our search for parishes with which to affiliate. We moved in January of 1993, so after having found one very fine parish, we had to find another. In each of these periods of searching we have found parishes that seem to be lost in a wasteland homiletically and liturgically. They were really discouraging. But in the midst of this wasteland, here and there we found gems—spiritually, homiletically, and liturgically. In these parishes, we found soil and sunshine for our faith to grow and enjoy itself.

Do you think the Network *and its members should be pro-active in reaching out to Protestant ministers and congregations?*

The *Network* and all Catholics should evangelize. No question about it. I think we should do everything possible to encourage Protestant clergy and even parishes to come home to Rome. Mainline Protestantism is definitely headed in the wrong direction. The evangelicals are on the right road, but how can we deny sharing with them the fullness of the faith that is in Catholicism? Moreover, they have a great deal with which to invigorate the Catholic Church.

They know the Word in a depth that escapes most Catholics. We should be aggressive about bringing them home. Absolutely.

So, there are my thoughts and our experiences. We are so glad that God has called us on this journey. It has been very tough at times, but the hard times have always been followed by times of blessings and many consolations in prayer and in the fellowship of the brethren.

Journeys Home

"I needed to realize once again that it was not my calling but the Lord who calls and it was not MY ministry."

by Sid Bruggeman

Give a quick outline of your pilgrimage ...

I grew up Lutheran. In the mid-seventies I became involved with the Charismatic movement, which resulted in becoming a licensed lay minister in the Christian Church (Disciples of Christ). I quit farming after eleven years, completed college and seminary, and was then ordained.

I serve a small Christian Church congregation, which up until a year ago was part of the Disciples of Christ (D. of C.) denomination. In Protestant fashion we departed because of the continued drift of the denomination toward "left wing" theology and politics. (ex., They handed out condoms at the national assembly as an aids awareness device.) Though I was originally drawn to the D. of C. because of my belief in unity, I could offer no worthy arguments for the congregation to stay. Their departure resulted in my departure also. I have no regrets. The Lord has used it to push me down the road.

How open were you to the Catholic faith because of your tradition?

My attraction to Catholicism has been a very slow process. My early Christian experience was filled with anti-Catholicism. The Lutheran pastor lectured us frequently concerning such "evil." Not knowing any Catholics, I had no reason not to take his warnings to heart. My perception of Catholicism could probably best be summarized with the term ignorance.

What were the primary issues that opened you to the Catholic faith?

As I grew older, ecumenical ideals followed by the Charismatic movement prevailed upon me. A Catholic priest in the Charismatic movement had a profound effect upon me and it was probably there that my journey began. I love history and studied Church history whenever possible. I was also a student of C.S. Lewis, not knowing his theology was more Catholic than Protestant. Later I read St. Augustine's *Confessions*. Seminary brought more, especially the study of the early Church Fathers.

In the study of 1 Corinthians 2, I came across Paul's statement, "For I have decided to know nothing among you except Jesus Christ and him crucified." This troubled me greatly. Protestantism seems only to know Christ resurrected. What did this mean to know Christ crucified? It nagged at me throughout seminary and into ministry. There is much that could be added here but let me only say that resolution came with Catholicism. The big shift came in the tandem events of enrolling our kids in a Catholic High School (not with any intent of becoming Catholic) and the exit of my congregation from the D. of C.

Through the Catholic school we encountered "fruitful" witnesses of the faith. The exit from the D. of C. brought home again the nagging problems of Protestantism, the continual splitting and theological gerrymandering. I was now an active party in the ongoing tragedy. I recall saying on occasions, "I feel like a spiritual orphan." Though I did not and still do not question my basic faith in Christ, I had this perception that the ground could shift under me at any time. It is like being a nomad or transient. When the environment around becomes unsuitable you just move. Thus was my theology.

What were the barriers and main issues?

My greatest issue (I thought) with Catholicism was Mary. As a Protestant I admired Mary as an example of faith and always thought that Protestants were disrespectful of her. But I also thought, in my ignorance of doctrine, that Catholics worshiped Mary as divine.

My greatest barrier, though, was probably my ego. I had always perceived Christianity as a call to sacrifice. But the last thing I ever expected to be asked to lay down was that which I believed was my calling, my ministry. I needed to realize once again that it was not my calling but the Lord who calls and it was not MY ministry. It came down to obedience. Jesus is either my Lord or He is not.

Where are you now in your journey? What are your plans for the future?

We are in the process of making a "Grace"-ful exit from Protestantism. (My conviction has long departed.) I am still active in ministry.

Concerning the future I am somewhere on the other side past great anxiety. Sometimes I think I am confused. But in general I feel at peace. I believe the important thing to do now (and always) is trust in the Lord. Though I am not certain at all about my role in the future, I perceive that I am seeing "in a mirror dimly." And that is okay.

What effect has this had on your family, your extended family, and friends?

My wife and children are supportive and intend also to join the Catholic faithful (with the exception of one son, whose Protestant girlfriend objects, but that discussion is not over). My extended family, congregation, and friends do not know though they probably suspect. I wish for my congregation and extended family to know the richness and wonder of the true Church. There are so many lies and feelings of prejudice out there, but it is still my prayer. However, I sense difficulty ahead.

How do you interpret what is happening and why?

I can only conclude that what has happened is a work of God's grace. I would feel presumptuous to state what the Lord may be doing. But my general speculation would be that Jesus' prayer "that they may be one" was, is and shall continue to be answered.

What has your experience been since coming into the Catholic Church?

Since I am not yet fully into the Catholic Church it may be premature to answer this. But one observation: I have a very supportive Bishop and a couple of supportive priests. But my general perception from other clergy is that they do not really take me seriously. Please understand, they have not been rude or such, but polite and somewhat distant. In their defense, I suppose they have good reason to wonder if "the leopard can change his spots." I mean, "Is this guy going to be Catholic or a "PROTEST-ant catholic." I understand a reasonable caution.

Do you think the Network and its members should be pro-active in reaching out to Protestant ministers and congregations?

I see the possible work of the *Network* in two forms. One: Keep doing what you are doing. It has been tremendously helpful to me becoming aware of other Protestant clergy making the same journey. I truly wondered at times if "I'd lost a few cards in the last shuffle." When a person is doing things or hearing things that other people do not, we many times correctly surmise they are mentally "off balance," to say it nicely.

Two: Help get the Church ready. I do not believe there will be a need to "proselytize." I suspect the Holy Spirit is ahead and already doing it. I think I am greatly blessed to experience God's wonderful grace in these matters. But I also know that God is "no respecter of persons." If He has moved upon those of us connected to the *Network*, then He is or is going to move upon many if not all others out there. I suspect the Church is not ready for many of "us." It needs to be or we might not shed our disruptive characteristics from Protestantism.

In October 1995, Sid officially resigned as pastor his congregation. Then on Christmas 1995 Sid, his wife Carol, and all four of their children were received into the Catholic Church. He is presently employed as a groundskeeper for a park and as a carpenter. He writes: "I miss being a pastor and from time to time feel sad about it. But I still would not go back nor do I have any less convictions about becoming Catholic; quite the opposite. If there would be nothing else for me to do in the Church than assist in Mass, pray, try to love the Lord and my neighbor, it is enough. I consider it a wonderful privilege and great undeserved honor just to be a Catholic."

"Although he would sometimes long for daily Mass, his conviction that it 'wasn't right' was an opinion I sought to reinforce."

Give a quick outline of your pilgrimage ...

My husband was raised Catholic. Although he had a sense of God's presence during the time of his First Communion, his young life was characterized by a nominal Catholicism that seemed lifeless. At about 17, he began searching in other religions and left home to continue that search. Eventually he met some hippie Bible Christians (Plymouth Brethren) and made a fresh commitment to the Lord. This small community dissolved a few years later. He became immersed in academics and uncommitted to any local church.

During graduate school, he experienced a revival in his walk with the Lord and temporarily returned to the Catholic Church and to daily Mass. Although he felt a wonderful closeness with the Lord, there were too many theological issues he could not resolve. One day he visited a nondenominational church where we met and were eventually married.

Although he would sometimes long for daily Mass, his conviction that it "wasn't right" was an opinion I sought to reinforce. His involvement in this on-fire evangelical church helped him sense a call to ministry, which eventually led him to enroll in an evangelical non-denominational seminary. After graduating from seminary, he served as a discipleship-training director at a homeless mission. A year or so later, he was called to pastor an American Baptist church.

He was a gifted bible teacher and studied for hours each day. His commitment to visitation and potluck dinners was not as strong, however, and he still had a hunger for a deeper communion with the Lord.

He started reading books on contemplative prayer, and it wasn't long before he was reading Catholic books on prayer. During a conference in St. Louis he visited a cathedral and called me to say he'd come home. From then on, his heart was determined, but ahead were many hours of study, as well as many hours of conflict between us.

What were the barriers and main issues?

The doctrinal barriers were the largest. His faith in Sola Scriptura was shaken by ministry itself, seeing so many people study the Bible without any visible change in their lives. He then immersed himself in studying the areas about which he had questions. Many nights we listened together to tapes by converts, and one by one the walls came down. Of course, the largest practical barrier was a job. We didn't feel that he could leave his pastorate without one. He applied to graduate school in Church History, but that did not work out. It took a little over a year for us to be in a position to finally leave pastoral ministry.

Where are you now in your journey? What are your plans for the future?

My husband has already entered the Catholic Church, and we had our marriage blessed in December. At Easter Vigil I'll be received into the church and our two kids will be baptized.

My husband has applied to a Ph.D. program in Sociology/Demography, his other field. But we hope to lead inductive Bible studies and to impart a love for the Scriptures, along with some practical "how-to" skills for this.

What effect has this had on your family, your extended family, and friends?

My husband's family, of course, was delighted, especially his mom. My family has been a mixed bag, from puzzled to hostile to very open (my mom). The transition has been hard on all of us.

We're relatively isolated now, since many friends no longer speak to us and also since we are no longer in ministry (this is not completely negative; after a public life, a season of regrouping quietly is helpful). Based on our experience, I would generally recommend to converts that if possible they leave the area where they were previously ministering. The imputed guilt (although false) of "betrayal" and "you hurt us" is difficult to deal with. Three of our friends remain open and dialogue with us; we are grateful for that. Others are still friends but treat our Catholicism as a landmine to step around.

How do you interpret what is happening and why?

The Lord is bringing the homeless back home. I think that Steve Wood's assessment in *Surprised by Truth* is accurate: the Jesus people, after years of spiritual homelessness (I can't tell you how widespread I know this feeling to be) are finally coming home to the Church.

What has your experience been since coming into the Catholic Church?

My initial experience with RCIA was difficult. The textbook we used had a very low view of Scripture, and *Humanae Vitae* was treated as a cause for dissent. But I was able to speak freely and have been accepted. I've also prayed each week for the Lord to show me something good in the material I've read. I now respect my priest who is teaching our class; I understand his love for the Church and the sacraments more; I am not so quick to judge. I find refuge in the vibrant Catholics I meet, and I have one close Catholic friend. I love the Mass. My husband is able to attend daily Mass. We are healing and hope to leave this fall for a doctoral program.

Do you think the Network and its members should be pro-active in reaching out to Protestant ministers and congregations?

I'm not sure about the extent to which we should "proselytize," but there are many who have questions, and knowing about the *Network* is really a service to them. They should know we are out there and available at the very least.

Because of the continued stress with extended family, this convert family has asked to remain anonymous. However, all the family are now members of an excellent local parish where the children attend school. The husband is continuing his doctoral studies. Their daughter will receive First Holy Communion this spring. The wife teaches a small group Bible study for women.

Journeys Home

"The main issue for me was Baptism ... This struggle was so intense that I quite literally feared for the souls of my children. Should I permit them to be baptized? (For then they might go through life thinking that they had been baptized into Christ, when, in fact, they had not.)"

by Bruce Sullivan

Give a quick outline of your pilgrimage ...

I was raised as a devout Southern Baptist. However, while in college, I joined the Church(es) of Christ (i.e. Stone-Campbell Movement). I was a member of the C. of C. for nine years and served as a minister for five of those years.

While I was not as dogmatic as many C. of C. preachers, I nonetheless had a very narrow definition of what qualified one to be a bona fide "Bible Christian" (I certainly did not consider Catholics to be Christians). My dream was to go to South America as a missionary in order to rescue Latinos from the clutches of Catholicism! It was while attempting to convert a devout Catholic family in our community that I was set on the pathway to Rome.

Upon graduating from Auburn University, I went to the Sunset School of Preaching in Lubbock, Texas. Upon graduation, we served in Upper East Tennessee with a congregation that wanted to send us to Brazil as missionaries. However, after about one year, our mission team disbanded, resulting in a change of plans. We then went to Greenville, North Carolina where I served as a campus minister. After six months, extreme financial duress compelled me to take a secular job in my wife's home state of Kentucky, where we have been for five years. I continued to serve on a part-time basis (as do most preachers in our rural setting) until certain Catholic apologists upset my "apple cart"!

How open were you to the Catholic faith because of your tradition?

While I always sought to be open to the truth, I never dreamed that it would come to me through the Catholic Church!

My background had created in me an extreme hatred of the Catholic Church. Why? Because I believed that not only had She corrupted the simple truths of the Gospel, but that She was literally damning billions to hell by Her teaching! Other "denominational churches" (C. of C. lingo) may have been in error, but the Catholic Church, in my mind, was utterly diabolical by design.

How, may you ask, could anyone ever entertain such wild ideas? Good question. Chalk it up to experiences with the Seventh-day Adventists in college, the pitfalls of private interpretation, a faulty ecclesiology, gross misinformation, incredible ignorance ... and a colorful imagination!

What were the primary issues that opened you to the Catholic faith?

A Catholic friend introduced us to the Church's teaching on contraception, which served to soften my heart somewhat towards the Catholic Church. That same friend subsequently gave me a copy of Karl Keating's *Catholicism and Fundamentalism*. My wall was breached!

That same friend introduced me to Father Benjamin Luther, a Catholic priest who was a former member of the C. of C.! He subsequently gave me a subscription to *This Rock* (along with three year's worth of back issues) and introduced me to the tape ministry of Scott and Kimberly Hahn. Scott and Kimberly Hahn then told me about the *Network*, etc., etc...

The key theological issue that was raised by Keating and that compelled me to press on was that of the Canon of Scripture. I could not come up with any convincing reasons for accepting the Scriptures apart from the teaching authority of the Catholic Church. Yet, how I arrived at the conclusion that the Scriptures are the Word of God would have to affect how I then approached those same writings. So, the issue of canon, and the related issue of Sola

Scriptura, proved to be the driving force behind my search.

In addition, I was deeply affected by an outpouring of God's grace that touched me in an area of my life that had tormented me for years—grace that came to me when I sought the intercession of our Blessed Mother and began to pray before the Most Blessed Sacrament.

What were the barriers and main issues?

Having a strong "Cambellite" (C. of C.) background, the main issue for me was BAPTISM. I believed that New Testament baptism was the immersion of a penitent believer, expressly for the purpose of the forgiveness of sin; anything else was simply not the "one baptism" of the New Testament. While I already agreed with the Catholic teaching on the meaning of baptism, I had a very hard time coming to grips with infant baptism and baptism by modes other than immersion. This struggle was so intense that I quite literally feared for the souls of my children. Should I permit them to be baptized? (For then they might go through life thinking that they had been baptized into Christ, when, in fact, they had not.)

Yes, it was a very difficult issue for me, but again by God's grace I recognized that my problems were more issues of lingering prejudices rather than theology.

I would be remiss if I failed to mention that Marian doctrines also posed quite a difficulty, but that too, by God's grace, was cleared up. Once I was able to set aside my misguided prejudice and *hear* what the Catholic Church truly taught and believed about Mary, I found my heart warmly opened to her.

Where are you now in your journey? What are your plans for the future?

I will be received into the Church at this year's Easter Vigil (1994)!!! As far as the future, that's a good question! Like most clergy converts, I have experienced something of an identity crisis. However, I am learning to glory in the vocation that God has given me. From this point forward, I just want Him to open and close the doors. Right now I have absolutely no idea what he has in store. I yearn to teach, to write, to do anything to build up others in the Faith. But, I will leave the details to Him.

What effect has this had on your family, your extended family, and friends?

My wife is very supportive, but not yet ready to enter the Church (though she is the one making sure our children learn their Catholic prayers!). Many people in our extended family sincerely think that I am leading my family towards damnation. Most of our friends are members of a very anti-Catholic fundamentalist denomination and, of course, think me a false teacher, etc. Most probably they think we are "moon-struck." However, for the most part, everyone is kind; just uncomfortable.

How do you interpret what is happening and why?

I simply believe that the power of the truth is compelling. God is trying to bring all men into the fullness of the Faith.

What has your experience been since coming into the Catholic Church?

It has been very strange!!! I have had Catholic laymen say, "Congratulations ... I think." They aren't even sure of their own faith, much less able to deal with a convert. It really is very sad.

I have had troubling exchanges with priests who espouse somewhat less than orthodox views. Catholic friends who openly disagree with the Church's teachings, etc have frustrated me.

HOWEVER, I have also been deeply challenged by the faithful. Holy priests have richly blessed me. I have made friendships with many "kindred spirits." It's just that most of them live so far away!!!

Do you think the Network and its members should be pro-active in reaching out to Protestant ministers and congregations?

Chalk it up to my fundamentalist's roots, but I believe that we ought to reach out to any and all who will listen. Cradle Catholics need to be evangelized. Protestant ministers need to be evangelized. I need to be evangelized!

No Protestant denomination possesses the fullness of the Faith as it is found in the one, holy, Catholic, and apostolic Church. This is not a matter of religious taste, it is a matter of the truth. While the Church certainly teaches that a man can be saved outside of the visible unity of the Church, it also teaches that it is wrong to presume upon God's grace. Obtaining the goal of eternal life is difficult enough for the Catholic who avails himself of the sacraments, how much more for the non-Catholic who rejects them.

Protestant ministers all present a partial or, at times, distorted Gospel. In so doing they jeopardize not only their own souls but the souls of those whom they shepherd. It is imperative that we do everything we can to bring them to the truth. Yes, they possess some truth—even much truth—but, the errors associated with Protestantism can and, I am afraid, will prove devastating to many souls.

Bruce has now been a Catholic for almost four years. His family is still on the journey. He now works as a salesman for an oil company which, to his great joy, is owned and managed by deeply committed Catholic businessmen.

Journeys Home

"Being already convinced that a person could be a Christian as a Catholic... I thought I should find out what Catholics really and officially believe."

by Dennis Kaser

Give a quick outline of your pilgrimage ...

I came from a non-churched family and spent years experimenting with "things spiritual." When I was 34, I made a commitment to Christ through the TV ministry of Billy Graham. I then joined a Baptist church and in two years enrolled in a Divinity College. While a student, I pastored three small churches, and then when I had completed the minimum requirements, I was ordained to the United Baptist Ministry. An unhappy experience in my next church led to my returning to high school teaching on Long Island, NY. I eventually joined a Presbyterian Church with evangelical leanings, and have served there as a part-time staff person and ordained elder. Through the past seven years I have had extensive involvement in the ministry of my church through preaching, teaching, visitation, etc.

How open were you to the Catholic faith because of your tradition?

My particular Protestant tradition tended to view Catholics as "not really Christians," and over the years I have inducted many ex-Catholics into the churches I have served. My pastoral experience, however, showed me that there are many truly Christian Catholic people. I used to read a newspaper column written by a local Monsignor and always found his insights helpful.

Presbyterians (PCUSA), being more liberal, tend toward more involvement in ecumenical services, retreats, etc., and so I came to have a nodding acquaintance with Catholic retreat facilities and local parish Priests. My view of the Catholic Church was that those born to it or already in it had a great treasure which they shouldn't cast aside. I didn't see any necessity for myself to become Catholic, especially since doing so would involve "adding so much" to the simple faith which I thought was all that was necessary. Of course, Mary was a big problem!

What were the primary issues that opened you to the Catholic faith? What were the barriers and main issues?

The influences that opened me to Catholicism were not primarily issues as such. Being already convinced that a person could be a Christian as a Catholic, and seeing that validated by several fellow teachers in my workplace, I thought I should find out what Catholics really and officially believe.

One of my school friends began giving me old copies of the Liguorian magazine and I was amazed that virtually everything in every issue was helpful to me in living my faith on a daily basis. Eventually I took out a subscription of my own, and began photocopying articles to share with my Catholic friends. Through the Liguorian I learned of the new Catechism of the Catholic Church and immediately ordered a copy.

About that time, my friends from school and I arranged to go together on a retreat to a Cenacle Retreat House. I thought, "Well, here I am with these experts on the Rosary, why don't I ask them to pray an abbreviated Rosary with me while I put away for the moment my difficulties with praying through Mary?" So, I did (fatal moment)! It didn't seem like "vain repetition" and it was a joy to share this moment of faith with my believing friends.

A few months later, at a private, quiet, retreat of my own I obtained a set of Rosary beads and a small booklet of prayers and procedures, with an audiotape, and began praying the Rosary (as of this writing it's been 265 consecutive days). As a result, my heart has grown several sizes in the direction of Mary—and, that barrier being down, I'm eagerly devouring the Catechism (page 630 at present).

Where are you now in your journey?

At present, I'm in a kind of limbo. Several months ago I resigned from active membership on the ruling Board of my church and "officially" I'm on a sabbatical for R&R. My primary fellowship is with my school friends at lunch where we share our journeys and talk of our faith together. This is my "year of Catholic experience." I'm attending Mass weekly in another community, subscribing to several other Catholic publications in addition to the Liguorian, and reading voraciously in Catholic directions (Tom Howard's books, the Hahn's book *Rome, Sweet Home*, and books by Romano Guardini, Thomas Aquinas, etc.).

What are your plans for the future?

My plans for the future are pretty hazy. I have about 9 more years in my teaching career and at the end of that time I will have a minimal pension. It seems to me from my limited experience as an infiltrator into Catholic parish life that there is a great need to get the Catechism into the hands, minds, and hearts of more people in the Church. Could my teaching experience be used in this? Would I have to become a deacon to be able to "do ministry" in a Catholic context? These are some of the questions that are cropping up.

It does seem that I have passed the point of no return on the road to Rome—I'm one of those who've been "surprised by truth." When I can take the step into the Church is very much up in the air, since my wife is rather confused about what is happening to me. She wants to follow, but things like this take longer for her.

What effects has this had on your family, your extended family, and friends?

My wife is the only one on the home and church front who knows about my journey in this direction. We are being very cautious so that no "scandal" or perceived "falling out" is connected with any move I may make. The great bulk of our social life together has been in connection with church people and church activities. The prospect of having to start all over socially is very daunting to my wife. Personally, I feel like a butterfly just emerging from the cocoon into a wide beautiful world and wanting to spread the new wings and fly into it. I feel ready but the Spirit is saying, "Wait, not yet." When I attend Mass I want to go forward with the faithful and receive the Lord in the fullness of His provision for his people ... How long, Lord?

Journeys Home

"As we began to read the Catechism and other Catholic works, my spirit and mind cried out, "YES! At last, the whole truth!" yet my heart quivered in fear."

by Kris and Marty Franklin

Give a quick outline of your pilgrimage ...

I was raised in a small fundamentalist church with no denominational ties. My mother was one of the founding members of the church. My faith was formed very early by frequent Bible reading, frequent attendance at church functions, daily prayer, and a strong emphasis on personal evangelism and missions. We were taught early on that only our doctrine was one hundred percent true— other Protestant churches were close (some Baptists, some Evangelicals, non-Pentecostal fundamentalists) but the rest were way off base and it was questionable whether people in those groups were truly "saved." When I was five years old I "asked Jesus to be my personal Savior." It wasn't long after that event that I began to evangelize the neighbor children, many of whom were Catholic.

From my tradition I learned that the Bible is the Word of God and could be fully trusted. I learned how to get to heaven (faith alone) and how to avoid hell (be born again). I learned that a lot of people were going to hell because they hadn't heard about Jesus and that the most important thing a Christian person could do was to be a missionary. I learned that sin hurts us and makes God unhappy, but that no matter what terrible sin a person committed, if he or she was truly "born again" it would not affect salvation. Aside from having faith, all the work of salvation was God's.

I learned all the stories of the Bible, memorized Scripture, and was encouraged to read the Bible for myself as soon as I was able. I learned to appreciate Christian music, and was taught to depend on God for everything. I learned that God hears the prayers of the "saved" but not the prayers of anyone else (unless that unsaved person was praying the "sinner's prayer.") I also learned that it was very easy to pick out people who were "saved" by how they lived and how they talked. For instance, someone who smoked was probably not "saved." Along with that, we were taught that just because someone called himself a Christian, it didn't mean he truly was.

My older brother was a missionary in Catholic countries for twenty years. My older sister and her husband were missionaries in New Guinea. For me, missions was a viable option for anyone who wanted to serve the Lord wholeheartedly, so early in our marriage Marty and I decided to pursue becoming missionaries. Since Marty is bilingual in Spanish, we assumed we too would end up in a Catholic country, saving the lost and bringing them home to real faith in Christ.

How open were you to the Catholic faith because of your tradition? How did you see the Catholic Church before?

To be honest, the Catholic Church was the last place we looked for truth. I was firmly prejudiced against it, having been taught from the time I was small that it was the largest and biggest tool of Satan to deceive people and keep them from Christ.

Our particular church put a great emphasis on end times issues. I remember well the day my mother informed me with sadness and sincerity that the anti-Christ would be a Catholic Pope. We were told that Catholics worshipped Mary, that they didn't know Jesus had risen from the dead (hence all those crucifixes), that the people in power deceived the people into giving a lot of money for building ornate churches, even in poor countries, that the Church taught salvation by works, that people might have a second chance after death (purgatory), and that the poor Catholics could never know for sure if they were saved and going to heaven, whereas we could KNOW. We were taught that Catholics only used memorized prayers and that this was a pagan practice. We were taught that the Catholic Church was the largest cult in the world. Catholics were people to be pitied and evangelized.

As I grew up I came in contact with Catholics who had a fervent, lively faith in Jesus Christ and thus was forced to lay aside the "Catholics aren't saved" idea. At least SOME Catholics were "saved." Why they stayed in the Church was beyond me, and though I was curious, I did not feel compelled in any way to investigate. I simply accepted the prejudice I'd received as fact.

What were the primary issues that opened you to the Catholic faith? What were the situations that brought you to your decision? Was there one key reason?

The primary issues which opened both Marty and myself to the Catholic Faith were myriad. First, we were serving as missionaries in Guatemala, along with missionaries from 40 other denominations. Obviously the message the Protestants were giving the people was anything but a unified whole. Seeing the reality of Protestantism up close in this way was disturbing.

Second, we began to see that Protestantism is elitist in that it requires that a believer be literate. Living in a country with upwards of fifty percent illiteracy made us wake up to the fact that for most of history, most people have been illiterate. Before the invention of the printing press, there were no Bibles to be had even for those who could read. Sola scriptura, or "the Bible alone" required that each individual "check out" whatever doctrine he heard being taught. With a Bible and the Holy Spirit, anybody could come to truth. So what about all those people who could not read?

It was chilling to realize that these people were completely at the mercy of the preacher. Would not the God of the universe, our Heavenly Father who wills that all be saved, make a way for every person, literate or not, to know the truth? And if a person did come to understand and accept Christ through faith, but could not read the Scriptures, how was he to grow in his faith, since Bible study was essential to that growth?

Third, we saw incredible abuses of "sola scriptura." Men with third-grade educations were setting themselves up as pastors and then surrounding themselves with people and calling it "church." Some of the Guatemalan pastors were barely literate. Of course no missionary thought this was a good thing, so there were groups in Guatemala set up to help these "pastors" learn better doctrine, study scripture, etc. But this caught our attention.

According to sola scriptura, all one needed was a Bible and the Holy Spirit. Now a theological grid was being added to the equation. Not only did the pastors need the Bible (and to be able to read it) but they needed a way of interpreting that scripture. Our next question was, "Whose?"

I had always been taught that the Catholic Church added things to the Bible, not only extra books that didn't belong, but doctrines, teachings that were unbiblical. It was the Word of God (Scripture) and nothing else.

In Guatemala we realized that if it were the Bible alone, than all any pastor would have to do was stand up, read from the Bible, and sit down, and the power of the Word would do the rest. Of course this never happens, and we realized that every time any pastor opens his mouth and proclaims "This is what it means," he is effectively adding to the Word of God.

Once again the question arose, "Whose addition is the truth?" If the Bible must be interpreted (as everyone agreed it did) then whose was correct? The old "scripture interprets itself" notion didn't wash at all. Always, without exception, there had to be an interpretive grid, a hermeneutic for the "how to" of interpretation, and this varied from group to group.

Marty and I realized that we were headed toward a form of Christian agnosticism, i.e., we can't really know all the truth, all that matters is a "personal relationship with Christ," so let's not talk about that which divides (everything!) and instead focus on what we have in common.

From this point, we began to study Church History, and to paraphrase Cardinal Newman, when we were over our heads in history, the Protestantism all washed away.

What were the barriers and main issues?

The biggest barriers to our being willing to examine Catholic teaching were ignorance, prejudice, and fear. Fundamentalists are raised with a healthy respect for Satan and his ability to deceive and mislead even the faithful. My husband was raised in the Episcopal Church but had a "born again" experience as a teen so he had been away from it for a long time. When we began first of all to read history, then to participate in liturgical worship at an Anglican Church, he felt a true sense of homecoming.

I too felt the homecoming, but I was afraid of it. We had been taught that man's nature is one of total depravity, that even reason is incompatible with faith because reason is subject to Satan's influence, to pride, self-deception, etc. As we began to read the Catechism and other Catholic works, my spirit and mind cried out, "YES! At last, the whole truth!" yet my heart quivered in fear.

There were no huge theological issues for us once we settled the issues of historicity and authority. Coming to understand the Christian Faith through Catholic eyes took some doing but we had lived overseas. We had to adjust to a different world view, and we knew that we had to come at our study of the Church by first asking the question, "What does the Church MEAN when she said this or that." For instance, when the Church teaches that Mary makes intercession for us, we had to dig deeper than our own instant response of "There is one mediator between God and man, the Man Christ Jesus." We had to recognize how Christ shares his mediatorship with ALL of His children in the very simple fact that we can pray for one another. As Protestants we too had been mediators for others, and had asked others to mediate for us in intercessory prayer. The Catholic view was MORE biblical, not less, and certainly not anti-biblical.

Catholic teaching is complete in every sense of the word. Once we took off our Protestant glasses and determined to at least put away our ignorance, we were astonished and delighted at what we found—the whole Truth and nothing but.

Where are you now in this journey? What are your plans for the future?

We were received into the Church on April 15, 1995 and we have never looked back!

We are gradually becoming involved in lay ministry in our local parish and of course we are constantly called upon to defend and explain the Faith to Protestants who want to know. I am teaching a class on Salvation History—the participants are very hungry for more information about their Faith.

Marty is studying to teach a class on the Sacraments next fall. It took us some time to become involved at this level—although we were Catholic-minded for some time before our reception into the Church. We felt it would take some time to become Catholic-hearted, and these past two years have been spent immersing ourselves in the joys of the Eucharist and life as a Catholic family.

What effects has this had on your family, your extended family, and friends?

For the most part my husband's family was not in the least bothered by our conversion, with the exception of Marty's twin brother who is Baptist. For the first time it has become somewhat strained for them to talk about spiritual matters but the relationship between them is solid. In time I believe it will become easier.

Half of my family is almost completely unable to cope with our decision to become Catholic. My brother didn't contact me for nearly a year afterwards and my relationship to my older sister has completely changed. Our being Catholic is the unmentionable topic. As far as they are concerned, we were deceived by the devil and went over the edge, dragging our children with us, and for them, this is nothing less than a total tragedy. In all seriousness, had we died it would have been easier on them. I don't say this flippantly, but rather to help others understand both the depth of anti-Catholicism that I grew up with and the width of the rift it has caused. Only the Holy Spirit can heal this kind of hurt.

Relations with Protestant friends vary depending on the degree of each person's anti-Catholicism. Some are very blase and tolerant (yet uncurious) about it, others avoid us in the grocery store. I would say most people are simply baffled, yet they don't ask questions either.

And then, of course, there is the good news that several of our friends are either already in the Church or on their way presently. They asked the questions and heard our answers, and allowed the Holy Spirit to lead them in Truth, too, regardless of the cost. We share their joy at the awesome discovery of Christ's True Bride.

How do you interpret what is happening and why? What is the Holy Spirit doing?

I would like to think that the Reformation is going to be undone in the centuries to come. I would like to think that this upswing in conversions among Protestant leaders is the beginning of a wave of Christian people coming HOME. Let us hope and pray and work toward this end.

What has your experience been since coming into the Catholic Church? What have you found?

The Church of Jesus Christ is like a woman in her late forties who over the years has given birth to and raised twenty children. She is worn out, she is tired, some days she isn't very pretty. In places she is flabby, in other places she is firm and hard and callused from so much work. Some of her children love and honor her. Some are rebellious. Some have forgotten and abandoned her. Some make her proud, some make her ashamed, but she loves them all.

The Church of Jesus Christ is the radiant, perfect Bride of Christ, the One for Whom He gave His life, the One He rose again to save. Regardless of how she looks on the outside, regardless of what some of her children say or how they behave, she is my mother. How I wish my sincere, Christ-loving Protestant friends and family would come home to Mom!

Do you think the Network and its members should be pro-active in reaching out to Protestant ministers and congregations?

I think it is absolutely essential that we at least plant the seeds. Only the Holy Spirit can lead a person to Truth, only the Holy Spirit can change a heart, and believe me, it takes a heart transplant for most Protestants to even consider the claims of Rome. As truly "bi-lingual Christians" we need to be not only a resource to those who are on the journey, but we need also to challenge those who are not on the journey into asking the hard questions which only the Catholic Church can answer adequately. If we are firmly convinced that the Catholic Church is the True Church of Jesus Christ, do we not owe it to other people to help them make that discovery as well?

Journeys Home

"If the extraordinary claims of the Catholic Church are true then all Christians should join it."

As a Calvinist minister who receives your newsletter through an anonymous benefactor, I was astonished by those survey responses that felt the *Network* should not evangelize. It is difficult for me to understand how anyone could go through the struggles associated with converting to the Catholic Church and then think that evangelizing is a bad idea. Here are five reasons why you should reach out to Protestant clergy and laity:

1. Truth matters. Recognizing the common love Catholics and Evangelical Protestants share for our one Lord does not negate our differences. If the extraordinary claims of the Catholic Church are true—then all Christians should join it. If the claims of the Catholic Church are false—then all Christians should leave it. This is not merely a question of style nor personal preference.

2. I make mistakes. The certainty that I have errors in my theology is matched by a desire to root them out. How can I do this if my brothers and sisters in Christ do not care enough about me to let me know I am wrong?

3. Pastor/Teachers will face a stricter judgement. If my own errors are bad enough, how can you stand by and let me teach those errors to others without gently correcting me as your brother in Christ. Is it charitable to let me face this greater judgment when it was in your power to help me? If Calvinists like myself are truly in error, who is better suited to reach us with the truth than those who have converted to Catholicism?

4. True Church unity demands it. If we are all to embrace One Faith we are constrained to earnestly contend for it.

5. You might learn something. Serious dialogue and debate with theologically literate brothers and sisters will inevitably lead to mutually greater clarity and depth in our knowledge of God.

As for me, give me John Calvin or John Paul II. Please don't present Catholicism as another entrée in the denominational cafeteria. Perhaps some Christians will be offended by passionate debate, but followers of a crucified Messiah should be made of stronger convictions.

May - July 1995

A Joyful Transfiguration

Greetings in the name of the Lord Jesus Christ!
As I begin this month's newsletter, I'm reminded of how Moses looked and must have felt as he descended Mount Sinai having stood in the presence of God. Moses literally glowed with joy! I'm also reminded of how Peter, James, and John must have felt as they came down from the Mount of Transfiguration experiencing the magnanimous presence of the Lord Jesus, in all his glory. I wonder if they had a glow about them, too?

Now I'm sure what I'm feeling is a mere fraction of the spiritual and emotional high these men of God experienced but nonetheless, I'm still brimming with excitement as a result of last weekend's *Defending the Faith Conference* and the *Network's* third *"How Should We Then Serve"* luncheon.

Oh sure, I know my own glow pales in comparison with those great biblical glows but, nonetheless, it was great! It was great to gather with new and old *Network* faces for pizza and Powerade after the final talk Friday night, in which Peter Kreeft waxed so eloquently. It was, also, great to gather Sunday afternoon with thirty *Network* members and spouses for lunch, and then several hours of individual sharing. With a mixture of laughter and tears we heard how the Lord had brought us each in different ways but yet to the one, holy, Catholic and apostolic Church. In some ways, it felt like a "Catholic's Anonymous" meeting as each of us said, "Hello, I'm ____ and I'm now a Catholic" and then proceeded to describe, sometimes in very difficult details, our journeys home. All in all, with the talks of the conference centered around the great gift of the new Catechism, combined with our *Network* gathering of brothers and sisters, it was truly a weekend of transfiguration!

But there was also a particularly somber note to the weekend. Several days before the conference, I received a fax from Dr. Ken-

neth Howell, a *Network* member, describing the unbelievable or-
deal he and his family had experienced over the past month. He
also expressed his gratitude for the prayers and encouragement of
the *Network.* As a fitting climax to his conference talk, Scott Hahn
read this letter to the entire group of 1500 gathered at the conference. Ken wanted me to include his letter in this newsletter so that
you might know how much he has appreciated your prayers and
also so you might be encouraged in your own journey of faith.

Dear Fathers, Brothers and Sisters in Christ:

*I write to you with a mixture of joy and sadness because I
cannot be with you at this year's Defending the Faith Conference. It was my intention to come at the gracious invitation of a
Catholic friend but Divine Providence has other plans for us
just now. My sadness is only ameliorated by the knowledge that
many of you as well as hundreds of others have faithfully prayed
for my physical and emotional recovery. My joy is deep because
I know that together we share in the common inheritance of God's
people and because of what God is doing among us to bring
together his lost sheep.*

*Since many of you have no doubt heard about my injury, I
thought I would relate the facts briefly so that you may know the
truth. On Saturday, June 3rd around 3:30 p.m. I was walking to
my office at Indiana University where I am currently a Visiting
Professor, when a young white male in his twenties attempted to
shoot me in the back with a 9 millimeter semi-automatic. After
the first shot, I turned to face him, and at that moment he fired a
second shot that struck me in the lower neck. I ran as fast as I
could with him firing three more shots at me, all of which missed.
With surgery to repair my vocal cords, this trauma has been
enormous for me and for my family. Yet we have sensed an unusual degree of the presence of God sustaining us. The love that
has been shown by friend and stranger alike has been overwhelming. Both Sharon's family and mine have been so supportive that
we hardly know any wants. We are currently convalescing in
Florida at the gracious invitation of my parents and older brother.*

*What has this to do with my journey toward the Catholic
Church? In my view, everything. As some of you know I have
been moving toward the Church over the past four or five years*

attempting to clear away obstacles to being received. This past year has been extremely difficult with the loss of my former teaching position, a major family move and a serious illness with one of my children. To this has been added great emotional strain on my precious wife and our children as we struggled in virtually every area of our lives. During this year my wife and I have often remarked that although things have been very difficult, they could get worse. Then with the shooting, they did.

Yet it is in the time of our deepest suffering when the reality of our Redeemer's love shines through. I have often felt keenly the presence of Christ and His holy angels surrounding me during this tragedy. In a real sense, I believe this may have been an answer to a prayer I said in 1993. During an Ignatian retreat I was meditating on our Redeemer's passion and the depth of his suffering for us. God brought to my mind 2 Cor. 4:10, "We always carry around in our body the dying of Jesus that the life of Jesus may also be manifested in our mortal bodies." I prayed that somehow I might be privileged to share in Jesus' suffering and bring his saving grace to the world. The events of this past year culminating in my being shot have brought me more deeply than I could have ever imagined into an experiential suffering of our Lord's passion.

Perhaps because I am an academic, I tend to process experiences rationally and analyze my life accordingly. Yet what happened to me defies rational explanation. Some things in our lives are simply there, not to be analyzed or categorized, but to open our hearts to the Spirit's deeper work. I can already see God working in our lives but how that shall fall out remains to be seen. One thing I know; I was spared for a purpose. A Catholic Sister in Canada wrote me just after the accident, "you must have some glorious mandate on your life seeing that you have been spared serious possibilities." I could no doubt think of many reasons why I have been spared (e.g. for my family) but am sure, whatever God wants from me, it has to do with the Church because my love for the Church, as the manifestation of Christ himself in this world, continually deepens in my heart. My longing for Christ in the Eucharist is profound and the day of first reception of this mystery will be a great joy to me. This came home to me when I was in the hospital.

After four days I was taken off the sedatives and regained consciousness to discover that my wife and oldest daughter had brought my Bible, Catholic missals and rosary to my bedside. They both knew what was dear to my heart. A Catholic friend brought another rosary, which I put around my neck. As I lay there half awake, I clung in tears to the crucifix which reminded me of the Savior's love and the prayer I had made to share his suffering.

I suppose the second purpose that has become clear has nothing to do with what I should do. Rather, it has everything to do with what I should be. One of the most wonderful byproducts of this accident has been the love that Christians of all stripes have poured out to our family. Conservative Presbyterians, Lutherans, Evangelicals, and Catholics have all overwhelmed us with love. I could not help but think to the vision of Vatican II when it speaks of Holy Mother Church yearning for her children to come home. I know where the center of gravity is but the love of God is emanating outwardly to God's children in every place and is being manifested in the most unexpected situations.

The unity of Christians in the Church and the incorporation of non-Christians will often take place through our willingness to share our Lord's passion. Our study of doctrine, our design of effective means of communication and our zeal for the Church are all instruments in God's hand. But, in the end, the redemption of the world happens today just as it did at Calvary. Or rather, I should say that the redemption of the world will come about through the extension and embodiment of what took place at Calvary. It is through our suffering that God manifests his saving grace to the world. God can do anything without me but he wants me to be everything for Him.

I must leave you now with the prayer that your journey and mine will be, as the Anima Christi says, more deeply into the Savior's passion. My family and I need the Saints' continued intercession and yours. Our future is very uncertain, not knowing whether we should continue to live in Bloomington or move to parts unknown. I wish you God's benediction and the deeper joy of embracing Christ.

Tuus frater intus Catholicus
Kenneth J. Howell

August 1995

Drooping Hands and Weak Knees

A s I sit in my office I struggle to survive in an island of jet lag. My son and I just returned from two weeks in Europe and now in two days, my wife and I will leave for Australia to speak at a Catholic Family conference. Through the jet lag, I'm trying to focus on a long list of tasks that need to be completed before I leave again. Many of these tasks involve the *Network* newsletter and planning for the Fall Retreat. But even with the tiredness, the power of the experience my son and I had, especially in England, is still strong.

Between doing business for Franciscan University and *Light and Life*, my son and I took excursions to more castles than we could count as well as the sites of the English martyrs. We stood in the halls of Oxford where John Henry Cardinal Newman, Edmund Campion, and others had studied while they were discerning God's call for their lives. We stood outside Lyford Grange, the house where Edmund Campion was celebrating a secret mass when he was betrayed, arrested and taken to the Tower of London. We toured the Tower and saw the prison cells with the inscriptions of St. Philip Howard, St. Thomas More, and St. John Fisher. We also saw the block upon which they were beheaded. We visited Arundel Castle, a center for recusant* Catholicism in the years after the Reformation.

All of these sites stood as a great challenge to me. I sometimes think I have sacrificed a lot in giving up my pastorate to come to the Catholic Church. But then I consider what other men and women have given up, like Edmund Campion, John Southford, Margaret Clitherow, Margaret Ward, Thomas A. Beckett, Thomas More or

---

* *Recusant: (rek' yoo zent) A person who refuses to obey an established authority; specifically in England in the 16th to 18th century, a Roman Catholic who refused to attend the services of the Church of England or to recognize its authority.*

John Fisher, and I realize that my own sacrifices and worries greatly pale in comparison. These men and women were driven to sacrifice all in defense of the Church they loved.

Standing on the coast near the place where Edmund Campion and others, knowing what would face them, secreted themselves back into England, the words of Hebrews 12 became very clear in a new way:

> *Therefore since we are surrounded by so great a cloud of witnesses, let us also lay aside every weight and sin which clings so closely and let us run with perseverance, the race that is set before us looking to Jesus, the pioneer and prefecture of our faith, before the joy that was set before him endured the cross, despising the shame, and is seated at the right hand of the throne of God.*
>
> *Consider Him who endured from sinners such hostility against himself so that you may not grow weary or faint hearted in your struggle against sin, you have not yet resisted to the point of shedding your blood.*
>
> *And have you forgotten the exhortation which addresses you as sons? My son, do not regard lightly the discipline of the Lord nor lose courage when you are punished by him, for the Lord disciplines him whom He loves and chastises every son whom he receives. It is for discipline that you have to endure. God is treating you as sons but what son is there whom his father does not discipline ...*
>
> *For the moment all discipline seems painful rather than pleasant. Later it yields the peaceful fruit of righteousness to those who have been trained by it ... . Therefore lift your drooping hands and strengthen your weak knees and make straight paths for your feet so that what is lame may not be put out of joint but rather be healed.*
>
> Hebrews 12:1-13

That line about "drooping hands" and "weak knees" really hits home, considering that for 40 years I hardly bent a knee in worship. And then once again that line "make straight paths for your feet" reminds me of those encouraging words from Proverbs 3:5,6 which challenge us to "trust in the Lord with all our heart and lean not onto our own understanding, in all our ways acknowledge him and he will direct our paths."

After being a Catholic now for over two and a half years I have encountered many surprises along the path. Through my readings and discussions, and particularly my experiences in the celebration of Mass and other sacraments, I have encountered countless truths that over and over again confirm that the Catholic Church is indeed the Church that Jesus Christ planted, with all of its warts, with all of its weaknesses, and especially with all of its sinners, especially, people like me. What a privilege of grace to share in its joy!

Journeys Home

November - December 1995

Friends Along the Journey

The *Network* Fall Retreat in Eureka Springs, Arkansas, was a wonderful success! The weather was great, the scenery was beautiful, the retreat center and hermitage were inspiring, and the fellowship was uplifting and greatly encouraging. Twenty-nine of us gathered in the small retreat house on the peak of an Arkansas mountain. The Spirit, who had drawn us together from divergent backgrounds and great distances was very present.

On Friday evening we enjoyed a private concert with John Michael Talbot, who shared his music and his own testimony and dreams for the *Network*.

On Saturday morning and early afternoon, Scott Hahn led us in open discussions about how we need to be open to let the Church bring renewal into our lives, and then how we can respond by helping to bring renewal in the Church. In the late afternoon we went on a pilgrimage to The Little Portion Hermitage. Then in the evening we had an open time of discussion where all topics were game. This discussion time was particularly meaningful as we tackled some very difficult and sensitive issues.

On Sunday morning the topic was *Network* Business. We talked about how we can improve the newsletter, communicate over the Internet, and further promote the work of the *Network*. One of the key purposes which we recognized about the *Network* was that of friendship. Remembering C. S. Lewis' description of "phileo" (friendship) in his book, *The Four Loves*, we were reminded that we are drawn together primarily because we stand side-by-side facing in the same direction. We share a common experience: a call by the Holy Spirit to journey from the comfort of our Protestant past into the Catholic Church. This journey can be unexpected, and in some ways frightening but it is the friendship of the journey that has drawn us together.

About a third of those who attended had not yet completed their journey into the Catholic Church. This made some of our discussions very interesting and at times heart wrenching. One of the issues that arose was centered around the fact that the *Network* includes believing brothers and sisters from a wide spectrum of theological perspectives. It is not our desire to narrow the focus of the *Network* to include only those who come from an evangelical side of the theological spectrum. However, the *Network* does primarily represent those who have left their Protestant background to become faithful Catholics—who did not become Catholic only to remain Protestant in spirit. The *Network* represents those who have surrendered to Jesus Christ and are deeply convinced in the authority of the Catholic Church centered around the Magisterium in union with the seat of Peter.

We are not men and women coming into the Catholic Church with the primary goal of changing the Catholic Church, nor insisting that it change to meet our own needs or foibles. Rather we recognize that the teachings of the Catholic Church, its history, and traditions are gifts of God's grace, which must be received with humility and surrender. To do otherwise is in fact to remain Protestant. The *Network* does not consist of former clergy who consider themselves gifts to the Church, with all of their training, experiences and successes, but rather men, women, and their families who accept the Church with all of its sacraments, Truth, traditions, and authority as Christ's gift to us.

We should enter the Church not with a long list of things we can give or with changes we can propose, but on our knees rejoicing that we through the grace of God have this great privilege of being a part of the body of Christ. And yes, this does require surrender and sacrifice. For a good number, if not most of the *Network* members, this may require the sacrifice of career and possibly pastoral ministry. To try to keep both—on the one hand proclaiming oneself a Catholic, while at the same time retaining, even in the least, one's image as a Protestant pastor if not one's position—is in fact not truly making the journey. It is like keeping one foot on the dock and the other one in the boat. Pretty soon this becomes very uncomfortable if not body wrenching.

Recently, I met with Bernard Cardinal Law of Boston to discuss the work and needs of the *Network*. He was very encouraging and supportive, and gave a clear indication that he wanted to work with us and with key bishops to help uncover opportunities for convert clergy in the Church. He particularly mentioned the possibility of the ministry of evangelism.

If we are to continue to win the support of the Church hierarchy, we need to assure them that we are willing, like the apostles who followed Christ, to leave behind whatever nets we once used and take up whatever new nets Christ may give us to serve him in his Church. We must show them that our conversions are sincere, and that we are team players who can be trusted. Let us keep each other in prayer, so that as friends on the journey we can together serve Him and His Church faithfully.

Thanksgiving... the Rest of the Story

As I'm re-reading historical sources, I continually find it eye-opening how much of our official American history has been re-written or at least revised when it comes to almost anything concerning the Catholic Church. Here is an interesting tid-bit I found in an old book entitled *Sketches of the Establishment of the Church in New England*, by Rev. James Fitton, published in Boston in 1877. He refers to a more general and better known *History of the United States* by Hildreth.

> In 1617, a French vessel was wrecked near Cape Cod, and all who reached the shore were massacred by the Indians, except three, who were sent from one Sachem to another in triumph. Two soon sank victims to disease and violence. The third, supposed to have been a priest, lived longer, and endeavored to convert the Indians and win them from vice; but their obdurate hearts were proof to all his appeals, and he frequently held up to them the terrors of eternity and the wrath of an offended God. Soon after his death, a pestilence swept over the land, which they looked upon as the result of his prayers, and as their tribes were reduced to a mere handful, they repented of their obduracy, and resolved to listen to the white men who should tell them of the Great Spirit. Thus was the field prepared for the future labors of Eliot.

> *In 1620 the Mayflower bore to the rocky shore, which had already received the name of Plymouth, the gloomy Separatists."*

In other words, if it weren't for the selfless missionary witness and subsequent death of a Catholic priest, the Mayflower pilgrims would not have been received quite so benevolently, and may have suffered the same fate as the turkeys!

January - February 1996

A Plethora of Needs

As I write this, there is an overflowing pile of unanswered letters and phone messages, from *Network* members as well as inquiring Protestant clergy, asking for advice or assistance.

Hardly a week goes by when I haven't received the names of new Protestant pastors or laymen on their journey towards the Catholic Church. Each of these names represents a plethora of needs and concerns and lately I've felt pretty sheepish about what the *Network* can do to help. We are making inroads and contacts, but we've decided that its time to take some strong steps towards making the *Network* more helpful.

In discussions with many of you, we have decided to begin the process of establishing the *Network* as a non-profit corporation. The following is the proposed purpose and goal statement for this new corporation:

GOAL: To assist the Catholic Church in fulfilling its mission of evangelization and its call for Christian unity, as most recently proclaimed by Pope John Paul II in his encyclical Ut Unum Sint.

PURPOSE: In cooperation with the Catholic Bishops, to help inquiring clergy and laity of other traditions return home and then be at home in the Catholic Church, by providing:

1. *Resources* that give clear expressions of Catholic Truth in ways that our separated brethren will hear and understand,

2. *Contacts, assistance and fellowship* for those who are considering coming into full communion with the Catholic Church,

3. ***Continued fellowship and encouragement*** for those who have entered the Church,

4. ***Vocational guidance, training and assistance*** for clergy and academic converts until they have been integrated into the Catholic community, and...

5. ***Opportunities*** for these new Catholics to share with the Catholic Church ideas for renewal and evangelization which the Holy Spirit had blessed in their previous experiences.

A Board of Advisors is being established, which will consist of a variety of lay and Clergy, including several Bishops. Some of the specific services we are proposing to provide through the *Network* will be:

1. the bimonthly Newsletter which contains articles written by *Network* members for other members on the journey;

2. the Internet Homepage where members and inquirers can discuss pertinent questions as well as explore the list of job postings;

3. brochures made available through local parishes and dioceses to separated brethren seeking help and assistance;

4. the Assistance Fund and Scholarship Fund, specifically established to help Protestant pastor converts become adequately trained to teach in a Catholic institution or to serve in a parish or diocesan ministry;

5. the Regional Annual Retreats and Conferences, as well as local Fellowship Groups; and, possibly, ...

6. an annual European Pilgrimage to a different location each year where sites of particular interest to converts are visited and contemplated from their new Catholic perspective.

As you can see, we envision the *Network* providing many services, which will not only help Protestant clergy and their families come home and then be at home in the Catholic Church, but also Protestant laity who also have much to give in service, but are finding the transition difficult.

Please pray for us as we patiently go through this process. At the present, the *Network* is completely out of funds. We're presently absorbing the costs for this newsletter, believing that the Lord will continue to bless this work. If you can contribute to at least cover newsletter printing and mailing costs this will greatly help. Once we have our own non-profit status, we will be looking for the names of potential benefactors who might have a heart to support this work.

Please tell others you know along the journey about the *Network*. I am constantly amazed when I meet new converts, like Chris and Janine LaRose, who had never heard of the *Network* or even the more well known converts like Tom Howard and Scott Hahn. We need to get the word out to our brethren who are searching and seeking, so that they know they are not alone on this journey.

The New Surge of Converts to Rome from Protestantism *by Kenneth J. Howell**

Conversions to the Catholic Church from the ranks of Protestantism are not new. But when, in the space of a few years, a critical mass of Protestant clergy and non-ordained church workers make arduous journeys toward Rome, the observer can't help taking notice. An organization called the *Network*, consisting of individuals and families, has emerged to offer solace and support for these journeys.

The *Network* is not to be confused with the Pastoral Provision, which is primarily oriented to enabling married Episcopal priests to enter the Catholic priesthood. The *Network*, in contrast, works with inquirers from all faith traditions. Headquartered in Steubenville, Ohio, under the leadership of former Presbyterian

---

* This article also appeared in the March 1996 issue of New Oxford Review.

minister, Marcus Grodi, the *Network* draws together a seemingly disparate collection of people who have been, are, or hope to be involved in the conversion process.

The ecclesial cultures from which the converts come span the gamut: fundamentalist, charismatic, evangelical, Calvinist, mainline Protestant, and even High-Church Anglican. The actual roads traversed are by no means identical, and the footprints that remain indicate many detours in the journeys. But most of these differences are due to individual inclinations and ecclesial backgrounds *from which* these pilgrims have come. The common elements in the stories arise from the object to which they are moving or have moved, elements that have four dimensions: ecclesial, historical, sacramental, and spiritual.

Members of the *Network* share the universal longing of all converts to Catholicism, to be united to the one universal Church. Many have noted a lack of legitimate authority in their churches. Dave, a former fundamentalist minister, and his wife Colleen began their journey to the Church when they saw how arbitrary were the doctrines and biblical interpretations of their background. The only ground for those doctrines and interpretations seemed to be Dave and Colleen themselves, or a group of independent Bible churches. The persistent problem of how to decide between competing interpretations of a text dogged them. Even those of more established traditions with credal and synodical statements asked how they could know that *these statements*, not others, represent the correct interpretations of the Bible. Others were troubled by the epistemological and moral relativism in contemporary American culture that has infected their churches.

Yet the search for legitimate, Christ-given authority is not a hankering after easy answers to perplexing problems. These pilgrims are aware of theological nuance, and embrace a truly catholic perspective that allows for theological diversity within defined parameters. But more than anything, they hear the authority of Christ speaking through the apostolic and Petrine ministry.

Most see the only hope for Christian unity in reunification with Rome. They have made their journey toward Rome, not only out of a recognition of the practical need for unity, but because the prayer of Jesus in John 17 has gripped them. Splintered Protestantism is an insurmountable obstacle to unity in their view. Christ prayed that his sheep might be one, and these pilgrims know that while they cannot unite ecclesial communities, they can take personal steps toward unity.

The journeys of *Network* members share a second feature, a growing awareness of the need for continuity with the early church. Bob, a charismatic pastor in New England, spent the better part of 25 years attempting to establish a "New Testament" church, a project undertaken many times since the Reformation. Imagine his consternation and then delight when he realized that the primitive church is to be found in the Catholic Church, now grown-up and well-developed but with observable links to Christ and his apostles.

As many *Network* members began to question their once cherished understandings of the Bible, they were also confronted with divergences between their Protestant churches and the witness of the Church Fathers. A former professor at a Calvinist seminary was dismayed when he discovered that St. Augustine was not the proto-Calvinist he thought. The Bishop of Hippo fully embraced the sacramentalism of the Catholic faith. Dismay turned to crisis when he realized that Augustine, so often invoked by Calvin, held to views of baptism, the Eucharist, and the papacy closer to Tridentine Catholicism than to the Genevan Reformation. Often pilgrims felt deprived of their Christian ancestry by a Protestant individualism that overlooks much of Christian history. Even such a well trained minister as Marcus Grodi felt at sea when preparing for Presbyterian worship, for he realized that he knew very little of the historic liturgies of the Church.

But is the Catholic Church really any closer to the ancient Church? Here was the problem John Henry Newman posed for himself over a century earlier. The members of the *Network* have arrived at Newman's conclusion: the Catholic Church is demonstrably closer to the ancient church than its Protestant counterparts. And, like the Oxford movement leader, they want to stand in the unbroken stream of tradition and draw from the rich variety of devotions and practices that have been handed down from the earliest days of the Church.

Yet the desire for unity or historical continuity doesn't fully explain the conversion of men and women who in some cases have relinquished comfortable salaries and satisfying ministries to enter the Catholic Church. Central to all their stories is the Eucharist. For those of High-Church Anglican background, the sacramental aspect of the journey poses only minor difficulties. But for most of the others, the Catholic doctrine of the Eucharist poses a major obstacle in their journey. They have been predisposed to reject any miraculous claims associated with the Lord's.

The real bodily presence of Christ provides the key entry point. For one convert, the words *hoc est corpus meum* (This is my body), uttered by Christ at the Last Supper, began to make sense only on the assumption that the eucharistic presence of Christ must be something more than God's omnipresence or the presence of the Holy Spirit. One of the more well publicized conversions has been that of former Presbyterian minister (now Franciscan University of Steubenville theology professor) Scott Hahn, who fell head over heels in love with Christ in the Eucharist. Others confirm that it was the assurance of an *objective* presence of Christ in the Mass that drew them inexorably to Rome's altars.

These converts soon realize that the power of the Eucharist is only a specific instance of something greater, the sacramental vision of Catholicism. For those whose church life has been devoid of any emphasis on the sacraments, a paradigm shift takes place. After considerable investigation, they begin to see the Church, the Bible, and indeed their entire experience of Christ in an embodied, mediated framework. This makes the sacrament of confession no longer a human presumption in their eyes, but an unmerited gift of Christ who absolves through His chosen ordained servants in the priesthood. They view life in sacramental terms: the invisible in the visible, the divine in the human, and the supernatural in the natural. And behind their adoption of the sacramental vision is an intense desire for a deeper spirituality.

Network members have repeatedly said that their journeys to the Church have been more than an intellectual quest, far more profound than a shift of theological allegiances. While for most, theological questions have been a prominent ingredient in their pilgrimage; many begin to travel the Roman road because they saw the promise of something deeper in their relationship with God. They are candid about their disappointment with the level of spiritual life in the average Catholic parish, but they are also fascinated by the beauty and power evident in the writings of spiritual guides in the Catholic Church. The many traditions of spirituality in the Church have drawn them into an authentic Catholic life. Paul became a Trappist monk from the ranks of Methodism after a long and fruitful career in seminary teaching. Others like John, a former Baptist minister, and his wife have joined secular orders in the Church to follow a Dominican rule while living in the world. The former Protestants testify that the level of spiritual depth in the Catholic tradition is unmatched. And, as might be expected, the uniquely Catholic practice of eucharistic adoration with all its attendant depth of spiritual love, has become a prominent part of the devotions of many of these renewed lovers of God.

The *Network* is barely two years old, but it already numbers over 200 members, with new inquires coming in weekly. It offers much needed advice and support to pilgrims. Through its newsletter and retreats, the *Network* converts and those still on or just beginning the journey in common purpose.

March - April 1996

A Long Awaited Transition

I am busting at the seams to tell you something! This edition of the newsletter has been delayed because I've been waiting for a few important ducks to get in order. It took some coaxing, but now that they're in line, I can tell you the good news.

First, the *Network* has a new name:

The Coming Home Network International

When we began three years ago, we called our growing fellowship the *Network* because we wanted to provide a network of support and encouragement for Protestant clergy and their families who were considering entering the Catholic Church. The name stuck, and the fellowship has grown enough for us to think seriously about keeping it going.

As I mentioned in the last newsletter, the number of letters, faxes, e-mails and phone calls I receive daily has continued to increase, particularly because of recent articles about the *Network* in *New Oxford Review* and *Sursum Corda* Magazine.

However, there are a gazillion "networks," most having something to do with either broadcasting or computers, so the name needed further definition. As I listen to your descriptions of why you have converted or are converting to the Catholic Faith, the most common metaphor I hear is that you feel like you are "coming home;" that you are returning home to the Church Christ founded and from which our ancestors had run away.

The name, the *Coming Home Network International,* more clearly describes what it is we're all about, particularly in line with the message of *Ut Unum Sint*: helping our separated brethren come home to the unity of the Church.

This fellowship is *International* because we have received inquiries from Canada, England, Australia, Israel, Africa, Guatemala and even the Philippines!

Now since this new name is a bit tedious, the short version will be the *CHNetwork*. Granted this still sounds a bit like an Internet server but then again, we'll hopefully have a strong presence on the Internet!

Second, as you notice, we've chosen a new symbol to represent the *CHNetwork*: a hand sketch of the Vatican. What better way to symbolize coming home to the Catholic Church then with the Church building which best represents our Catholic home: the Vatican, the location of the Seat of Peter.

Third, with great excitement I can now tell you that I am going to be able to direct this fellowship full time! Ever since coming into the Catholic Church, God has been more than generous, providing lots of opportunities to serve Him and support my family. Most recently, I have been serving as the Executive Director of Christian Outreach for Franciscan University. However, as my responsibilities at the University increased, I was forced to spend less and less time responding to the needs of the *Network* which continue to pile up on my desk.

I am always deeply moved by your letters. Some of you are facing difficult, life-changing decisions. I don't consider myself a qualified spiritual nor vocational director, nor do I view myself as your "pastor." However, what your letters and requests challenge me to be is your advocate and encourager: to prayerfully carry your requests and concerns before the Father, and then before the Magisterium of the Church, to help the Church hear and respond to your needs, and hopefully to help open doors so you can find opportunities to continue serving the Lord in ministry while also supporting your families.

A good portion of my time will now focus on fund development, not only to cover administration costs, like printing the newsletter and putting food in my kids' mouths, but also to establish a substantial Assistance Fund. This fund is crucial to providing new clergy converts and their families enough breathing room so they can adequately discern, under the guidance of qualified spiritual and vocation directors, how God might be calling them to serve now that they are Catholics. You will hear more about this as it develops.

Presently I am working through the legal and accounting details of transforming the *CHNetwork* into a non-profit corporation. Please pray for us and for all the members of the *CHNetwork*. As you are reading this, there are an amazingly large number of Protestant clergy and laity struggling with difficult questions about their present denominations and ministerial positions, some with the shocking realization that God may be calling them into the Catholic Church. As most of you know intimately, this questioning can lead to decisions that will drastically change their lives! As members of the *CHNetwork*, we must continue to stand beside one another in faith, hope, and charity, for we have walked along very similar paths, all of which have led or are leading to the same place: home to the Catholic Church.

A Great Many Priests Convert To the Faith!

The twelve summoned the body of disciples and said,
   'It is not right that we should give up preaching
   The word of God to serve tables.
Therefore, brethren, pick out from among you
   Seven men of good repute,
   Full of the Spirit and of wisdom,
   Whom we may appoint to this duty.
But we will devote ourselves to prayer
   And to the ministry of the word.'
And what they said pleased the whole multitude...
These they set before the apostles,
   And they prayed and laid their hands upon them.
And the word of God increased;
   And the number of the disciples
   Multiplied greatly in Jerusalem,
   AND A GREAT MANY OF THE PRIESTS
   WERE OBEDIENT TO THE FAITH.
   Acts 6. 1-7, (Liturgical readings for Sat., April 20, 1996)

Did you ever notice that it is AFTER Luke describes the delineation of ministry tasks between the Apostles and the newly ordained lay leaders, or "deacons," that he mentions that "a great many priests" are converting to the Faith! Could it be that many Jewish priests were interested in, even convinced by the claims of this new movement within Judaism, but were holding back because they weren't sure what they would do if they converted or how it would affect their lives? For these trained and ordained Jewish clergy, conversion would mean the loss of their pastoral careers. Since Jewish priests were generally married, conversion would also mean the loss of their means of supporting their wife and children. Conversion would mean complete rejection by their family and friends, leading possibly to severe persecution. This therefore isn't just a modern phenomenon. Conversion always requires great sacrifice.

Later after the pharisee Saul converted, "the Jews plotted to kill him" (Acts 9.23) who was once their champion persecutor of this growing sect. In Saul's case, it is also interesting to note that when "he attempted to join the disciples ... they were all afraid of him, for they did not believe that he was a disciple" (Acts 9.26). He needed an advocate, Barnabas, who was already accepted by the disciples, who could then stand by and for him before this first Magisterium.

This is the charism of the *Coming Home Network International*, with St. Barnabas as our patron: to stand beside and for Protestant clergy and laity, and their families, who are responding to the leading of the Holy Spirit, to accept great change and sacrifice, to leave the comfortable and familiar, to come home to the Catholic Faith.

May we be "sons of encouragement" to these men, women and their families, as Barnabas was to Saul.

St. Barnabas pray for us!

June - August 1996

Getting Organized and Serious:

WE NEED YOUR HELP!

A s I write this, many exciting things are coming together for the *CHNetwork*. Thank you for your prayers, your letters of encouragement, and for your financial support.

On June 1, after much prayer and with the trusting support of my wife, Marilyn, I officially separated from Franciscan University to become the *CHNetwork's* full-time director. Then, also, on that day, as if God were testing our faith, I found out that I needed immediate back surgery! This required spending most of June on my back recovering. But thanks to the blessed miracles of modern science, everything went terrifically and I'm "back" better than ever.

But the most exciting thing that happened on that day was the reception of Dr. Kenneth Howell into the Catholic Church! After a long and difficult journey (which you can read about in more detail in Part One) Ken came home. Since his conversion also cost him his teaching position, he has agreed to work with me at least part time as the associate director of the *CHNetwork*. He brings a tremendous quiver of skills to this work, particularly in the areas of writing, editing, theology and pastoral care. Please pray for him as he continues to discern his future.

On the third weekend of June, we had our 4th Annual "How Should We Then Serve?" Luncheon. More than 30 *CHNetwork* members and friends gathered for fellowship, sharing, and a discussion of the new future for the *CHNetwork*. It looks like this annual luncheon will become our official Annual Meeting, so I pray that more of you can make it next year.

As we took turns sharing our experiences along the journey, we once again recognized how blessed, yet how difficult, the journey can be. The whole gathering reconfirmed in spades the importance of our fellowship in the *CHNetwork*.

Last week, Ken and I joined Scott Hahn and Jeff Cavins at EWTN to film a segment about the *CHNetwork* for the *Abundant Life Show*. This is scheduled to air in the fall. Each of us shared briefly our reasons for coming home to the Catholic Church, and then together we discussed the work of the *CHNetwork*. We are also scheduled to appear on *Mother Angelica Live* in December! Hopefully, these programs will not only get the word out about our work but also help develop the needed donation base to make this apostolate viable.

Obviously, funding becomes a bigger issue now that we have to feed our families through this apostolate, but God has always been more than generous. He has brought us safely through the treacherous transition from the Protestant pastorate into the Catholic Church, constantly providing opportunities both for ministry and for financial support. We believe deeply that Christ has called us into this apostolate, and we believe his promise with all our hearts: "I will never leave you nor forsake you."

I would ask you three things, besides your prayers:

1. **Tell others about the work of the *Coming Home Network International***, inviting them to become a member. There are three levels of membership, and therefore room for everyone. So invite anyone you might know—inquiring Protestant clergy or laity, fallen away or lax Catholics, or on-fire cradle Catholics—to adopt in prayer the work of the *CHNetwork*, and consider contributing to its work.

2. **Tell your parish priest about the *CHNetwork*** and then ask him if you could have an evening to promote the work and needs of the *CHNetwork*. One possibility would be to schedule an opportunity for you to speak on your own conversion to the Catholic Church, say some Sunday evening in the parish, and then take an offering especially for the Assistance Fund. All donations to the *CHNetwork* are tax-deductible.

3. **Please consider including the *CHNetwork* in your regular giving**. I've never been comfortable asking for donations, even back during the old stewardship sermon days. But if the *CHNetwork* is to have a future and particularly if it is going to be able to assist converts in the transition, I need to bite the bullet and ask.

Being full time with the *CHNetwork* allows Ken and me to:

1. Work with the bishops and other Church leaders to develop vocational opportunities for the many clergy converts with their diversity of skills and training.

2. Distribute financial assistance from our Assistance Fund to converts who desperately need help while they become settled in the Church.

3. Provide free tapes and books to all inquiring Protestant clergy or laity so they can have the necessary information to work through the myriad of hurdles along the way home.

4. Plan and facilitate regional retreats and gatherings.

5. Compile and edit the bimonthly *Coming Home Newsletter,* as well as other evangelistic literature.

6. Respond to the daily deluge of letters, e-mail, and phone calls, which up until now have piled up on my desk.

7. Follow-up on *CHNetwork* members who are at different places along the journey home, through letters, e-mail, phone calls and even visits if possible.

8. Manage the administration and financial aspects of this non-profit corporation.

9. Plan and implement fundraising activities.

10. Continue speaking in parishes and conferences on issues related to coming home to the Catholic Church.

Hopefully, Ken will be able to continue assisting in all these areas. Please let us know if you identify any potential donors we can contact.

Please keep us in your prayers, and if there is anything that the *CHNetwork* can do or should be doing to assist you in your journey home, please don't hesitate to contact us, by phone, mail or e-mail.

An Eye-opening Trend: Congregations Switching Denominations!

On the front cover of a recent issue of the *Wall Street Journal* (Friday, June 14, 1996) I came across an extremely interesting article entitled "Father Bell's Curve," by Calmetta Y. Coleman, a Staff Reporter.

The primary focus was on the conversion of Rev. Chuck Bell from being the pastor of a Vineyard Christian Fellowship Church to becoming Father Seraphim Bell, an Eastern Orthodox priest. Besides this strange transition in itself, what was particularly newsworthy was that after Rev. Bell announced to his congregation that "God had called him to a radically different brand of Christianity—Eastern Orthodoxy," he then proceeded to tell them that he believed that "God wanted them to join it, too."

The church went through a radical transformation. The once charismatic congregational more accustomed to Christian "rock music, public prophesying and speaking in tongues gave way to liturgical readings, lit candles and kissed paintings of the Virgin Mary." Great turmoil erupted, but nearly half of the congregation decided to follow their pastor out of charismatic fundamentalism into Eastern Orthodoxy.

In the rest of the article, the author widens her focus to illustrate that this is not a one-time but a reoccurring phenomenon in American Christianity. Listen to her analysis:

> *Throughout non-Catholic Christianity, churches are being born again, especially among independent churches. Even among some centralized denominations, the switch is occur-*

ring. There are Baptist churches becoming Presbyterian, Lutheran churches going charismatic, Pentecostal churches turning Episcopalian and so on. The number of denominational switches reaches well into the hundreds, and religious experts say the pace is accelerating.

The United Church of Christ, with 6,180 churches, reports that an average of 29 churches a year have left to join other groups or to become independent since it began keeping such records in 1993. The denomination even held a consultation in January to discuss the flight of its churches.

The Charismatic Episcopal Church, for one, has benefited from the trend. Since 1992, the young denomination, based in San Clemente, Calif., has grown to more than 100 churches from five. Most new comers are charismatic and Pentecostal churches looking for more structured practices, says Kenneth Tanner, a denomination spokesman.

Often, churches bolt because of a denomination's position on issues such as abortion or homosexuality. But increasingly, the precipitating event is a minister's revelation of belonging to the wrong church. In the past, such a minister would have quietly left his congregation to take up residence where he felt God had called him. But these days, he simply tells his church, "this is really not where we belong," says Lyle Schaller, a retired Methodist minister who has studied trends among denominations. That forces a congregation to choose between its denomination and its spiritual leader, and neither option is easy. Parishioners loyal to their beliefs must find a new congregation. They also face ostracism from members of their old congregation. After Kenneth Hoffmann retained the Lutheran faith that his Winter Springs, Fla., church had dropped, he found his old friends critical of him. To them, he says, "everything that was Lutheran was bad"—including him.

On the other hand, those who follow their minister into a new denomination must learn and accept a whole new set of rituals and beliefs. The moment that Chicago's Life Center Church of Universal Awareness joined the Pentecostal Church of God in Christ, Jesus was promoted from wise teacher and good man to Son of God—a troubling development for those

*who didn't believe it. When Lord of Life Lutheran Fellowship in
Winter Springs, Fla., ditched that denomination in favor of charismatic worship, the minister announced that any baptism performed on infants suddenly didn't count—prompting members
such as 91-year-old Marion Marx to be rebaptized.*

*In religions where property is church owned, such as Catholicism, a priest who tried switching flags could be sent packing. But the very quality that makes a number of Protestant denominations attractive to parishioners—a lack of central authority—can make these churches unstable. The minister can
become a papal figure, his whims unchecked by any higher authority and his hold over the congregation more powerful than
that of the denomination. "With the weakened role of denominational heritage, the minister gets elevated in terms of the kind of
influence he can have" says Wade Clark Roof, professor of religion and society at the University of California, Santa Barbara.*

*Another factor is that the beliefs of some of the faithful
have begun to change with the latest fashions. "People are now
choosing [religion] on the basis of current hopes and aspirations as opposed to inherited decisions from parents and grandparents," says William McKinney, dean of Hartford Seminary
in Connecticut.*

Most of us are probably unaware of this growing phenomenon,
which I believe actually points to a much larger, deeper phenomenon of which most of you who are converts are well aware. When
I was a Presbyterian pastor, my churches were generally made up
of lots of "ex-" everybody else: ex-Episcopalians, ex-Lutherans,
ex-Baptists, ex-Disciples of Christ, ex-Methodists, and, of course,
ex-Catholics. Individuals, couples and whole families who had
become dissatisfied with their present denominations or congregations went church hoping for a more acceptable church home. Inter-denominational transfers had become increasingly common. In
fact, we even used universally accepted forms specifically designed
to pass between churches to make sure that two or more churches
weren't carrying the same theological vagabonds on their rosters.

But what this article most clearly identifies is the growing phenomenon of not individual laymen, but pastors—educated, well-informed leaders—becoming dissatisfied and pulling their entire congregations with them to go denominational hoping.

This seems to point to a deeper reality that many of these pastors and their flocks may not see. I didn't see it during the first part of my journey towards the Catholic Church: the Protestant experiment is a failure. What they are doing is no different than what has been done over and over again for the past 500 years, if not from the beginning: the relentless search for the perfect church, without weeds and only wheat.

The primary charism of the *Coming Home Network International* is to help these brothers and sisters, who are dissatisfied and searching, to discover the riches and truth of the Catholic Church— by no means a perfect church (She has us, enough said)—and then truly come home.

Journeys Home

November - December 1996

Believe that You may Understand

"He who created all things from nothing
Would not remake his ruined creation without Mary.
For God begot the Son,
Through whom all things were made,
And Mary gave birth to Him
As the Savior of the world.
Without God's Son, nothing could exist;
Without Mary's Son, nothing could be redeemed."
St. Anselm, Archbishop of Canterbury, (1033-1109)

I find it interesting, if not down right humorous, that the day I finally get around to writing this column for the newsletter is the Feast of Mary's Immaculate Conception, the Catholic teaching which stands out as probably the most consistent bugaboo for Protestants considering the Catholic Church. A part of me, responding to those residual Protestant attitudes still haunting my subconscious, would like to leave this doctrine up on the "nice shelf," out of the normal day in, day out trampings of my Christian walk. I still feel that nagging voice, that demanding criteria: "Show it to me in Scripture!" But then the battle rages on with an immediate response: "Show me where in Scripture it says that I've got to show you in Scripture?!"

Actually I find another quote from St. Anselm very enlightening on this and many other subjects:

"I do not seek to understand that I may believe,
but I believe that I may understand:
for this I also believe,
that unless I believe I will not understand."

Isn't this true of all that we understand in our Christian faith? What little I truly understand about the Trinity or the divinity of Christ comes basically from my belief that the Holy Spirit can be trusted to lead the Church into all truth, and, therefore, interpret Scripture and Tradition correctly. Apart from this belief, we are left with a modern "Christianity" that includes Unitarianism or "Jesus only" fundamentalism, as well as modern forms of Arianism, Modalism, even polytheism.

What is truly amazing when we honestly consider God's choice of Mary is that we are faced with the reality that God's plan was dependent upon Mary's choice of God. In God's unfathomable wisdom, He chose to make His plan subject to the will of a young Palestinian peasant girl. The mystery we encounter here is summarized in the exchange between the angel and Mary:

> *"For with God nothing will be impossible."*
> *And Mary said, "Behold, I am the handmaid of the Lord;*
> *Let it be to me according to your word."*

These words are very important to those of you who are struggling in your journey home to the Catholic Church, particularly as you look to the future—as you wonder how you will not only support your family if you leave your ministry, but how you will be able to continue to serve the Lord in the Catholic Church. These words give you both a promise and a premise.

The promise is one we fully believe as Christians, but must be willing to act on: that all things are possible with God. He can do a whole lot more for us, and better than we can ever imagine. (Neither Kenneth Howell nor I dreamed when we left our pastorates that we would one day be sitting with Mother Angelica on her Live television program proclaiming the gospel to possibly 35 million viewers!)

The premise is that in Mary, God has given us a perfect example of how we are to respond to God's grace. All that she was and ever would be was a gift of God's grace, and her necessary response to receive all that He might give and accomplish through her was total trust and surrender. Her words, "Let it be to me according to thy word," are to be our unfettered answer to God's Call.

Now, even Mary had questions about how the impossible becomes possible, but when reminded that God is greater than any impossibility, she responded in the only way we must respond to God's infinite greatness: obedient surrender. It is only then that He can freely work in and through and for us.

As you approach the Christmas season, may Mary's words be like the hound of heaven, pursuing you, beckoning you to step out in faith, trusting the Holy Spirit as he calls you home.

"To Believe in Christ Means to Desire Unity; To Desire Unity Means to Desire the Church."

Simply stated, the Goal of the *Coming Home Network International* is to help reverse the deleterious effects of the Reformation! I realize this may seem a bit audacious and even to some a bit presumptuous but having spent the first forty years of my life fanning the flames of autonomy, I would like to spend the next forty, God willing, bringing healing.

Though the Catholic Church of the sixteenth century was surely in need of renewal, the methods of renewal initiated by the Reformers, which involved condemning and abandoning the Mother Church and her authority to start new ones of their own creation, have caused great and continuing disunity and confusion. Millions of men, women and children have been led out of the Church, away from the sacramental graces and the guidance of magisterial authority.

The devil thought he was destroying the Church by leading millions away, but God always "works all things for the good of those who love God and are called according to his purpose" (Romans 8.28). Those that left the Church continued to follow Christ with sincere hearts and, with particular devotion to the written Word of God, built churches and denominations and established standards of faith designed to lead their followers toward holiness and salvation. But even as thousands were being drawn away from the Church, millions more were being brought in by zealous evangelization, especially as a result of the apparitions of Our Lady of Guadalupe in Mexico City.

The fact is that, as is stated in the *Catechism of the Catholic Church,* quoting the Vatican II "Decree on Ecumenism":

> *The ruptures that wound the unity of Christ's Body—here we must distinguish heresy, apostasy, and schism—do not occur without human sin ... However, one cannot charge with the sin of the separation those who at present are born into these communities [that resulted from such separation] and in them are brought up in the faith of Christ, and the Catholic Church accepts them with respect and affection as brothers ... All who have been justified by faith in Baptism are incorporated into Christ; they therefore have a right to be called Christians, and with good reason are accepted as brothers in the Lord by the children of the Catholic Church.*
>
> *Furthermore, many elements of sanctification and of truth are found outside the visible confines of the Catholic Church: 'the written Word of God; the life of grace; faith, hope, and charity, with the other interior gifts of the Holy Spirit, as well as visible elements.' Christ's Spirit uses these Churches and ecclesial communities as means of salvation, whose power derives from the fullness of grace and truth that Christ has entrusted to the Catholic Church. All these blessings come from Christ and lead to him, and are in themselves calls to 'Catholic unity.'*
>
> *'Christ bestowed unity on his Church from the beginning. This unity, we believe, subsists in the Catholic Church as something she can never lose, and we hope that it will continue to increase until the end of time.' Christ always gives his Church the gift of unity, but the church must always pray and work to maintain, reinforce, and perfect the unity that Christ wills for her. This is why Jesus himself prayed at the hour of his Passion, and does not cease praying to his Father, for the unity of his disciples: 'that they may all be one. As you, Father, are in me and I am in you, may they also be one in us, ... so that the world may know that you have sent me.' The desire to recover the unity of all Christians is a gift of Christ and a call of the Holy Spirit.*

(Catechism, 817-820)

We in the *Coming Home Network International* see these words as our charge. We recognize that the work of unity is primarily a work of Jesus Christ, for as he said, "apart from me, you can do nothing." The *CHNetwork* desires only to be a channel of his grace, responding to those the Holy Spirit is calling to listen to the Catholic Church and come home.

For many, conversion requires great sacrifice, even repentance for active promotion of schism and heresy. But ultimately this requires of all who come the willingness to accept the same requirements Christ gave to the rich young man in Mark 10: "go, sell what you have, and give to the poor, and you will have treasure in heaven; and come, follow me." Therefore, the *Coming Home Network International* desires in prayer to help everyone and anyone to come home to the "One, Holy, Catholic and Apostolic Church."

Because of the different needs and concerns brought about by the journey home, we have established **three types of membership in the *CHNetwork***:

Primary Membership is for former clergy and their families who are somewhere along the journey into the Catholic Church. The needs of this group are particularly acute, requiring for many the loss of job, family, friends and vocation. As those whose transition often requires the most sacrifice, their testimonies are particularly encouraging to Catholics who have always had the Faith, but may have taken it for granted.

Secondary Membership is for laity of other traditions and their families, who also are somewhere along the journey. Though this group generally does not suffer the same sacrifices as clergy converts, yet these also may suffer the loss of friends and family, as well as the stress and confusion that comes from adopting new traditions and practices.

Tertiary, or Associate Membership, is for Catholic laity, priests, deacons, religious and bishops who support the *CHNetwork* with their prayers and generous contributions. The suc-

cess of the *CHNetwork* depends upon the encouragement
and support of this group.

Though the transition from separation into full communion can
literally only take moments, the full transition mentally and emotionally can take years, and involve many "dark nights of the soul."
Therefore, we strongly encourage members to gather in local fellowship groups for prayer and fellowship, for small group studies
of Scripture and Church tradition, and for reaching out with the
truth of the Catholic faith to friends and relatives outside the Church.

We believe this work of ours together is a grand and blessed
work, particularly at this time at the close of the millenium. Pope
John Paul II believes with great hope that the year 2000 will be a
blessed year of jubilee! As he so strongly states in his most recent
encyclical, *Ut Unum Sint* ...

> *The unity of all divided humanity is the will of God. For this
> reason he sent his Son, so that by dying and rising for us he
> might bestow on us the Spirit of love. On the eve of his sacrifice
> on the Cross, Jesus himself prayed to the Father for his dis-
> ciples and for all those who believe in him, that they might be
> one, a living communion. This is the basis not only of the duty,
> but also of the responsibility before God and his plan, which
> falls to those who through Baptism become members of the Body
> of Christ, a Body in which the fullness of reconciliation and com-
> munion must be made present. How is it possible to remain di-
> vided, if we have been "buried" through Baptism in the Lord's
> death, in the very act by which God, through the death of his
> Son, has broken down the walls of division? Division "openly
> contradicts the will of Christ, provides a stumbling block to the
> world, and inflicts damage on the most holy cause of proclaim-
> ing the Good News to every creature.*
>
> *The Lord of the Ages wisely and patiently follows out the
> plan of his grace on behalf of us sinners. In recent times he has
> begun to bestow more generously upon divided Christians re-
> morse over their divisions and a longing for unity. Everywhere,
> large numbers have felt the impulse of this grace, and among
> our separated brethren also there increases from day to day a*

movement, fostered by the grace of the Holy Spirit, for the resto-
ration of unity among all Christians ... This unity bestowed by
the Holy Spirit does not merely consist in the gathering of people
as a collection of individuals. It is a unity constituted by the
bonds of the profession of faith, the sacraments and hierarchi-
cal communion...

For the Catholic Church, then, the communion of Chris-
tians is none other than the manifestation in them of the grace
by which God makes them sharers in his own communion, which
is his eternal life ... To believe in Christ means to desire unity; to
desire unity means to desire the Church; to desire the Church
means to desire the communion of grace which corresponds to
the Father's plan from all eternity. Such is the meaning of Christ's
prayer: 'Ut Unum Sint.'

(Ut Unum Sint, 6-9)

To this end, under the maternal intercession of Mary, Mother
of the Redeemer, and the paternal care of St. Joseph, do we in the
Coming Home Network International dedicate our lives.

Journeys Home

Appendix A:
Pillar of Fire, Pillar of Truth[*]

The Catholic Church and God's Plan for You

Whether or not you are Catholic, you may have questions about the Catholic faith. You may have heard challenges to the Catholic Church's claim to be the interpreter and safeguard of the teachings of Jesus Christ.

Such challenges come from door-to-door missionaries who ask, "Are you saved?," from peer pressure that urges you to ignore the Church's teachings, from a secular culture that whispers "There is no God."

You can't deal with these challenges unless you understand the basics of the Catholic faith. This booklet introduces them to you.

In Catholicism you will find answers to life's most troubling questions: Why am I here? Who made me? What must I believe? How must I act? All these can be answered to your satisfaction, if only you will open yourself to God's grace, turn to the Church he established, and follow his plan for you (John 7:17).

---

[*] Included by permission: *Catholic Answers*, San Diego, 1993.

An Unbroken History

Jesus said his Church would be "the light of the world." He then noted that "a city set on a hill cannot be hid" (Matt. 5:14). This means his Church is a *visible* organization. It must have characteristics that clearly identify it and that distinguish it from other churches. Jesus promised, "I will build my Church and the gates of hell will not prevail against it" (Matt. 16:18). This means that his Church will never be destroyed and will never fall away from him. His Church will survive until his return.

Among the Christian churches, only the Catholic Church has existed since the time of Jesus. Every other Christian church is an offshoot of the Catholic Church. The Eastern Orthodox churches broke away from unity with the pope in 1054. The Protestant churches were established during the Reformation, which began in 1517. (Most of today's Protestant churches are actually offshoots of the original Protestant offshoots.)

Only the Catholic Church existed in the tenth century, in the fifth century, and in the first century, faithfully teaching the doctrines given by Christ to the apostles, omitting nothing. The line of popes can be traced back, in unbroken succession, to Peter himself. This is unequaled by any institution in history.

Even the oldest government is new compared to the papacy, and the churches that send out door-to-door missionaries are young compared to the Catholic Church. Many of these churches began as recently as the nineteenth or twentieth centuries. Some even began during your own lifetime. None of them can claim to be the Church Jesus established.

The Catholic Church has existed for nearly 2,000 years, despite constant opposition from the world. This is testimony to the Church's divine origin. It must be more than a merely human organization, especially considering that its human members—even some of its leaders—have been unwise, corrupt, or prone to heresy.

Any merely human organization with such members would have collapsed early on. The Catholic Church is today the most vigorous church in the world (and the largest, with a billion members: one sixth of the human race), and that is testimony not to the cleverness of the Church's leaders, but to the protection of the Holy Spirit.

Four Marks of the True Church

If we wish to locate the Church founded by Jesus, we need to locate the one that has the four chief marks or qualities of his Church. The Church we seek must be one, holy, catholic, and apostolic.

The Church Is One
(Rom. 12:5, 1 Cor. 10:17, 12:13, CCC* 813–822)

Jesus established only *one* Church, not a collection of differing churches (Lutheran, Baptist, Anglican, and so on). The Bible says the Church is the bride of Christ (Eph. 5:23–32). Jesus can have but *one* spouse, and his spouse is the Catholic Church.

His Church also teaches just one set of doctrines, which must be the same as those taught by the apostles (Jude 3). This is the unity of belief to which Scripture calls us (Phil. 1:27, 2:2).

Although some Catholics dissent from officially-taught doctrines, the Church's official teachers—the pope and the bishops united with him—have never changed any doctrine. Over the centuries, as doctrines are examined more fully, the Church comes to understand them more deeply (John 16:12–13), but it never understands them to mean the opposite of what they once meant.

The Church Is Holy
(Eph. 5:25–27, Rev. 19:7–8, CCC 823–829)

By his grace Jesus makes the Church holy, just as he is holy. This doesn't mean that each member is always holy. Jesus said there would be both good and bad members in the Church (John 6:70), and not all the members would go to heaven (Matt. 7:21–23).

But the Church itself is holy because it is the source of holiness and is the guardian of the special means of grace Jesus established, the sacraments (cf. Eph. 5:26).

The Church Is Catholic
(Matt. 28:19–20, Rev. 5:9–10, CCC 830–856)

Jesus' Church is called catholic ("universal" in Greek) because it is his gift to all people. He told his apostles to go throughout the world and make disciples of "all nations" (Matt. 28:19–20).

---

* *Catechism of the Catholic Church.*

For 2,000 years the Catholic Church has carried out this mission, preaching the good news that Christ died for all men and that he wants all of us to be members of his universal family (Gal. 3:28).

Nowadays the Catholic Church is found in every country of the world and is still sending out missionaries to "make disciples of all nations" (Matt. 28:19).

The Church Jesus established was known by its most common title, "the Catholic Church," at least as early as the year 107, when Ignatius of Antioch used that title to describe the one Church Jesus founded. The title apparently was old in Ignatius's time, which means it probably went all the way back to the time of the apostles.

The Church Is Apostolic
(Eph. 2:19–20, CCC 857–865)

The Church Jesus founded is apostolic because he appointed the apostles to be the first leaders of the Church, and their successors were to be its future leaders. The apostles were the first bishops, and, since the first century, there has been an unbroken line of Catholic bishops faithfully handing on what the apostles taught the first Christians in Scripture and oral Tradition (2 Tim. 2:2).

These beliefs include the bodily Resurrection of Jesus, the Real Presence of Jesus in the Eucharist, the sacrificial nature of the Mass, the forgiveness of sins through a priest, baptismal regeneration, the existence of purgatory, Mary's special role, and much more— even the doctrine of apostolic succession itself.

Early Christian writings prove the first Christians were thoroughly Catholic in belief and practice and looked to the successors of the apostles as their leaders. What these first Christians believed is still believed by the Catholic Church. No other Church can make that claim.

Pillar of Fire, Pillar of Truth

Man's ingenuity cannot account for this. The Church has remained one, holy, catholic, and apostolic—not through man's effort, but because God preserves the Church he established (Matt. 16:18, 28:20).

He guided the Israelites on their escape from Egypt by giving them a pillar of fire to light their way across the dark wilderness (Exod. 13:21). Today he guides us through his Catholic Church.

The Bible, sacred Tradition, and the writings of the earliest Christians testify that the Church teaches with Jesus' authority. In this age of countless competing religions, each clamoring for attention, one voice rises above the din: the Catholic Church, which the Bible calls "the pillar and foundation of truth" (1 Tim. 3:15).

Jesus assured the apostles and their successors, the popes and the bishops, "He who listens to you listens to me, and he who rejects you rejects me" (Luke 10:16). Jesus promised to guide his Church into all truth (John 16:12–13). We can have confidence that his Church teaches only the truth.

The Structure of the Church

Jesus chose the apostles to be the earthly leaders of the Church. He gave them his own authority to teach and to govern—not as dictators, but as loving pastors and fathers. That is why Catholics call their spiritual leaders "father." In doing so we follow Paul's example: "I became your father in Jesus Christ through the gospel" (1 Cor. 4:15).

The apostles, fulfilling Jesus' will, ordained bishops, priests, and deacons and thus handed on their apostolic ministry to them—the fullest degree of ordination to the bishops, lesser degrees to the priests and deacons.

The Pope and Bishops
(CCC 880–883)

Jesus gave Peter special authority among the apostles (John 21:15–17) and signified this by changing his name from Simon to Peter, which means "rock" (John 1:42). He said Peter was to be the rock on which he would build his Church (Matt. 16:18).

In Aramaic, the language Jesus spoke, Simon's new name was *Kepha* (which means a massive rock). Later this name was translated into Greek as *Petros* (John 1:42) and into English as Peter. Christ gave Peter alone the "keys of the kingdom" (Matt. 16:19) and promised that Peter's decisions would be binding in heaven. He also gave similar power to the other apostles (Matt. 18:18), but only Peter was given the keys, symbols of his authority to rule the Church on earth in Jesus' absence.

Christ, the Good Shepherd, called Peter to be the chief shepherd of his Church (John 21:15–17). He gave Peter the task of strengthening the other apostles in their faith, ensuring that they taught only what was true (Luke 22:31–32). Peter led the Church in proclaiming the gospel and making decisions (Acts 2:1– 41, 15:7–12).

Early Christian writings tell us that Peter's successors, the bishops of Rome (who from the earliest times have been called by the affectionate title of "pope," which means "papa"), continued to exercise Peter's ministry in the Church.

The pope is the successor to Peter as bishop of Rome. The world's other bishops are successors to the apostles in general.

How God Speaks to Us

As from the first, God speaks to his Church through the Bible and through sacred Tradition. To make sure we understand him, he guides the Church's teaching authority—the magisterium—so it always interprets the Bible and Tradition accurately. This is the gift of infallibility.

Like the three legs on a stool, the Bible, Tradition, and the magisterium are all necessary for the stability of the Church and to guarantee sound doctrine.

Sacred Tradition
(CCC 75–83)

Sacred Tradition should not be confused with mere traditions of men, which are more commonly called customs or disciplines. Jesus sometimes condemned customs or disciplines, but only if they were contrary to God's commands (Mark 7:8). He never condemned sacred Tradition, and he didn't even condemn all human tradition.

Sacred Tradition and the Bible are not different or competing revelations. They are two ways that the Church hands on the gospel. Apostolic teachings such as the Trinity, infant baptism, the inerrancy of the Bible, purgatory, and Mary's perpetual virginity have been most clearly taught through Tradition, although they are also implicitly present in (and not contrary to) the Bible. The Bible itself tells us to hold fast to Tradition, whether it comes to us in written or oral form (2 Thess. 2:15, 1 Cor. 11:2).

Sacred Tradition should not be confused with customs and disciplines, such as the rosary, priestly celibacy, and not eating meat on Fridays in Lent. These are good and helpful things, but they are not doctrines. Sacred Tradition preserves doctrines first taught by Jesus to the apostles and later passed down to us through the apostles' successors, the bishops.

Scripture
(CCC 101–141)

Scripture, by which we mean the Old and New Testaments, was inspired by God (2 Tim. 3:16). The Holy Spirit guided the biblical authors to write what he wanted them to write. Since God is the principal author of the Bible, and since God is truth itself (John 14:6) and cannot teach anything untrue, the Bible is free from all error in everything it asserts to be true.

Some Christians claim, "The Bible is all I need," but this notion is not taught in the Bible itself. In fact, the Bible teaches the contrary idea (2 Pet. 1:20–21, 3:15–16). The "Bible alone" theory was not believed by anyone in the early Church.

It is new, having arisen only in the 1500s during the Protestant Reformation. The theory is a "tradition of men" that nullifies the Word of God, distorts the true role of the Bible, and undermines the authority of the Church Jesus established (Mark 7:1–8).

Although popular with many "Bible Christian" churches, the "Bible alone" theory simply does not work in practice. Historical experience disproves it. Each year we see additional splintering among "Bible-believing" religions.

Today there are tens of thousands of competing denominations, each insisting its interpretation of the Bible is the correct one. The resulting divisions have caused untold confusion among millions of sincere but misled Christians.

Just open up the Yellow Pages of your telephone book and see how many different denominations are listed, each claiming to go by the "Bible alone," but no two of them agreeing on exactly what the Bible *means*.

We know this for sure: The Holy Spirit cannot be the author of this confusion (1 Cor. 14:33). God cannot lead people to contradictory beliefs because his truth is one. The conclusion? The "Bible alone" theory must be false.

The Magisterium
(CCC 85–87, 888–892)

Together the pope and the bishops form the teaching authority of the Church, which is called the magisterium (from the Latin for "teacher"). The magisterium, guided and protected from error by the Holy Spirit, gives us certainty in matters of doctrine. The Church is the custodian of the Bible and faithfully and accurately proclaims its message, a task which God has empowered it to do.

Keep in mind that the Church came before the New Testament, not the New Testament before the Church. Divinely-inspired members of the Church wrote the books of the New Testament, just as divinely-inspired writers had written the Old Testament, and the Church is guided by the Holy Spirit to guard and interpret the entire Bible, both Old and New Testaments.

Such an official interpreter is absolutely necessary if we are to understand the Bible properly. (We all know what the Constitution *says*, but we still need a Supreme Court to interpret what it *means*.)

The magisterium is infallible when it teaches officially because Jesus promised to send the Holy Spirit to guide the apostles and their successors "into all truth" (John 16:12–13).

How God Distributes His Gifts

Jesus promised he would not leave us orphans (John 14:18) but would send the Holy Spirit to guide and protect us (John 15:26).

He gave the sacraments to heal, feed, and strengthen us. The seven sacraments—baptism, the Eucharist, penance (also called reconciliation or confession), confirmation, holy orders, matrimony, and the anointing of the sick—are not just symbols. They are signs that actually convey God's grace and love.

The sacraments were foreshadowed in the Old Testament by things that did not actually convey grace but merely symbolized it (circumcision, for example, prefigured baptism, and the Passover meal prefigured the Eucharist. When Christ came, he did not do away with symbols of God's grace. He supernaturalized them, energizing them with grace. He made them more than symbols.

God constantly uses material things to show his love and power. After all, matter is not evil. When he created the physical universe, everything God created was "very good" (Gen. 1:31). He takes such delight in matter that he even dignified it through his own Incarnation (John 1:14).

During his earthly ministry Jesus healed, fed, and strengthened people through humble elements such as mud, water, bread, oil, and wine. He could have performed his miracles directly, but he preferred to use material things to bestow his grace.

In his first public miracle Jesus turned water into wine, at the request of his mother, Mary (John 2:1–11). He healed a blind man by rubbing mud on his eyes (John 9:1–7). He multiplied a few loaves and fish into a meal for thousands (John 6:5–13). He changed bread and wine into his own body and blood (Matt. 26:26– 28). Through the sacraments he continues to heal, feed, and strengthen us.

Baptism
(CCC 1213–1284)

Because of original sin, we are born without grace in our souls, so there is no way for us to have fellowship with God. Jesus became man to bring us into union with his Father. He said no one can enter the kingdom of God unless he is first born of "water and the Spirit" (John 3:5)—this refers to baptism.

Through baptism we are born again, but this time on a spiritual level instead of a physical level. We are washed in the bath of rebirth (Titus 3:5). We are baptized into Christ's death and therefore share in his Resurrection (Rom. 6:3–7).

Baptism cleanses us of sins and brings the Holy Spirit and his grace into our souls (Acts 2:38, 22:16). And the apostle Peter is perhaps the most blunt of all: "Baptism now saves you" (1 Pet. 3:21). Baptism is the gateway into the Church.

Penance
(CCC 1422–1498)

Sometimes on our journey toward the heavenly promised land we stumble and fall into sin. God is always ready to lift us up and to restore us to grace-filled fellowship with him. He does this through the sacrament of penance (which is also known as confession or reconciliation).

Jesus gave his apostles power and authority to reconcile us to the Father. They received Jesus' own power to forgive sins when he breathed on them and said, "Receive the Holy Spirit. Whose sins you forgive are forgiven them, and whose sins you retain are retained" (John 20:22–23).

Paul notes that "all this is from God, who has reconciled us to himself through Christ and given us the ministry of reconciliation... So, we are ambassadors for Christ, as if God were appealing through us" (2 Cor. 5:18–20). Through confession to a priest, God's minister, we have our sins forgiven, and we receive grace to help us resist future temptations.

The Eucharist
(CCC 1322–1419)

Once we become members of Christ's family, he does not let us go hungry, but feeds us with his own body and blood through the Eucharist. In the Old Testament, as they prepared for their journey in the wilderness, God commanded his people to sacrifice a lamb and sprinkle its blood on their doorposts, so the Angel of Death would pass by their homes. Then they ate the lamb to seal their covenant with God.

This lamb prefigured Jesus. He is the real "Lamb of God," who takes away the sins of the world (John 1:29). Through Jesus we enter into a New Covenant with God (Luke 22:20), who protects us from eternal death. God's Old Testament people ate the

Passover lamb. Now we must eat the Lamb that is the Eucharist. Jesus said, "Unless you eat my flesh and drink my blood you have no life within you" (John 6:53).

At the Last Supper he took bread and wine and said, "Take and eat. This is my body ... This is my blood which will be shed for you" (Mark 14:22–24). In this way Jesus instituted the sacrament of the Eucharist, the sacrificial meal Catholics consume at each Mass.

The Catholic Church teaches that the sacrifice of Christ on the cross occurred "once for all"; it cannot be repeated (Heb. 9:28). Christ does not "die again" during Mass, but the very same sacrifice that occurred on Calvary is made present on the altar. That's why the Mass is not "another" sacrifice, but a participation in the same, once-for-all sacrifice of Christ on the cross.

Paul reminds us that the bread and the wine really become, by a miracle of God's grace, the actual body and blood of Jesus: "Anyone who eats and drinks without recognizing the body of the Lord eats and drinks judgment on himself" (1 Cor. 11:27–29).

After the consecration of the bread and wine, no bread or wine remains on the altar. Only Jesus himself, under the appearance of bread and wine, remains.

Confirmation
(CCC 1285–1321)

God strengthens our souls in another way, through the sacrament of confirmation. Even though Jesus' disciples received grace before his Resurrection, on Pentecost the Holy Spirit came to strengthen them with new graces for the difficult work ahead.

They went out and preached the gospel fearlessly and carried out the mission Christ had given them. Later, they laid hands on others to strengthen them as well (Acts 8:14–17). Through confirmation you too are strengthened to meet the spiritual challenges in your life.

Matrimony
(CCC 1601–1666)

Most people are called to the married life. Through the sacrament of matrimony God gives special graces to help married couples with life's difficulties, especially to help them raise their children as loving followers of Christ.

Marriage involves three parties: the bride, the groom, and God. When two Christians receive the sacrament of matrimony, God is with them, witnessing and blessing their marriage covenant. A sacramental marriage is permanent; only death can break it (Mark 10:1–12, Rom. 7:2–3, 1 Cor. 7:10–11). This holy union is a living symbol of the unbreakable relationship between Christ and his Church (Eph. 5:21–33).

Holy Orders
(CCC 1536–1600)

Others are called to share specially in Christ's priesthood. In the Old Covenant, even though Israel was a kingdom of priests (Exod. 19:6), the Lord called certain men to a special priestly ministry (Exod. 19: 22). In the New Covenant, even though Christians are a kingdom of priests (1 Pet. 2:9), Jesus calls certain men to a special priestly ministry (Rom. 15:15–16).

This sacrament is called holy orders. Through it priests are ordained and thus empowered to serve the Church (2 Tim. 1:6–7) as pastors, teachers, and spiritual fathers who heal, feed, and strengthen God's people—most importantly through preaching and the administration of the sacraments.

Anointing of the Sick
(CCC 1499–1532)

Priests care for us when we are physically ill. They do this through the sacrament known as the anointing of the sick. The Bible instructs us, "Is anyone among you suffering? He should pray... Is any one among you sick? He should summon the presbyters [priests] of the Church, and they should pray over him and anoint him with oil in the name of the Lord, and the prayer of faith will save the sick person, and the Lord will raise him up. If he has committed any sins, he will be forgiven" (Jas. 5:14–15). Anointing of the sick not only helps us endure illness, but it cleanses our souls and helps us prepare to meet God.

Talking with God and His Saints

One of the most important activities for a Catholic is prayer. Without it there can be no true spiritual life. Through personal prayer and the communal prayer of the Church, especially the Mass, we worship and praise God, we express sorrow for our sins, and we intercede on behalf of others (1 Tim. 2:1–4). Through prayer we grow in our relationship with Christ and with members of God's family (CCC 2663–2696).

This family includes all members of the Church, whether on earth, in heaven, or in purgatory. Since Jesus has only one body, and since death has no power to separate us from Christ (Rom. 8:3–8), Christians who are in heaven or who, before entering heaven, are being purified in purgatory by God's love (1 Cor. 3:12–15) are still part of the Body of Christ (CCC 962).

Jesus said the second greatest commandment is to "love your neighbor as yourself" (Matt. 22:39). Those in heaven love us more intensely than they ever could have loved us while on earth. They pray for us constantly (Rev. 5:8), and their prayers are powerful (Jas. 5:16, CCC 956, 2683, 2692).

Our prayers to the saints in heaven, asking for their prayers for us, and their intercession with the Father do not undermine Christ's role as sole Mediator (1 Tim. 2:5). In asking saints in heaven to pray for us we follow Paul's instructions: "I urge that supplications, prayers, intercessions, and thanksgivings be made for everyone," for "this is good and pleasing to God our Savior" (1 Tim. 2:1–4).

All members of the Body of Christ are called to help one another through prayer (CCC 2647). Mary's prayers are especially effective on our behalf because of her relationship with her Son (John 2:1–11).

God gave Mary a special role (CCC 490–511, 963–975). He saved her from all sin (Luke 1:28, 47), made her uniquely blessed among all women (Luke 1:42), and made her a model for all Christians (Luke 1:48). At the end of her life he took her, body and soul, into heaven—an image of our own resurrection at the end of the world (Rev. 12:1–2).

What is the Purpose of Life?

Old catechisms asked, "Why did God make you?" The answer: "God made me to know him, to love him, and to serve him in this world and to be happy with him forever in the next." Here, in just 26 words, is the whole reason for our existence. Jesus answered the question even more briefly: "I came so that [you] might have life and have it more abundantly" (John 10:10).

God's plan for you is simple. Your loving Father wants to give you all good things—especially eternal life. Jesus died on the cross to save us all from sin and the eternal separation from God that sin causes (CCC 599–623). When he saves us, he makes us part of his Body, which is the Church (1 Cor. 12:27–30). We thus become united with him and with Christians everywhere (on earth, in heaven, in purgatory).

What You Must Do to Be Saved

Best of all, the promise of eternal life is a gift, freely offered to us by God (CCC 1727). Our initial forgiveness and justification are not things we "earn" (CCC 2010). Jesus is the mediator who bridged the gap of sin that separates us from God (1 Tim. 2:5); he bridged it by dying for us. He has chosen to make us partners in the plan of salvation (1 Cor. 3:9).

The Catholic Church teaches what the apostles taught and what the Bible teaches: We are saved by grace alone, but not by faith alone (which is what "Bible Christians" teach; see Jas. 2:24).

When we come to God and are justified (that is, enter a right relationship with God), nothing preceding justification, whether faith or good works, *earns* grace. But then God plants his love in our hearts, and we should live out our faith by doing acts of love (Gal. 6:2).

Even though only God's grace enables us to love others, these acts of love please him, and he promises to reward them with eternal life (Rom. 2:6–7, Gal. 6:6–10). Thus good works are meritorious. When we first come to God in faith, we have nothing in our hands to offer him. Then he gives us grace to obey his commandments in love, and he rewards us with salvation when we offer these acts of love back to him (Rom. 2:6–11, Gal. 6:6–10, Matt. 25:34–40).

Jesus said it is not enough to have faith in him; we also must obey his commandments. "Why do you call me 'Lord, Lord,' but do not do the things I command?" (Luke 6:46, Matt. 7:21–23, 19:16–21).

We do not "earn" our salvation through good works (Eph. 2:8–9, Rom. 9:16), but our faith in Christ puts us in a special grace-filled relationship with God so that our obedience and love, combined with our faith, will be rewarded with eternal life (Rom. 2:7, Gal. 6:8–9).

Paul said, "God is the one who, for his good purpose, works in you both to desire and to work" (Phil. 2:13). John explained that "the way we may be sure that we know him is to keep his commandments. Whoever says, 'I know him,' but does not keep his commandments is a liar, and the truth is not in him" (1 John 2:3–4, 3:19–24, 5:3–4).

Since no gift can be forced on the recipient—gifts always can be rejected—even after we become justified, we can throw away the gift of salvation. We throw it away through grave (mortal) sin (John 15:5–6, Rom. 11:22–23, 1 Cor. 15:1–2; CCC 1854–1863). Paul tells us, "The wages of sin is death" (Rom. 6:23).

Read his letters and see how often Paul warned Christians against sin! He would not have felt compelled to do so if their sins could not exclude them from heaven (see, for example, 1 Cor. 6:9–10, Gal. 5:19–21).

Paul reminded the Christians in Rome that God "will repay everyone according to his works: eternal life for those who seek glory, honor, and immortality through perseverance in good works, but wrath and fury to those who selfishly disobey the truth and obey wickedness" (Rom. 2:6–8).

Sins are nothing but evil works (CCC 1849–1850). We can avoid sins by habitually performing good works. Every saint has known that the best way to keep free from sins is to embrace regular prayer, the sacraments (the Eucharist first of all), and charitable acts.

Are You Guaranteed Heaven?

Some people promote an especially attractive idea: All true Christians, regardless of how they live, have an absolute assurance of salvation, once they accept Jesus into their hearts as "their personal Lord and Savior." The problem is that this belief is contrary to the Bible and constant Christian teaching.

Keep in mind what Paul told the Christians of his day: "If we have died with him [in baptism; see Rom. 6:3–4] we shall also live with him; if we persevere we shall also reign with him" (2 Tim. 2:11–12).

If we do *not* persevere, we shall *not* reign with him. In other words, Christians can forfeit heaven (CCC 1861).

The Bible makes it clear that Christians have a moral assurance of salvation (God will be true to his word and will grant salvation to those who have faith in Christ and are obedient to him [1 John 3:19–24]), but the Bible does not teach that Christians have a guarantee of heaven. There can be no absolute assurance of salvation. Writing to Christians, Paul said, "See, then, the kindness and severity of God: severity toward those who fell, but God's kindness to you, provided you remain in his kindness, otherwise you too will be cut off" (Rom. 11:22–23; Matt. 18:21–35, 1 Cor. 15:1–2, 2 Pet. 2:20–21).

Note that Paul includes an important condition: "provided you remain in his kindness." He is saying that Christians can lose their salvation by throwing it away. He warns, "Whoever thinks he is standing secure should take care not to fall" (1 Cor. 10:11–12).

If you are Catholic and someone asks you if you have been "saved," you should say, "I am redeemed by the blood of Christ, I trust in him alone for my salvation, and, as the Bible teaches, I am 'working out my salvation in fear and trembling' (Phil. 2:12), knowing that it is God's gift of grace that is working in me."

The Wave of the Future

All the alternatives to Catholicism are showing themselves to be inadequate: the worn-out secularism that is everywhere around us and that no one any longer finds satisfying, the odd cults and movements that offer temporary community but no permanent home, even the other, incomplete brands of Christianity. As our tired world becomes ever more desperate, people are turning to the one alternative they never really had considered: the Catholic Church. They are coming upon truth in the last place they expected to find it.

Never Popular, Always Attractive

How can this be? Why are so many people seriously looking at the Catholic Church for the first time? Something is pulling them toward it. That something is truth.

This much we know: They are not considering the claims of the Church out of a desire to win public favor. Catholicism, at least nowadays, is never popular. You cannot win a popularity contest by being a faithful Catholic. Our fallen world rewards the clever, not the good. If a Catholic is praised, it is for the worldly skills he demonstrates, not for his Christian virtues.

Although people try to avoid the hard doctrinal and moral truths the Catholic Church offers them (because hard truths demand that lives be changed), they nevertheless are attracted to the Church. When they listen to the pope and the bishops in union with him, they hear words with the ring of truth—even if they find that truth hard to live by.

When they contemplate the history of the Catholic Church and the lives of its saints, they realize there must be something special, maybe something supernatural, about an institution that can produce holy people such as St. Augustine, St. Thomas Aquinas, and Mother Teresa.

When they step off a busy street and into the aisles of an apparently empty Catholic church, they sense not a complete emptiness, but a presence. They sense that *Someone* resides inside, waiting to comfort them.

They realize that the persistent opposition that confronts the Catholic Church—whether from non-believers or "Bible Christians" or even from people who insist on calling themselves Catholics—is a sign of the Church's divine origin (John 15:18–21). And they come to suspect that the Catholic Church, of all things, is the wave of the future.

Incomplete Christianity Is Not Enough

Over the last few decades many Catholics have left the Church, many dropping out of religion entirely, many joining other churches. But the traffic has not been in only one direction.

The traffic toward Rome has increased rapidly. Today we are seeing more than a hundred and fifty thousand converts enter the Catholic Church each year in the United States, and in some other places, like the continent of Africa, there are more than a million converts to the Catholic faith each year. People of no religion, lapsed or inactive Catholics, and members of other Christian churches are "coming home to Rome."

They are attracted to the Church for a variety of reasons, but the chief reason they convert is the chief reason *you* should be Catholic: The solid truth of the Catholic faith.

Our separated brethren hold much Christian truth, but not all of it. We might compare their religion to a stained glass window in which some of the original panes were lost and have been replaced by opaque glass: Something that was present at the beginning is now gone, and something that does not fit has been inserted to fill up the empty space. The unity of the original window has been marred.

When, centuries ago, they split away from the Catholic Church, the theological ancestors of these Christians eliminated some authentic beliefs and added new ones of their own making. The forms of Christianity they established are really incomplete Christianity.

Only the Catholic Church was founded by Jesus, and only it has been able to preserve all Christian truth without any error— and great numbers of people are coming to see this.

Your Tasks as a Catholic

Your tasks as a Catholic, no matter what your age, are three:

Know your Catholic faith. You cannot live your faith if you do not know it, and you cannot share with others what you do not first make your own (CCC 429). Learning your Catholic faith takes some effort, but it is effort well spent because the study is, quite literally, infinitely rewarding.

Live your Catholic faith. Your Catholic faith is a public thing. It is not meant to be left behind when you leave home (CCC 2472). But be forewarned: Being a public Catholic involves risk and loss. You will find some doors closed to you. You will lose some friends. You will be considered an outsider. But, as a consolation, remember our Lord's words to the persecuted: "Rejoice and be glad, for your reward is great in heaven" (Matt. 5:12).

Spread your Catholic faith. Jesus Christ wants us to bring the whole world into captivity to the truth, and the truth is Jesus himself, who is "the way, and the truth, and the life" (John 14:6). Spreading the faith is a task not only for bishops, priests, and religious—it is a task for all Catholics (CCC 905).

Just before his Ascension, our Lord told his apostles, "Go, therefore, and make disciples of all nations, baptizing them in the name of the Father, and of the Son, and of the Holy Spirit, teaching them to observe all that I have commanded you" (Matt. 28:19–20).

If we want to observe all that Jesus commanded, if we want to believe all he taught, we must follow him through his Church. This is our great challenge—and our great privilege.

Journeys Home

Appendix B
Resources for the Journey Home

The following list of books is provided to help those on the journey understand more clearly the various dogmas, practices and customs of the Catholic Church. The sad reality is that too few Protestants have actually read books written by Catholics about the Catholic Church. They have relied too often on books written by people who have only seen the Church from the outside or who have left the Church sometimes with great bitterness and anger. But is this reliable? If you were a Methodist wanting Catholics to understand the basics of the Methodist faith, wouldn't you want them to read books written by sincere Methodists? For this reason we present the following list of Catholic books produced by sincere Catholics who love the Church and love the Lord who established Her.

This is in no way a comprehensive list. Rather it represents our personal choices of books that we and others in the *Coming Home Network International* have found particularly helpful. The two main criteria for these choices were: 1) faithfulness to the historic magisterial teachings of the Catholic Church and 2) ease of understanding.

Apologetics

Nevins, Albert J. *Answering A fundamentalist.* (Huntington: Our Sunday Visitor, 1990). Each of the sixteen chapters focuses on dispelling common fundamentalist misunderstandings about the Catholic Faith through logic and reasoning rooted in Scripture and Apostolic Tradition.

Keating, Karl. *Catholicism and fundamentalism* (San Francisco: Ignatius Press, 1988). This book, which very effectively refutes the common fundamentalist misconceptions of and attacks on the Catholic Church, has served as the initial stepping stone for many modern converts.

Apostolic Succession

Kocik, Thomas M. *Apostolic Succession in an Ecumenical Context* (New York, Alba House, 1996). A very thorough and enjoyable study of the historical roots and present implications of Apostolic Succession.

Canon of Scripture

Short treatments on the Canon can be found in some of the stories in *Surprised by Truth* (Patrick Madrid, ed.) (See under Testimonies).

Catholicism: Basic Stuff

Foy, Felician A. and Avato, Rose M., eds. *Our Sunday Visitor's Catholic Almanac* (Huntington: Our Sunday Visitor, 1997) Published yearly, this is a must reference book for your desk. Probably the most complete one-volume source of facts and information on the Catholic Church.

Stravinskas, Peter M.J. *The Catholic Encyclopedia* (Huntington: Our Sunday Visitor, 1995) A thorough one-volume compendium of everything Catholic.

Catholicism: Selected Official Church Documents

Catechism of the Catholic Church. (Rome: Libreria Editrice Vaticana, 1994). This is the first universal catechism since the Council of Trent in the sixteenth century. This is the standard source for learning dogma for the post-Vatican II Catholic. Everyone should have one at home.

The Companion to the Catechism of the Catholic Church. (San Francisco, Ignatius Press, 1994). A convenient compendium of all the texts referred to in the footnotes of the new Catechism.

Denzinger, Heinrich. *The Sources of Catholic Dogma* A translation by Roy J. Deferrari of the 30th ed. of Denzinger's *Enchiridion Symbolorum.* (New York: B. Herder Book Co. 1957). The standard source of official documents used by Catholic theologians. Difficult to obtain today but can sometimes be located in libraries or used book stores.

Flannery, Austin O.P, ed *Vatican II*, 2 volumes (Northport: Costello Publishing Co. 1987). The official documents of the Second Vatican Council and many other magisterial pronouncements.

Neuner, Josef, and Roos, Heinrich. *The Teaching of the Catholic Church* (New York: Alba House, 1967) An excellent selection of Church documents arranged topically.

The following Encyclical letters by Pope John Paul II are extremely important for understanding the essential issues facing the modern Church.

Dominum et Vivificantem: On The Holy Spirit in the Life of the Church and the World (Boston: St Paul Books and Media, 1986).

Redemptoris Mater: On the Blessed Virgin Mary in the life of the Pilgrim Church (Boston: St Paul Books and Media, 1987).

Christifideles Laici: The Lay Members of Christ's Faithful People (Boston: St Paul Books and Media, 1988).

*Veritatis Splendor: The Splendor of Truth (*Boston: St Paul Books and Media, 1993).

Terio Millennio Adveniente: On The Coming of the Third Millennium (Boston: St Paul Books and Media, 1994).

Ut Unum Sint: On Commitment to Ecumenism (Boston: St Paul Books and Media, 1995).

Catholicism: Surveys of Church Teachings

*(Many of the specific topics in this resource
list are treated in these surveys.)*

Adam, Karl. *The Spirit of Catholicism* (Steubenville: Franciscan University Press, 1996 edition) A classic study of the essence of Catholicism that is well worth reading.

Baker, Fr. Kenneth. *Fundamentals of Catholicism,* 3 vols. (San Francisco: Ignatius Press, 1985) A very thorough discussion of all the major teachings of the Catholic Church in a very readable and conversational style.

De Lubac, Henri. *Catholicism: Christ and the Common Destiny of Man* (San Francisco: Ignatius Press, 1988) This book and the following one represent classic Catholic teaching by an eminent French Jesuit who is one of the premier theologians of the twentieth century. Challenging material but well worth the effort.

De Lubac, Henri. *The Splendor of the Church* (San Francisco: Ignatius Press, 1988) Like the previous volume, this book is richly grounded in the Church Fathers.

Gibbons, James (Cardinal). *The Faith of Our Fathers* (Rockford: Tan Books & Publishers, 1980) A classic study first published in 1876 that reads as freshly as if it were written yesterday. Cardinal Gibbons was one of America's greatest bishops.

Howard, Thomas. *On Being Catholic* (San Francisco: Ignatius Press, 1997) In this very unique book, Dr. Howard gives lay meditations on Catholic teaching and practice, opening up in practical and simple terms the richness at work in virtually every detail of Catholic prayer, piety, liturgy and experience.

Kreeft, Peter. *Fundamentals of the Faith* (San Francisco: Ignatius Press, 1988) In this very helpful book by this prolific convert to the Catholic faith Dr. Kreeft considers all the fundamental elements of Christianity and Catholicism, explaining, defending, and showing their relevance to our life and the world's yearnings.

Newman, John Henry Cardinal. *An Essay On The Development of Doctrine* (Notre Dame: University of Notre Dame Press, 1986). Newman's classic study in which he originally set out to prove that the Anglican Church was the "via media" or middle way between the Catholic Church and Protestantism, but in the process became convinced that only in the Catholic Church is found the fullness of the deposit of faith as delivered by Jesus to his apostles. This book has proved a great source of inspiration and conviction for many a convert.

Ott, Ludwig. *The Fundamentals of Catholic Dogma* (Rockford: Tan Books & Publishing, 1960 4th ed). A translation of a pre-Vatican II theology that was standard in the German-speaking Church. Pithy but an excellent reference manual.

Schreck, Alan. *Basics of the Faith: A Catholic Catechism* (Ann Arbor: Servant Books, 1987) A highly readable guide to the basic teachings of the Catholic Church.

Schreck, Alan. *Catholic and Christian: An Explanation of Commonly Misunderstood Catholic Beliefs.* (Ann Arbor: Servant Books, 1984). An extremely well written presentation of all the basic Catholic beliefs that are so often misunderstood.

Schreck, Alan. *Your Catholic Faith* (Ann Arbor: Servant Books, 1989) A concise, question-and-answer Catechism that is particularly helpful for parents trying to teach their children the basics.

Sheed, Frank. *Theology and Sanity.* (San Francisco: Ignatius Press, 1947, 1978). One of Sheed's most popular books, this is the ideal volume for helping the layman to take a more active role in the Church by showing him the practical aspects of theology and the role it has in the life of Christian believers.

Trese, Leo. *The Faith Explained* (Manila: Sinag-Tala, 1995) A concise and straightforward account of Catholic teachings.

Wuerl, Bishop Donald W.; Lawler, Ronald; Lawler, Thomas Comerford, eds. *The Teaching of Christ: A Catholic Catechism for Adults* (Huntington: Our Sunday Visitor, 1976, 1983, & 1991) A cooperative work of a large number of faithful Catholic scholars, this is more than a catechism. This invaluable tool is a precise and clear presentation of a complete vision of Catholic faith and life.

Celibacy of the Clergy

Cochini, Christian. *Apostolic Origins of Priestly Celibacy.* Translated by Nelly Marans. (San Francisco: Ignatius Press, 1990) The definitive scholarly examination of the topic of clerical celibacy in the first seven centuries of the Church's history.

Church Fathers (Selections of Texts)

Bettenson, Henry, ed. *The Early Christian Fathers* (New York: Oxford University Press, 1986 8th impression)

Bettenson, Henry, ed. *The Later Christian Fathers* (New York: Oxford University Press, 1970) This and the preceding volume are chronologically arranged with a topical index in each volume.

Jurgens, William. *The Faith of the Early Fathers.* 3 vols. (Collegeville: The Liturgical Press, 1970) A rich source of quotations from the Fathers that is enhanced by a systematic doctrinal index at the end of each volume.

Russell, Claire. *Glimpses of the Church Fathers* (London: Scepter Press, 1994) A very thorough and handy one-volume selection of the writings of the Fathers of the Church arranged chronologically and topically.

Church History (Catholic historians)

Belloc, Hilaire. (Rockford: TAN Books and Publishers, Inc., 1992) Belloc is a forgotten gem of English literature. A personal friend of Chesterton, Belloc was at one time considered the rising star of English writers, but as his writings became more candid defenses of the Catholic Church, he became less and less popular until today he is almost forgotten. However, I have found every one of his books a powerful correction for the revisionist histories so many of us received not only in our Protestant seminaries but in American public schools. The following books reprinted by TAN are all excellent reads giving the Catholic perspective on particularly the English Reformation:

Europe and the Faith
The Crusades
How the Reformation Happened
Characters of the Reformation
The Great Heresies
Survivals and New Arrivals

Bokenkotter, Thomas, *A Concise History of the Catholic Church* (New York: Image Books, 1979) A short but insightful history of the Catholic Church from the earliest times to the twentieth century.

Laux, Fr. John. *Church History* (Rockford: TAN Books, and Publishers, Inc., 1989 ed.) A thorough and thick one-volume classic presentation of the history of the Catholic Church written expressly for students and for adults.

Marty, Martin E. *A Short History of American Catholicism* (Tyler Texas: Thomas More Publishing, 1995)

Maynard, Theodore. *The Story of American Catholicism* (New York: The Macmillan Company, 1942). An out of print gem but well worth searching for. Essentially a retelling of American history filling in the many Catholic gaps left out by historical revisionists.

Schreck, Alan. *The Compact History of the Catholic Church* (Ann Arbor: Servant Books, 1987). A lively and readable intoduction to the life of the Church throughout the ages.

The Eucharist

Gaudoin-Parker, Michael. *The Real Presence Through the Ages* (New York: Alba House Press, 1993) Selections from Church Documents, from the Early Christian centuries to the present with informative introductions.

O'Connor, James. *The Hidden Manna A Theology of the Eucharist* (San Francisco: Ignatius Press, 1988) A must-read in-depth presentation and commentary on substantial excerpts from the major sources of the Church's Tradition, focusing on the real Presence, extending all the way back to apostolic times.

Shea, Mark P. *This Is My body: An Evangelical Discovers The Real Presence* (Huntington, IL: Our Sunday Visitor, 1992)

Justification

Decree on Justification Council of Trent.

Sungenis, Robert. *Not by Faith Alone - Biblical Study of the Catholic Doctrine of Justification* (Santa Barbara: Queenship Publishing Co, 1997). An excellent, thorough presentation of all the issues involved in and surrounding the justification debate.

Liturgy

Howard, Thomas. *Evangelical Is Not Enough* (San Francisco: Ignatius Press, 1984). A persuasive account by a former evangelical of the liturgical riches of ancient catholic worship.

Jungman, Josef A. *The Early Liturgy: To The Time of Gregory the Great.* Translated by Francis A. Brunner. (Notra Dame: University of Notre Dame Press, 1959)

Stravinskas, Peter M.J. *The Bible and the Mass* (Ann Arbor: Servant Publications, 1989)

Mary and the Saints

Breen, Sr. Eileen. *Mary the Second Eve: Selections from the Writings of John Henry Newman* (Tan Publishers, 1982)

Madrid, Patrick. *Any Friend of God's Is a Friend of Mine A Biblical and Historical Explanation of the Catholic Doctrine of the Commuion of the Saints* (San Diego: Basilica Press, 1996) A short but lucid explanation of how Catholics and Protestants differ in their understanding of the communion of the saints.

Miravalle, Mark I. *An Introduction to Mary* (Ann Arbor: Servant Books, 1990). This book was most helpful in clearing up my own misconceptions about the Catholic Church's teachings on Mary.

Miravalle, Mark I, *Mary Coredemptrix, Mediatrix and Advocate* (Santa Barbara: Queenship Publishing Co, 1993). Miravalle is one the world's leading Marian scholars who teaches at the Franciscan University in Steubenville. This and the next two books are very important for understanding Mary's place in salvation history.

Miravalle, Mark I., ed. *Mary Coredemptrix, Mediatrix and Advocate: Theological Foundations Towards a Papal Definition* (Santa Barbara: Queenship Publishing Co, 1995).

Miravalle, Mark I., ed. *Mary Coredemptrix, Mediatrix and Advocate: Theological Foundations II Papal, Pneumatological, Ecumenical* (Santa Barbara: Queenship Publishing Co, 1996).

Moral Theology

May, William E. *An Introduction to Moral Theology* (Huntington: Our Sunday Visitor, 1994 revised edition).

Papacy

Butler, Scott; Dahlgren, Norman; and Hess, David. *Jesus, Peter & the Keys: A Scriptural Handbook on the Papacy* (Santa Barbara: Queenship Publishing Co, 1996) An extensive collection of exegetical and historical sources that bear on the Petrine doctrine.

This book contains most of the important data which any view of the Papacy must explain.

Jaki, Stanley L. *And On This Rock* 2nd ed. (Manassas,: Trinity Communications, 1987) Fr. Jaki examines puts these words of Christ into their full biblical perspective and geographical context, offering the reader a novel insight into the primacy of Peter.

Jaki, Stanley L. *The Keys of the Kingdom* (Chicago: Franciscan Herald Press, 1986) Here Fr. Jaki gives a very thorough analysis of historical, biblical, patristic and medieval texts on the keys of the kingdom.

Morrissey, Gerard. *Defending the Papacy* (Front Royal: Crossroads Books, 1984)

Prayer and the Rosary

Belmonte, Charles and Socias, James, eds. *Handbook of Prayers* (Princeton: Scepter Press, 1992) A very helpful compilation of Catholic prayers, devotions and blessings.

Chautard, Dom Jean-Baptiste. *The Soul of the Apostolate* (Rockforf: TAN Books and Publishers, reprint of 1946 edition). A powerful, life-changing book that was the bed side reading of many popes. This classic underscores the importance of the inner life of prayer as the foundations for all acts of service.

Guardini, Romano. *The Art of Praying* (Manchester, NH: Sophia Institute Press, 1994 ed). A reprint of a classic practical presentation of the nuts and bolts of Catholic Prayer.

Guardini, Romano. *The Rosary of Our Lady* (Manchester, NH: Sophia Institute Press, 1994 ed). A spirit-filled explanation of the Rosary that will lead you to deeper experience of grace. Probably best read after learning to pray the Rosary.

Scanlan, Michael. *Rosary Companion* (Steubenville: Franciscan University Press, 1993) A simple, very practical aid to understanding the scriptural background to the Rosary.

A free tape may be obtained from the Mary Foundation which teaches you how to pray the Rosary. You can access their webpage at: <http://www.catholicity.com>

The Reformation

Adam, Karl. Translated by Cecily Hastings. *The Roots of the Reformation.* (New York: Sheed & Ward, 1951). An unbelievably powerful 94-page candid summary of the issues that led to the Reformation and their implications for today.

Belloc, Hilaire. *How the Reformation Happened,* (Rockford: TAN Books and Publishers, Inc., 1992). A very enjoyable and eye-opening presentation of a Catholic perspective on the English Reformation.

Daniel-Rops, Henri. Translated by Audrey Butler. *The Catholic Reformation*, 2 vols. (New York: Image Books, 1963).

Daniel-Rops, Henri. *The Protestant Reformation,* 2 vols. (New York: Image Books, 1963). A clasic retelling of all the issues, people and events of the Reformation period.

Sacraments

Stravinskas, Peter M.J. *Understanding the Sacraments* (Ann Arbor: Servant Publications, 1984). The single shortest and best study guide on all seven sacraments.

Wuerl, Donald. *The Church and Her Sacraments* (Huntington: Our Sunday Visitor, 1990) A very brief but lucid explanation by the Bishop of Pittsburgh.

Sacramentals, Customs and Traditions

Dues, Greg. *Catholic Customs and Traditions: A Popular Guide* (Mystic: Twenty-Third Publications, 1990) A simple, clear, concise presentation of common Catholic customs.

Richter, Klemens. *The Meaning of the Sacramental Symbols* Translated by Linda M. Maloney (Collegeville: The Liturgical Press, 1990) A comprehensive examination of the symbols of worship, tracing their origins, what they have meant through the ages, and whether their meaning is clear for Christians today.

Sacred Tradition

Shea, Mark P. *By what Authority? An Evangelical Discovers Catholic Tradition* (Huntington: Our Sunday Visitor, 1996) Interspersed with his own journey from evangelicalism to the Catholic Church, Mark Shea skillfully explains how and why Sacred tradition occupies a central role in divine Revelation.

Scriptures and Scripture Studies

One of the most common requests we receive is for recommendations for reliable Scripture translations, commentaries, and bible studies. Unfortunately, too many of the notes in many Catholic study bibles present hypothetical higher-critical opinions in a matter-of-fact way, giving lay readers the idea that these opinions are accepted facts. The following translations and commentaries avoid this speculation as well as the influence of modern political correctness.

The Holy Bible, Revised Standard Edition Catholic Edition (San Francisco: Ignatius Press, 1966).

The Holy Bible, Revised Standard Edition Catholic Edition (London: Scepter Press, 1966).

The Navarre Bible Commentaries (Dublin, Ireland: Four Courts Press, 1992) These New Testament commentaries contain both the Latin and the RSVCE texts accompanied by running commentary.

Fuentes, Antonio. *A Guide To The Bible* (Houston, TX: Lumen Christi Press, 1987) An excellent one-volume Catholic over-view of the Bible.

Spiritualities in the Catholic Church

Aumann, Jordan. *Christian Spirituality in the Catholic Tradition* (San Francisco: Ignatius Press, 1985) A broad survey of how different Catholic orders (groups) have lived out the Gospel of Jesus Christ.

Aumann, Jordan. *Spiritual Theology* (Chicago: Christian Classics, 1980) A perceptive survey of spiritual growth from one f the leading spiritual theologians in the Catholic Church.

Testimonies of Converts

Baram Robert, ed. *Spiritual Journeys Toward the Fullness of Faith* (Boston: Daughters of St. Paul, 1988). Twenty-seven men and women share their faith journeys home to the Catholic Church.

Chervin, Ronda, ed. *The Ingrafting* (New Hope: Remnant of Israel, 1993) The Conversion stories of Ten Hebrew-Catholics.

Currie, David. *Born Fundamentalist Born Again Catholic* (San Francisco: Ignatius Press, 1996)

Guindon, Kenneth R. *The King's Highway*. (San Francisco: Ignatius Press, 1996) The testimony of a man born Catholic who left the Church and tried other religions for 30 years, including 16 years as a Jehovah's Witness, and then found his way back to the Catholic Church through his study of scripture.

Hahn, Scott & Kimberley. *Rome Sweet Home* (San Francisco: Ignatius Press, 1993) One of the most well publicized conversion stories in the late twentieth century.

Howard, Thomas. *Lead, Kindly Light* (Steubenville: Franciscan University Press, 1994) A short but wonderful account of one evangelical's journey to Rome in the spirit of John Henry Newman.

Madrid, Patrick, ed. *Surprised By Truth* (San Diego: Basilica Press, 1994) Eleven modern conversion accounts that are both packed with biblical, theological, and historical proofs for Catholicism and at the same time very winsome and entertaining.

Merton, Thomas. *The Seven Story Mountain* (Harcourt Brace and Co, 1948) A classic of a secular man turned Trappist monk.

Newman, John Henry. *Apologia pro Vita sua* originally published in 1880, this classic narrates the conversion of one of the greatest English cardinals in the nineteenth century.

Ray, Stephen K. *Crossing the Tiber* (San Francisco: Ignatius Press, 1997) A moving account of the conversion of an evangelical, thoroughly documented with over 400 biblical and patristic quotations and commentary.

Appendix C
How to become a member of The Coming Home Network International and support its work

The *Coming Home Network International* is comprised of three types of memberships. Our primary membership is for former clergy and their families who are somewhere along their journey into the Catholic Church. Secondary membership is for laity of other traditions and fallen away Catholics, who again are somewhere along their journey into the Catholic Church. The Tertiary or Associate membership is for Catholic laity, priests, deacons, religious, bishops and even Cardinals who support the *CHNetwork* in their prayers and generous contributions.

Members are encouraged to form local fellowship groups for prayer, fellowship, small group studies of Scripture or Church teachings, as well as for reaching out with the truth of the Catholic faith to friends and relatives outside the Church.

The goal of the *CHNetwork* is to assist the Catholic Church in fulfilling its mission of evangelization and its call for Christian unity, as most recently proclaimed by Pope John Paul II in his encyclical *Ut Unum Sint.*

One of the strongest desires of all members of the *CHNetwork* is to help all Catholics appreciate the wonderful faith they have always had and sometimes have taken for granted.

How Can I Help?

There are several ways in which you can support the work of the *Coming Home Network International*:

- **Become a member of the *CHNetwork*.** As a member you receive the newsletter and information about how to inter- connect with others on the journey around the world. You also can attend regional retreats, gatherings and pilgrim- ages. An annual suggested donation of $25 helps cover the costs of printing and mailing the newsletter plus other ad- ministrative and apostolic expenses.

- **Pray for the *CHNetwork*, its staff and members.** All members are encouraged to pray regularly for all the needs of the *CHNetwork*, and to present these needs at least one hour each month before the Blessed Sacrament.

- **Make a contribution to the *CHNetwork*.** The *Coming Home Network International* is a nonprofit Catholic lay apostolate, solely funded through the contributions of its members and friends. **All donations are tax deductible and greatly appreciated.**

- **Tell others about our work, and encourage them to sup- port it.** Let your priest and bishop know about our apostolate. Often when clergy of other traditions become interested in finding out about the Catholic faith, they do not know where to turn. We want to help them.

- **Distribute our brochures, newsletter, and even a copy of this book to clergy and laity of other traditions.** Most members of other traditions have been misinformed about the teachings of the Catholic faith. Following the model of

St. Francis de Sales who committed his life to bringing thousands of Calvinists back to the Catholic faith after the Reformation, we believe the loving communication of the truth will win hearts back to the Church.

- **Schedule one of our staff members or a member of the *CHNetwork* to speak at your parish or at a conference.** Both Marcus Grodi and Kenneth Howell, as well as other clergy and lay converts in the *CHNetwork*, are experienced speakers and enjoy sharing their conversion stories as well as other topics to strengthen the faith of Catholic laity.

- **The *Coming Home Network International*** depends almost entirely on gifts from individuals like yourself to continue our work. Your generous donation allows us to provide financial and spiritual assistance to those seeking the truth of the Catholic Faith.

How Can I Become A Member?

If you are interested in becoming a member of the *CHNetwork* complete the survey on the following page and return it to the address below. A $25 annual donation is greatly appreciated to cover the costs of printing and mailing the newsletter, as well as other administrative and apostolic expenses. We can also be contacted through e-mail at mgrodi@clover.net.

The Coming Home Network International
P. O. Box 8290
Zanesville, OH 43702

Journeys Home

CHNetwork Membership Survey

Name: _____

Address: _____

City: _____

State:_____ Zip:_____ Country: _____

E-Mail: _____

Hm Phone:_____ Wk Phone: _____

Fax: _____

Denominational Information
(In which denomination were you ...)

Baptized: _____

Ordained:_____ Date: _____

Presently a Member of:

_____

Previously a Member of:

_____

Please describe your present relationship to the Catholic Church:

_____

_____

_____

_____

_____

Family Information

Spouse's Name: _____

His/Her Current Denomination:

_____

Children & Their Denominations:

_____

_____

_____

_____

_____

Please describe your spouse's relationship to the Catholic Church:

_____

_____

_____

_____

_____

Can we release your name to other members and inquires? _____

The Coming Home Network International
P. O. Box 8290
Zanesville, OH 43702
740-450-1175

http://www.chnetwork.org